The Book of Gates
A MAGICAL TRANSLATION

Commentary by Josephine McCarthy
Translation by Michael Sheppard
Illustrations by Stuart Littlejohn

TaDehent Books
Exeter

For more information, please visit www.quareia.com

Translation copyright 2017 © Michael Sheppard
Commentary copyright 2017 © Josephine McCarthy
Original paintings copyright 2017 © Stuart Littlejohn

All rights reserved

Without limiting the rights under copyright reserved above, no part of this publication may be reproduced, stored in, or introduced into a retrieval system, or transmitted, in any form or by any means (electronic, mechanical, photocopying, recording or otherwise) without prior permission of the copyright owner and the publisher of this book.

First edition published by Quareia Publishing UK 2017

Second edition published by TaDehent Books 2022
Exeter UK

ISBN (Hardback) 978-1-911134-68-8
ISBN (Paperback) 978-1-911134-69-5
ISBN (Ebook) 978-1-911134-70-1

Dedicated to Josephine Stockdale, Robert Henry, and David Blank, three magicians of great stature who successfully faced the Gates in life and then in death; and to the original text's unknown authors, whose tow-ropes have now lasted over thirty-three centuries.

Thanks to Aaron Moshe and Catherine for making this project possible.

A special thanks to archaeologist François Olivier of Meretseger Books, who made his private collection of photographs available for use.
www.meretsegerbooks.com

Contents

Introduction	7
Translator's Introduction	25
First Hour	29
Second Hour	43
Third Hour	61
Fourth Hour	81
Fifth Hour	101
Sixth Hour	129
Seventh Hour	147
Eighth Hour	167
Ninth Hour	183
Tenth Hour	197
Eleventh Hour	217
Twelfth Hour	243
Glossary	269
Bibliography	319
Biographies	321

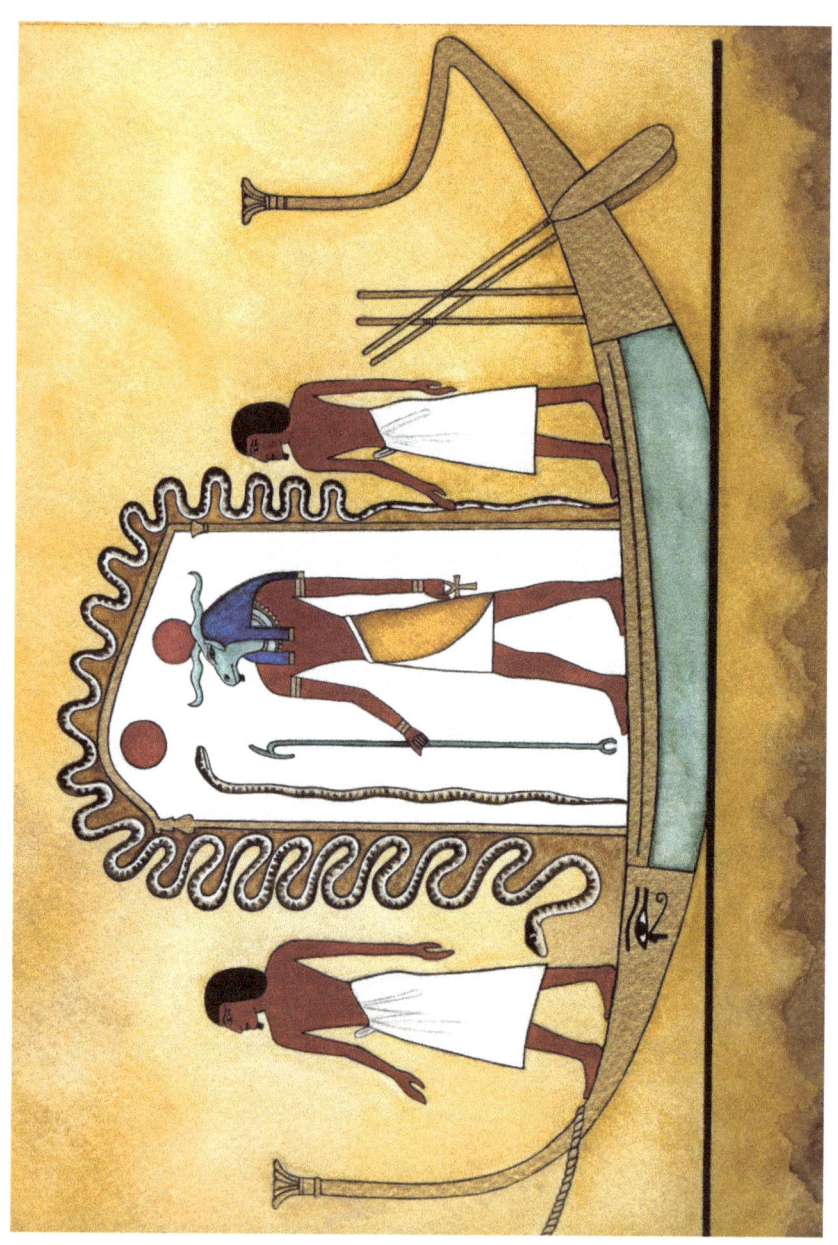

The Barque of Re

Introduction

The Book of Gates is a powerful and profound royal magical funerary text that emerged during Egypt's New Kingdom (sixteenth to eleventh century B.C.). It first appeared in use at the end of the eighteenth dynasty and continued in use until the twentieth dynasty. Using images and text, it maps out the descent of Re into the Underworld and through twelve hours and gates.

Though many other 'Books of the Dead' existed in ancient Egypt, *The Book of Gates* stands out for its absolute magical detail and the coherence of its Mysteries. Each hour marks a stage in the transition of a soul's passage and evolution through the Duat, while casting light into dark corners of the Duat to show you who—or what—is waiting there, what happens there, why, and how. It is a remarkable text, within which magicians can find the roots of many different magical Mysteries to do with the passage of the dead, and of Re, through the Underworld.

It is unlike the other funerary texts that we know about, such as *The Amduat*, *The Coffin Texts*, or *The Book of the Dead*—the main players—which consist more of spells to avoid adversaries. *The Book of Gates* is a magically intelligent, subtle, and highly sophisticated Underworld text seemingly reserved specifically for the monarch. It dispenses with the overcomplicated drama of *The Amduat*; and it has nothing to do with the more degenerate collections of spells in *The Book of the Dead*, which were widely used by anyone who could afford them. Instead it focuses on the evolution of the soul through descent, rebirth, ascension, and becoming as gold: one with the gods.

And that is where it becomes interesting for the living magician. Hidden in its many layers is the path for a living magician towards Justification—the transformation from mundane lead into the gold of a Godly One through stages of magical Justification.

Structure

The Book of Gates is written in Middle Egyptian, and contains a hundred scenes spread out over twelve sections, one for each hour. Each hour is divided into three horizontal sections, and ends with a gate. There are also some repeating numerical patterns: twelve (hours), nine (Ennead), and seven (completion/resurrection).

The language and vocabulary in *The Book of Gates* is extraordinary in its expression and complexity. There are many puns, and multiple layers of meaning that can apply equally to a living candidate of the Mysteries as well as to a dead one.

The gates themselves are different from other funerary texts, like *The Amduat*, in that they appear at the end of each hour rather than the beginning, and they are described in detail.

Eleven of the gates present as the power of a goddess, protected by a serpent on the door, two Uraeus serpents, two guardians, and nine mummies. The first hour and gate, however, are very different.

The first hour and gate are set in the Western Desert, the Zemit, known to adept magicians as the Inner Desert. The First Gate is the threshold between the Zemit and the Duat, the Inner Desert and the Underworld. After passing through the First Gate into the realms of the Underworld, the deceased—or living—candidate begins their long descent into the depths of the various aspects and areas of the Duat. The First Gate is guarded by a single vast serpent described, simply, as the Guardian of the Desert.

What also makes *The Book of Gates* stand out from other funerary texts is its use of deity names—or rather its lack of them. Few deities appear in the *Gates*. In *The Amduat* and *The Book of the Dead*, the pertinent deities are clearly shown and named; in *The Book of Gates*, the key players are often Finished Ones, or Justified humans. Similarly, most of the many characters depicted in the *Gates* are obviously human, not gods. Many times the name of a deity *seems* to appear, but the god determinative is missing. This is saying that a character or power is like that deity, but not the deity itself; it is showing you the power and dynamics present in that scene.

Similarly, in *The Amduat*, the Solar Barque's crew consists of quite a collection of deities, but in *The Book of Gates*, its crew is simply Sia, 'Perception,' known to magicians as 'inner senses,' and Heka, 'Magic': the two powers needed by the candidate to traverse the *Gates* safely.

The Judgement Hall of Osiris appears inside the fifth gate, and instead of the familiar scene we see in other funerary texts, of the heart being weighed against a feather of Ma'at on the scales, in *The Book of Gates* the candidate/deceased is themselves depicted as the fulcrum of the scales: their inherent Ma'at stands before Osiris for acceptance.

Discovering the Gates

I first came across *The Book of Gates* unknowingly in the winter of 2011 while exploring tombs in the Valley of the Kings in Egypt. In one of the tombs I visited, which was visually unimpressive and cramped, something tweaked my magical antenna. The tomb was busy with tourists, packed with everyone jostling to find space. So I could not penetrate through the distractions to listen to the quiet voice doing the tweaking. This was the tomb of Ramesses I—decorated only with *The Book of Gates*.

I came out of the tomb and searched for the last one I wished to visit. I was not sure which tomb would be best to use my final ticket on, so I closed my eyes and magically sought for where I should go next. Many 'lights' were shining in that valley, but one shone much brighter than others, so I aimed for it. It was a tucked away tomb that no one seemed to be visiting. A relief: I needed to get away from the herds of tourists and their noise.

The tomb's magic was evident the moment I started down its passageway. It was a large and impressive tomb, with a stillness and power above and beyond all the others I had visited. Its walls were alive with a balanced, finely-tuned magic that I can describe only as beautiful. It was the tomb of Twosret (KV14), a queen who briefly became Pharaoh at the end of the nineteenth dynasty. Her tomb was quickly usurped by Sethnakht, the first king of the

The Judgement Scene of the Book of Gates in the Tomb of Horemheb (KV57)

twentieth dynasty, and Twosret's images were plastered over and replaced with images of him.

It is a long and beautiful tomb, orientated west, with two burial chambers. While the corridors are decorated with *The Book of the Dead* and *The Amduat*, the two burial chambers are decorated with *The Book of Gates*, and with the closing scenes of *The Book of Caverns*.

I spent a long time in that tomb, and was truly astonished at the level of magic that flowed through it despite its troubled history and ransacking. I did not know about *The Book of Gates*; I just bathed in the magic and marvelled at the high quality paintings.

Years later, when I was coming to the end of writing the Quareia magical course in the autumn of 2016, the editor of the course, Michael Sheppard, told me that there was a book I should get and take a close look at. I had made use of some Egyptian funerary texts in the course to introduce students to the magic of Egypt, but I was unfamiliar with *The Book of Gates*. He contacted me one day and said, "The Book of Gates, get it, you will be astonished. It is like Cliff Notes for the Quareia course."

I was used to the Egyptian Underworld books, which are mostly collections of spells aimed at pushing the dead through death as safely as possible. But the *Gates* was a totally different animal. The closer I looked, the more astonished I became. What I was looking at was a very ancient version of the mystical magical process that takes someone from the beginnings of serious mystical magical development through to magical Justification and beyond, yet presented in an Underworld 'funerary' text. Michael Sheppard and I decided at that point to publish this book once the course was finally finished, as we were in the last month of work on Quareia.

It was not till we had just started work on *The Book of Gates* that I realized, on very close inspection, that this was not only a book for the dead, but also a book for the living. The living Justification process was hidden beneath the funerary layer—something common in old magical texts, and which can be found in such texts until at least the sixteenth century A.D..

The steps towards Justification, and the magical processes outlined in the *Gates*, were very, very similar to the steps that Quareia students are guided to take on their path to Justification. They were steps that many other adept magicians in the Western magical tradition will recognize. Those steps have survived, largely intact, hidden away, buried deep in magical writings that have walked down through time.

A closer look

Superficially, *The Book of Gates* is about the passage of the solar deity, Re, through the Duat (the Underworld), and what he has to say to the dead as they go through their various stages of development in the Duat. It talks about the various things that can happen to the dead, depending on what stage of development they are at, and how their life actions have defined what will happen to them as they undergo the different stages of transformation.

As the dead pass through the gates of the Duat, they are taken apart and slowly put back together. Those who succeed in this process rise with Re to traverse the sky and become reborn with the dawning of the sun.

Various characters in the Duat are introduced, nearly all of whom have names which merely reflect their function. The same is true of the 'adversaries' of those who are 'developing,' who are also looked at: what they do, why they do it, and who they are. The candidate traversing the *Gates* is given clues on how to develop beyond their adversaries—advice more pertinent to the living than the dead.

This is a subtle but important aspect of the *Gates* which is also reflected in other true magical texts that have travelled down through time to us today. Beings are mostly not given names, but identified by function. This is often a subtle clue that you are dealing with a real magical text. In *The Book of Gates*, this is often done by using deity names without god determinatives—hieroglyphs at the end of names that tell readers the name belongs to a deity.

We also come across people 'resting' or 'waiting' in the Duat until they are ready to move forward and continue their journey, and people helping, advising, and accompanying the dead through certain sections of the process.

Beneath this surface layer hides another, a layer that speaks to living people attempting to undergo the Justification-in-Life process, known in magic as the *ascent*, or the alchemical 'Lead to Gold' process well known in some corners of adept magic to this day. It is an initiation-through-life process that guides the magician, or king, through various stages of development towards the goal of becoming Justified while still living—a Justification subsequently tested in death.

This is fascinating because in Ancient Egypt, while there are many records of rituals that revolve around temples—rituals involving priests, priestesses, and the general public—there is nothing specific in any texts that refers to an esoteric initiatory process. This has led many Egyptologists to hold the opinion that such a process did not exist in Egypt—and for the longest time, this opinion was also mine.

However, over time, and through close examination of various structures and texts, as an adept I was able to begin to recognize not only references to initiatory processes hidden in funerary texts, but also to understand their delivery methods. Whereas the Greeks hinted heavily about their esoteric initiatory processes, the Egyptians opted for a more silent, hidden approach.

To date I have seen evidence of such Egyptian initiatory processes only in funerary texts. Why?

In today's world, anyone with the inclination and focus can embark on the path of the Mysteries. However in Ancient Egypt, that role was pretty much the focus of the monarch, and occasionally some other outstanding individual, usually one close to the monarch. Such things do not need writing down, as they are passed on from mouth to ear, and taught practically rather than written down explicitly.

The Justification-in-Life process is tested and confirmed in death, and as such, advice was placed on the walls to remind the dead of what was before them. The fact that it was only used for a brief time in Egyptian history fascinates me, and we will probably never discover the details of exactly how and why it appeared, then disappeared. What we do know, as adepts, is that so far the *Book of Gates* is the earliest in-depth presentation of the Path of Gold.

Justification?

Justification is an alchemical process by which the magician is slowly transformed from the heavy state of mundane 'lead' into Divine 'gold'—the root of Hermetic alchemy. This theme has survived for millennia, flowing out of Egypt through the Greeks, then carried in texts from the Near East into Europe. It is a theme that appears in both mystical Christian and Greek Hermetic texts; fragments of it also appear in Jewish Kabbalistic texts.

When the Justified magician dies, the process of Justification is revisited in stages by a journey through the *Gates*, where the adept is tested, judged, and challenged to confirm their in-life Justification. In Egyptian texts, those who have undergone the process are pronounced *True of Voice*, and groups of Justified individuals are known as the Ma'ati—which Michael translates as "the Righteous." (See the Glossary for details.)

The True of Voice title, like all things magical, gradually became debased currency, and by the twentieth dynasty and beyond, into the Late Period, it was not much more than a 'status in death' title for high-ranking officials and rich nobles. (Today's version of that degeneration is experienced by people who pay a small fortune to go on a weekend magical retreat and come out with a certificate that says they are an adept.)

> Workers of Truth:
>   When they are on Earth,
>   They are striving for their godhoods.
> They are those who are summoned to a post of the Earth,
>   To the enclosure (called) Living In Truth.
> Scrutinized for them is their Truth,
>   Before the Great God who causes the destruction of sin.
>
>   —from the Seventh Hour, Scene 43.

The Book of Gates for magicians

Many of the most profound aspects of the magical Mysteries can be found in ancient and classical texts, and they all serve in their own way as pointers, reminders, and breadcrumbs to the deeper side of magic and the Mysteries. Many of the keys of the Mysteries were embedded in various texts, often hidden in layers for magicians and mystics to find in the future, and to ensure their survival and continual working.

Often these texts are obscure, and their secrets are hidden under layers of allegory and image, their authors having been confident that future magicians, priests, priestesses, and mystics would have the knowledge and skill to decipher the hidden meanings and put them to work. Such texts ensured the survival of their lines of knowledge, and placed the keys to the Mysteries in the path of the future so that when the time was right and there was great need in the world, they would be rediscovered, understood again, and worked with.

This method of sending wisdom into the future by preserving and hiding keys is also known in the Tibetan Buddhist culture in the form of *Terma* or 'treasures': hidden scrolls meant to be found in times of great need, which would be discovered by a seeker and would trigger an awakening of the Mysteries.

However, besides turning the deceased's tomb or coffin into a miniature universe of the Mysteries to help them partake of the pattern as they traverse death, *The Book of Gates* has another deeper, more profound purpose. That purpose is to be a complete magical-mystical pattern externalized in text and images that can act as a living machine of the Mysteries.

A complete copy of *Gates* in a sealed tomb, or on the walls of a mortuary temple, ticks away as a living universe that affects everything and everyone around it. It keeps the inner knowledge alive and working. Stepping into a tomb or temple that contains the *Gates* pattern is like stepping into a continuously working ritual that is constantly renewing itself, thousands of years after its creation. And this is the most profound aspect of the *Gates*, which often passes unnoticed with these sorts of texts: more than preserved knowledge or a book of guidance, it is a living, working magical pattern travelling down through time.

The complexity, detail, and brilliant magical accuracy in *The Book of Gates* makes it a fascinating text for magicians to study; but more importantly its many hidden layers hold a wealth of knowledge for magicians,

Introduction   15

knowledge that reaches deep into the Underworld, high up to the stars, and, in its hidden aspect, educates the magician about the different steps and phases of magical and mystical development. Unlike other funerary texts of the time, it reaches far beyond the magic of the dead and their passage through the Underworld; it also speaks to the magical aspirant seeking to reach far beyond dabbling in spells, who wishes to climb the Ladder of the Mysteries. It teaches and advises, reflects and demonstrates; and its living magical pattern triggers the magician, pushing them along the Path of Hercules.

How to work with this book

In his English translation of *The Book of Gates*, Michael has tried to stay very close to the literal meaning of the text while still exposing its underlying, hidden, and obscure connotations. Where he could not do this in the translation itself, he has written explanatory footnotes.

Alongside his translation is my commentary. This peels back some of the text's more hidden and obscure magical meanings. It is a careful look through adept eyes, and relies on a knowledge of the timeless Mysteries that emerge again and again in adept Western magic.

I also used a specific method of reading the *Gates* to unlock its Mysteries. This method, detailed below, is particularly useful for studying mystical and esoteric texts, and is quite similar to how the Ancient Egyptians themselves approached their texts—particularly those designed to hide special meanings from mundane eyes.

In today's world, where many have been educated in the undergraduate university system, we are used to everything being straightforward, footnoted, and indexed. B comes after A, and everything is quantifiable. The Mysteries have never worked like that. They are not simple experiments that can be reproduced and verified; nor can information be simply and clearly stated in bullet points.

This makes it difficult for modern readers lacking a classical education to navigate the complexities of more ancient texts. In a classical education, the reader is taught to spot the puns, allegories, hidden meanings, and different layers woven into a story. Without such an understanding, the reader can often end up utterly perplexed as they try to penetrate a seemingly incomprehensible text. Which is exactly the point: the text's complexity protects it from profane eyes.

This is demonstrated beautifully in this delightful quote from Jābir ibn Ḥayyān, the eighth-century Islamic alchemist also known as Geber:

> "The purpose is to baffle and lead into error everyone except those whom God loves and provides for."
>
> —from *Kitab Al-Ahjar, The Book of Stones*, by Jābir ibn Ḥayyān.

The method I used to read this text is known in Jewish Kabbalah as *PaRDeS*. (In the Quareia system of magical training, the student magician is taught in detail how to read ancient, classical, and historical texts using this method.) *PaRDeS* stands for:

Peshat The most superficial, literal interpretation, the first layer, the most mundane meaning.

Remez The allegorical or symbolic meaning hiding just beneath the mundane layer.

Derash The layer of the seeker, where comparative meaning can be drawn from a similar situation or presentation, i.e. "this is like..."

Sod The hidden esoteric meaning that comes to light through inspiration or mystical revelation.

As you can imagine, this method is extremely troublesome for someone who has been taught to pay attention only to facts and bullet points. It is also wide open to abuse: it is very difficult to challenge or analyse a person's 'inspiration' or 'revelation'...

Nevertheless, when a profound, ancient, magical-mystical text like *The Book of Gates* turns up under the nose of a magician who has been working practically within the Mysteries for decades, it is a wonderful confirmation that they are on the right path. The outer form may change, but the magical dynamics stay the same.

The Mysteries never really change as they travel down through time. A twenty-first-century magician can spot in ancient texts the same magical dynamics that they are currently working with. This is a mark of the true Mysteries: direct recognition throughout the generations.

> Behind the veil of all the hieratic and mystical allegories of ancient doctrines, behind the darkness and strange ordeals of all initiations, under the seal of all sacred writings, in the ruins of Nineveh or Thebes, on the crumbling stones of old temples and on the blackened visage of the Assyrian or Egyptian sphinx, in the monstrous or marvellous paintings which interpret to the faithful of India the inspired pages of the Vedas, in the cryptic emblems of our old books on alchemy, in the ceremonies practised at reception by all secret societies, there are found indications of a doctrine which is everywhere the same and everywhere carefully concealed.
>
> —Alphonse Louis Constant/Eliphas Levi, French Occultist (1810–1875)

The Egyptians used many different strategies to hide meanings in their texts. The more important the text, the more strategies they employed.

In *The Book of Gates*, lots of methods were used. As well as the one we now call *PaRDeS*, it uses puns, allegories, mirror writing, and lots of playing around with words and images. The Egyptians were clever, pragmatic, and playful—we even see a Duat serpent with a smiley face!

In my analysis of the *Gates* I have employed all these reading methods; and these, coupled with magical knowledge, has let me tease out the text's more important aspects for magical readers, while still respecting the necessity of silence to protect its deepest Mysteries.

You will quickly come to realize, as you read through this book, that it does not describe a linear path through the Duat; rather it meanders through each hour, and talks about the different hidden corners of the Duat and the various beings who work there. It is particularly slow to reveal that it talks to living initiates as well as dead ones. As you are introduced to the various characters who populate the Duat, you will start to realize that some are deity powers and others Underworld beings; and that some are dead human workers while others are living humans operating in vision, in magical service.

For those with eyes to see and ears to hear, the meanings and details outlined in the *Gates* will slowly emerge, as will its function and purpose in today's magical world for the living magician. It is not right or balanced within the laws of Ma'at to uncover completely the Mysteries of the *Gates*, or to give step-by-step instructions to work with them as a living adept. Those are for you to discover. If it is right for you to walk the *Gates* in life, then its methods will make themselves known to you.

Just reading and understanding the text will have a talismanic effect. It is a complete, healthy, and functioning magical pattern which has survived for millennia. As such, it brings change to the magician just by nature of its presence in your consciousness. Reading it will change you slowly over time. Fragments of its Mysteries will spring open in your mind for decades to come. And at the right times, its dynamics will present to you not just in quiet, thoughtful moments, but also in the physical world by way of encounters, experiences, and events.

Historical background

For those interested, here is a short look at the historical provenance of the *Gates* and the events leading up to their appearance, which may have had a direct bearing on the necessity of their emergence from hiding.

The Book of Gates first appeared in royal tombs in the aftermath of the Amarna period, at the end of the eighteenth dynasty, in the New Kingdom. When it appeared it was already a mature, knowledgeable, and complete system, not an evolving funerary text. Nor was it a development of *The Amduat*, the most popular royal funerary text of the time. It is patently obvious that this system was previously known and recorded, yet it had not been used in royal tombs until its first appearance in the tomb of king Horemheb (KV57), who reigned from c. 1319 B.C. to 1292 B.C..

To understand why *The Book of Gates* emerged at this time, we have to look at what had just happened to Egypt and its magical implications. The mess caused by the Amarna period is likely what prompted the use of the *Gates*, not only to reestablish the state religion within the orbit of the monarchy, but also to reestablish and protect a religious magical pattern that had just been torn apart. Looking at the events leading up to the appearance of the *Gates* gives us the historical background to its emergence, and provides a deeper magical understanding of why it had to appear.

Until Akhenaten, the monarch was the captain of the ship of Egypt, steering the nation through its challenges both in life and in death. He had not only temporal responsibilities, but also religious and magical ones. The king was deeply embedded in the mystical and magical aspects of Egypt's religion, and his—or her—upkeep of Ma'at in all things was supposed to keep the gods happy and the nation prosperous. The king was the chief juggler of power on all levels.

Akhenaten swept all that away by experimenting with monotheism, ignoring state and international matters, and disregarding the welfare of his people. We see from paintings and records that Akhenaten's main temple, to the Aten, the sun-disc, was open to the skies and filled every day with food offerings. Nine hundred offering tables were discovered in archaeological explorations, and these are depicted in tomb paintings as being piled high with fresh food. It makes for an image of a prosperous, happy world.

All worship of the families of deities was dispensed with, temples were disbanded, priests removed, and the age-old religious system of Egypt was cast to the winds. Everyone, without exception, worshipped Akhenaten and his family as gods, who in turn worshipped the Aten.

It is pertinent to point out here that religious and mundane life were heavily intertwined, as were magic and religion. They were all part of the fabric of Egyptian life and culture. Pull out one element, and the whole thing unravels. Akhenaten ignored his borders, his people, and the religious structure of his culture. He cast aside the rule of Ma'at to pursue his own obsessions.

The direct result of his actions towards his people became more apparent in 2002 as a result of the archaeological excavation of some burials around Amarna, the new city that Akhenaten built in the desert. The burials contained a higher than usual number of young people: children, adolescents, and young adults. A large percentage of them showed marked signs of *cribra orbitalia* and *hyperostosis spongiosa*, the physical signs of chronic scurvy and anaemia. These were a people slowly starving to death while Akhenaten's temple altars overflowed with food offerings to the Aten.[1]

---

[1] Kuckens 2013

Akhenaten's new monotheistic Egypt, then, was hardly the idyllic life portrayed in the period's tomb paintings. It was a time of chaos, political collapse, religious collapse, starvation, and deadly disease. Archaeological examination has now revealed traces of the bubonic plague in fossilized fleas, evidence which backs up descriptions of the disease in contemporary medical papyri.

It is also worth noting that during the reign of Akhenaten, in the war between the Egyptians and Hittites that went on for two centuries, Hittite soldiers were documented as catching a disease from the Egyptian soldiers that sounds very much like smallpox. This is now considered the first recorded smallpox outbreak.

Once Akhenaten was dead, his new religion was torn apart. Under the boy king Tutankhamen, the old religion started the long haul back to restoration.

However, Tutankhamen was only nine or ten when he became king, and he was a sickly child who died in his late teens from illness, accident, foul play, or some combination of the three. The kingdom was economically and politically weak, fragmented, and chaotic, and its people were malnourished, diseased, and economically crippled.

The next king was Ay. Ay was thought to be the brother of Queen Tiye, mother of Akhenaten, and he had also been Tjaty—Vizier—to Tutankhamen. He lasted only four years before he died. He had appointed Nakhtmin as his heir, but Horemheb took control and became king, after which things began to change rapidly. Horemheb had been commander-in-chief of Tutankhamen's army and his chief advisor.

The names Akhenaten, Ay, Tutankhamen, and Nakhtmin were wiped from the records. And three of them had their tombs trashed, though Tutankhamen's was spared and protected.

When you look at the tombs of Ay and of Tutankhamen, it is clear that they were both done by the same crew of artists. The tombs have very little religious painting: in fact in both tombs the bare minimum was done, and it was more decorative than religious. They used only the first opening part of *The Book of the Dead*, and did not display any of the Mysteries.

When you step back and look at the whole picture, you see a cursory return to the Mysteries, but no deep use of them. Was that intentional for these tombs, or had knowledge and skills been lost in the Amarna period? We don't know, and in the complex mess that was Egypt at that time, it was likely a very tangled situation.

But when we get to Horemheb, everything changes—and this is where *The Book of Gates* emerges. Horemheb, who in the reign of Tutankhamen was titled Iry-Pat, "hereditary prince," quickly and fully reinstated the Egyptian religion, as well as the offices and privileges of the Place of Truth (*st mAat*) on the west bank of Thebes (Deir el-Medina). This is important, as it tells us that the status of the Duat Mysteries were of the utmost importance to the new ruler.

The Place of Truth was the workmen's community close to the Valley of the Kings which oversaw the creation of the royal tombs and all the funerary goods. The workmen were highly skilled, and mainly priests and priestesses. They were a self-contained unit that saw to the creation and magical enlivening of the Mysteries of the royal tombs. They were educated and deeply involved in the magical-religious pattern of the Egyptian religion.

Whether the texts of *The Book of Gates* were held in their own House of Life (i.e. temple library) or in the nearby temple of Karnak on the east bank, we don't know. But either way, the highly magical *Book of Gates* was brought out for use in Royal tombs for the first time in the reign of Horemheb: his tomb was the first in which the *Gates* appeared fully.

Horemheb's long-serving Tjaty was Paramesse, a high priest of Amun. He was the overseer of the priests of Upper and Lower Egypt, and a very capable administrator. He also became Horemheb's successor, as he lacked an heir. Paramesse, being a high priest of Amun, certainly would have had knowledge of, and access to, *The Book of Gates*, and he was probably instrumental in reestablishing the Egyptian religion. He had control, through his duties as Tjaty and priestly overseer, of how the ship of the state religion was steered.

On Horemheb's death he became Pharaoh and was the start of the Ramessid line of kings. To emphasize his responsibilities as the priestly monarch who reestablished the foundations of spiritual and magical Egypt, his Golden Horus name was Semenmaathettawy, which means "Making Ma'at Firm Throughout the Two Lands."

He ruled only briefly, as he was already an old man when he came to the throne. Horemheb had enjoyed a long rule of approximately twenty-five years, and before that he and Paramesse had worked side-by-side in the army. They grew old together and died within two years of each other. Paramesse, as Ramesses I, had a small tomb, but it too featured *The Book of Gates* exclusively.

Ramesses I's son, Seti I, became king after the very brief reign of Ramesses I, and he ruled for approximately eleven years before his son, Ramesses II, a.k.a. Ramesses the Great, became one of Egypt's all-time powerful rulers. It is through Seti I that we really come to know the *Gates*, as the text was inscribed on his stunning sarcophagus, on his tomb walls, and in his mortuary temple at Abydos. Seti I also completed his father's mortuary chapel at Abydos, and this return of focus to Abydos is another of the breadcrumbs in the story of the *Gates*.

Abydos is a very ancient centre connected to the Mysteries of Osiris, and a place that contains the Osirion, the enigmatic underground ritual chambers of the Osiris Mysteries, the north tunnel of which is decorated with *The Book of Gates*. Reconnecting the royal line to Abydos, and its long and deep history of the hidden Osiris Mysteries, was a very clear magical and religious statement: the monarchs were returning to the old mystical ways in an outright rejection of the heresies of Akhenaten.

This is clearly shown in the choices Seti I made for his tomb and mortuary temple. His tomb features *The Book of Gates*, but also *The Book of the Heavenly Cow*, a story of the destruction of mankind, where humans rebel against Re. Re instructs Hathor/Sekhmet to punish those responsible, but she goes on a wild rampage, killing everything in her path. Remember, Sekhmet is a goddess of war and disease. After a time of plague and smallpox, I am sure the message of the Heavenly Cow was at the forefront of everyone's mind. In the story she is tricked into getting drunk on wine that looks like blood, which turns her from being a raging lioness back into the more peaceful Hathor.

So here we have *The Book of Gates*, which on one level is a map and advice for the dead as they navigate the Duat. But more importantly it is a book of the Mysteries, a book of ascent, and of becoming "gold, as a godly one"—something closely connected to the Mysteries of Osiris at Abydos, which centred on the transformation of the king from noble human to ascended god. The *Gates* was a text reserved only for monarchs who had become "as gold," Justified, a godly one, one who had become Osiris, then merged with the Divine power of Re.

Coupled with the warnings in the Book of the Heavenly Cow, we have a clear statement of intent: the Mysteries are back, and with a harsh warning attached.

Where the text was used

As stated earlier, the first appearance of *The Book of Gates* was in Horemheb's tomb. The tomb was not finished, so the artwork remains in various stages of completion. It then appeared in the Tomb of Ramesses I, where it was the only funerary text used. After Ramesses I, the next monarch to use it was his son, Seti, who put parts of it in various places, including on his sarcophagus, in his tomb, and in his mortuary temple at Abydos.

It is worth mentioning here that the alabaster sarcophagus of Seti I was really something very special. Nearly the whole of *The Book of Gates* was engraved into it, and the engravings were then filled with Egyptian Blue pigment.

His sarcophagus is now kept in the Sir John Soane's Museum in London, England. As an aside, when Soane brought the sarcophagus to England, he threw a party to show off his latest acquisition, a party which went on for three days. He filled the sarcophagus with oil lamps, and the translucent alabaster shone like a giant lampshade, its intricate scripts and images coming to life.

The use of translucent alabaster, as opposed to the more usual granite or sandstone, is interesting. Justified Ones are said to shine with their brightness, a theme which appears repeatedly in *The Book of Gates*. I suspect that the sarcophagus was constructed to light up when the bright soul of Seti was put in it.

Parts of the *Gates* were also painted on Seti's tomb walls: in the pillared chamber, on a gate, in a side chamber, and in the burial chamber. He also included scenes from *The Amduat*, which appear in the stairwell, corridor, and side chambers. *The Book of the Dead* was used in the stairwell along with *The Amduat*, as was *The Book of the Heavenly Cow* and *The Litany of Re*.

This pattern of using scenes from different funerary texts continued through the next few royal tombs of Ramesses II, Merneptah, and Ramesses III. The *Gates* continued to feature strongly in the Ramessid tombs. Ramesses VII was the last to use the *Gates*, having just the first two hours in a corridor. Some small scenes from the *Gates* do appear again in various later royal and non-royal tombs, but its use as a main tomb text ended with Ramesses VII.

A note for Quareia magicians

For those of you reading this, the various stages of development in the Quareia course's magical training also appear in the *Gates*, if you look closely.

In this introduction I have purposely not pointed out various very interesting and pertinent magical gems hidden away in the *Gates*, but if you look carefully, and use the skills you will have learned in your training, then they will reveal themselves to you. Remember to use the *PaRDeS* method of reading, and to pay attention.

You should recognize a great deal in the *Gates*, and find that certain sections draw you more than others. Where there is developing for you to do, or work in service in the Duat, it will make itself known. Such is the nature of this amazing, profound, and living magical pattern!

Josephine McCarthy, February 2017.

Translator's Introduction

When Pythagoras came to the temples of Egypt demanding to know their secrets, the priests would not tell him; instead they sent him off on a journey on foot. We, who are more the spiritual descendants of Greeks than Egyptians, must expect much the same treatment when we go knocking on the gates of their Mysteries.

For you readers who have worked with a grimoire or two, many of this book's methods of knowledge transmission will seem quite familiar, and what you suspect you are looking at may well be what is intended. Treat this book exactly as you would treat a grimoire. For those of you who are uninitiated into the grimoire tradition, you may be in for a bit of a shock...

The fashion with books at the moment is to control tightly the reader's journey, and to do as much of the legwork as possible so that the book's central point is received in the strongest possible way. *The Book of Gates* does not do this. One of the most surprising features of ancient Egyptian funerary literature is just how gnomic it is. Rather than defining the whole mental landscape to be transmitted and commanding "behold," it prefers to give just enough information to spark the correct experience in the listener. For the mystically inclined, this is a feature.

As such, I have tried not to be more specific in my English than is the original Egyptian. For instance, where the original text indicates a relationship between two clauses by simple juxtaposition, then, tempting as it was to turn them into a nice, precise English sentence by interposing an and, but, while, or because, I usually contented myself with a comma or semicolon, keeping my translation as open to the reader's interpretation as the original, so far as this was possible.

This, and some other idiosyncrasies—such as keeping verbs, where I could, at the beginnings of clauses—may also suggest a little of the original text's flavour.

I must also talk a bit about puns. *The Book of Gates* uses a lot of them; generally, though not exclusively, for mystical rather than comic effect. Such puns are mainly untranslatable. Instead, where a pun unlocks the text's main meaning, it is indicated by alternate readings separated by slashes. Less important puns are footnoted or explained in the glossary. Many Egyptian prepositions also receive alternate readings in this translation where this may help the reader more deeply understand the text.

I have tried to compensate a little for the Egyptian text's inscrutability by being extremely consistent with the English words used to translate it. If you want to see what Egyptian word generally lurks behind its English translation, then look up the English word in the glossary. Where I depart from this consistency, I have tried always to provide a footnote. Words in bold type are a particular invitation to use the glossary.

The main primary source for this translation was the nearly-complete version of *The Book of Gates* on the alabaster sarcophagus of Seti I, now in Sir John Soane's Museum, London, whose engravings were reproduced in their entirety by Bonomi and Sharpe (1864). However, the sixth hour is not depicted on the coffin, and the seventh and eighth hours have been preserved only partially on the coffin's lid. The primary source for the sixth hour, therefore, was the copy on the walls of Seti I's tomb, which are reproduced in its entirety by Hornung (1991, pp. 128–133). For the seventh and eighth hours, primacy was given to what portions of them remain on the coffin's lid, and the blanks were filled in from the composite hieroglyphic text of Hornung and Abt (2014). Hornung's hieroglyphic text was also used to fill in occasional blanks in the other hours where the coffin's carvers appear to have run out of space to put their text, and his translation was used to check my work.

Egyptian funerary texts were not just manuals for the dead; they were also studied in life. Every time you revisit them, you discover new things. *The Book of Gates* greatly rewards this sort of rereading, more so than any other funerary text I have ever encountered. Such study supports a successful spiral!

Michael Sheppard, Easter Sunday, 2017.

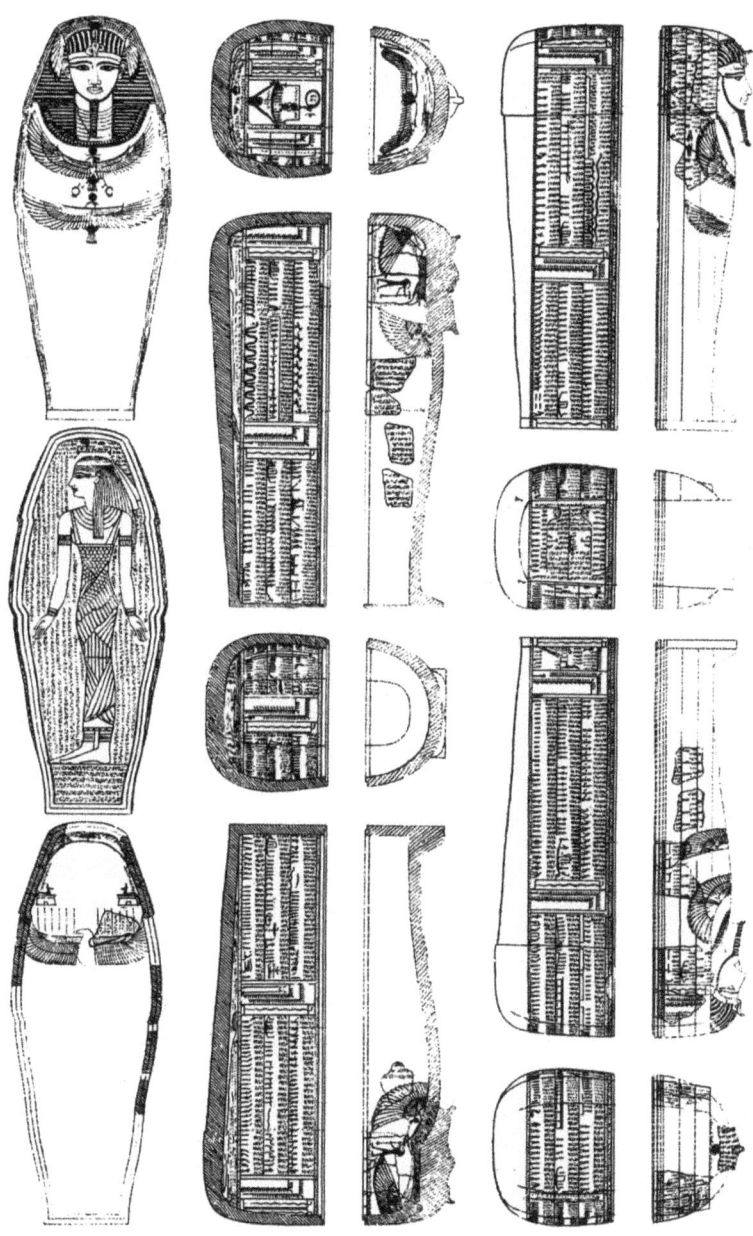

The Alabaster Sarcophagus of Seti I (Bonomi and Sharpe 1864).

First Hour

Scene 1

Twelve figures walking along towards the horizon in the Desert:

Gods of the Desert.

The accompanying text reads:

Who developed from/into Re,
  From/into his Akhet,
Who came forth from/into his Eye.

He ordains for them a hidden place
  For their selection/dismemberment:[2] the humans, the gods;
Even all living things.
  Everything created by this Great God.

This god, he ordains the designs[3]
  After he has penetrated into the Earth,
  Which he created/winnowed for his Western Eye.[4]

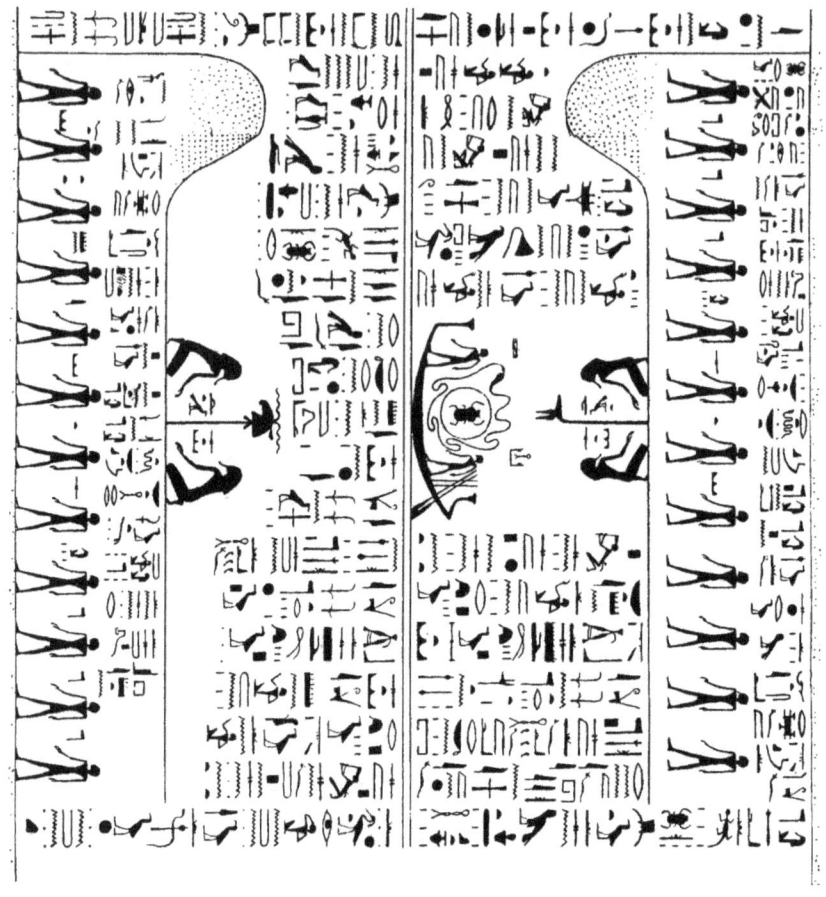

First Hour on Seti I's coffin (Bonomi and Sharpe 1864).

---

²*stp*. The word can mean "selection" and also "dismemberment": the original word is deliberately ambivalent. What makes a soul one of the select or one of those requiring deconstruction is a major topic in this book.

³i.e. he is assigning the conditions of the dead souls in the Duat according to what has to happen to them.

⁴The sense is that Re created everything with his Eastern, Creative Eye in order for it to pass through his Western, Destructive Eye. This introduces the theme of the cycle of creation and destruction.

Commentary

In this opening scene, we are introduced to the Inner Desert and the "winnowed" creations of Re. The Inner Desert is a threshold place both in death and in vision. It does not refer to a physical desert; it is a place people traverse in death and pass through on their way into life, and it is where visionaries, mystics, and magicians go in visions and dreams to work or interact with various powers and beings. The Inner Desert is *zmjt* "Zemit," the threshold place; and the Duat is the Underworld.

Zemit is also the inner visionary place where the magician undergoes trials and tests as they seek adepthood and *Justification* in life: the trial of death-in-life. This is the key to the Mysteries of the *Gates* for magicians wishing to pursue Justification in life, or true adeptship. Traversing the trials of the Inner Desert in vision triggers trials in the life of the adept candidate. The Inner Desert is guarded by fierce entities that repel, block, challenge, help, and give safe passage to those who penetrate its depths.

The opening scene also features those to whom the gates are especially pertinent: those who are the results of Re's winnowing. The fact that "winnow" is nearly the same word as "create" in Egyptian speaks to their deep insight regarding the inner mechanics of life. It also begins one of the allegorical themes that runs throughout the *Gates*, that of bread-making and its connection with Osiris.

When you winnow, you toss grain in the air to separate the wheat from the chaff. This mirrors the deeper magical dynamics of creation where air/breath/utterance comes into play, and it also points to one of the main themes of the *Gates*, which is *sorting people out*: the chaff is separated out, and the wheat is kept.

This process is mirrored in the Neith creation myth, in which Neith creates Re, then uses the leftover bits to create Apep. The grain becomes one power and the chaff becomes the antagonistic power. As an aside for those readers with a good grasp of Kabbalah, you may spot echoes of the Sefirot and Qliphoth here in the *Gates*, as it contains a deeper undercurrent of the Kabbalistic process of creation and destruction.

The Western Eye of Re is also deeply significant here. In Egyptian magic the right is the west, the position of the scales, of harvest, and of completion; which is why the gates to death are in the west.

The Western Eye of Re, the right eye, is the unchanging eye of the continuous cycle of creation and destruction. And the magician's right eye is the one that casts into the inner worlds of creation and destruction. The magician's left eye is the injured and restored eye: a process connected to Osiris, renewal, rebirth, and Justification. It is the eye of time and magic.

So Re defines an inner place where his creations/seeds go after death, and he tells the "gods of the Western Desert" that he has assigned this place for all living things to pass through when they die. The Zemit is where seeds and chaff are winnowed: as it is in creation, so it is in destruction.

Scene 2

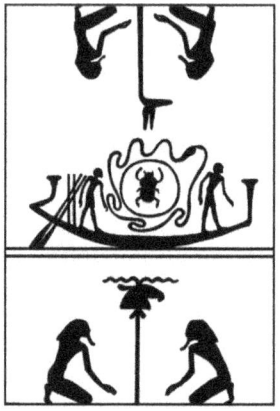

In the centre, the Sun Barque. A scarab beetle inside the sun disc, with a serpent coiled around it, its tail in its mouth. At the prow of the boat, Perception; at the stern of the boat, Magic. Above the Sun Barque, standing in the Desert, a staff with a jackal's head, with two kneeling figures either side of it. Left of the staff, Duat personified; right of the staff, Desert personified.

The accompanying text reads:

>Says Re to the Desert:
>
>"Be bright,[5] Desert!
>   It shines at/by you,
>   What is in me.
>
>Dismembering of people who are filled/finished![6]
>   No dismembering of you who are gods:
>Breath for you, in whom am I;

>Brightness for you, Underworlders!
>My Akhet is *yours*; I ordain *their* dismemberment:
>>There is a selection for them, and for all.[7]
>I have hidden you from those atop the Earth;[8]
>>Provided is the Ribbon for the Best of the Desert!"[9]

Say these, who are of the gods:

>"Influential is this bread,[10]
>>The ordaining words of the Great God,
>>When he exalts/refines his members.
>Come then to us,
>>We who have come forth from in him.
>Oho! For who is in his sun-disc?
>>It is the Great God, of myriad developments."[11]

Their gifts are as bread and beer.[12]

Commentary

The use of the word "bright" is important. Magically, when something is brightened, it is awakened by the creator power and brought into active use. The Inner Desert is activated to receive the "people who are finished."

---

[5] We will meet the theme of brightness again and again in this text.

[6] We will meet a theme of emptiness and fullness in this book; these are the people who are both "finished" and full of...something.

[7] The sense seems to be that all beings who travel through the Duat must undergo a selection process, but the "Underworlders"..."in whom am I" (Re) have nothing to fear; only those who are "finished" are due for dismemberment.

[8] i.e. those walking about on the surface of the Earth, as opposed to being under it in the Duat.

[9] This book is filled with puns. Here the pun is between two senses of *tpw*: "those *atop* the Earth," and "the *best of* the Desert." We will see a great deal of punning, including visual puns, with the word *tp*, "head, top, best of," in the scenes to come.

[10] Reading *wsr t tn* instead of *wsrt tn*, "this neck is..." The second reading, which is Hornung's, also makes sense of the scene: the "neck" in question is the *wsr* staff in the scene.

[11] All things trace their beginnings back to Divinity.

[12] The first instance of a theme which will deepen and develop greatly as we journey through the book.

This brightness is depicted in sacred art as halos, or light emanating from a person or deity's body and/or eyes. Making the Desert bright means that it is being brought into action: power is awakened in the Desert, and the newly dead are brought into awareness in preparation for the trials of the Duat.

There is a distinction made between the created, the "people who are finished" who undergo life, death, and trials, and the "Gods of the Desert." These are deities in the Desert who do not partake of the trials process, or Justified humans (Michael translates their title as "the Righteous") who have already done so successfully and have become "of the gods."

This can refer to adepts, kings, priests, or priestesses who have undergone Justification and become "as gods." They have vanquished death while still alive, and serve in the Inner Desert as guides. These are often referred to in magic as inner contacts, inner adepts, or, in more old-fashioned language, Masters. These inner adepts may still be living and serving in vision, or they may be out of the death/life cycle and serving in the inner worlds.

Those still living are "hidden" from the world of the living to serve in the Inner Desert. Visionary adepts often find themselves suddenly called to work in vision, or overcome with an overwhelming need to sleep. When they wake, they often feel as though they have been working hard and are even more exhausted: they were working in vision alongside the gods of the Desert in service, briefly, in the Inner Desert.

The Ribbon gives us another clue about the nature of those in the Desert whom the text describes as "the Best." The Ribbon is connected to serpent power, is usually red, and is worn on the head of the Justified. It is also often seen on the heads of goddesses in wall paintings.

In a living adept candidate's final round of magical trials and tests, they are placed in a visionary situation that is triggered by Renenutet, the cobra goddess. The name of the adept is recorded, and they are birthed into their new life as a Justified adept.

Part of this process involves placing on their head what appears in vision as a red ribbon. This is an outer depiction of the power of the cobra goddess Renenutet, and is gifted to the adept by Isis. It is a reforming of the adept's *measure*. In their trials, their life measure—their harvest—was torn apart and renewed in a different form. It also links the protective power of Renenutet to the adept. Renenutet is the goddess of the harvest in all senses, of crops, of pregnancy (she is also the ninth month), of life, and of the naming of that

First Hour

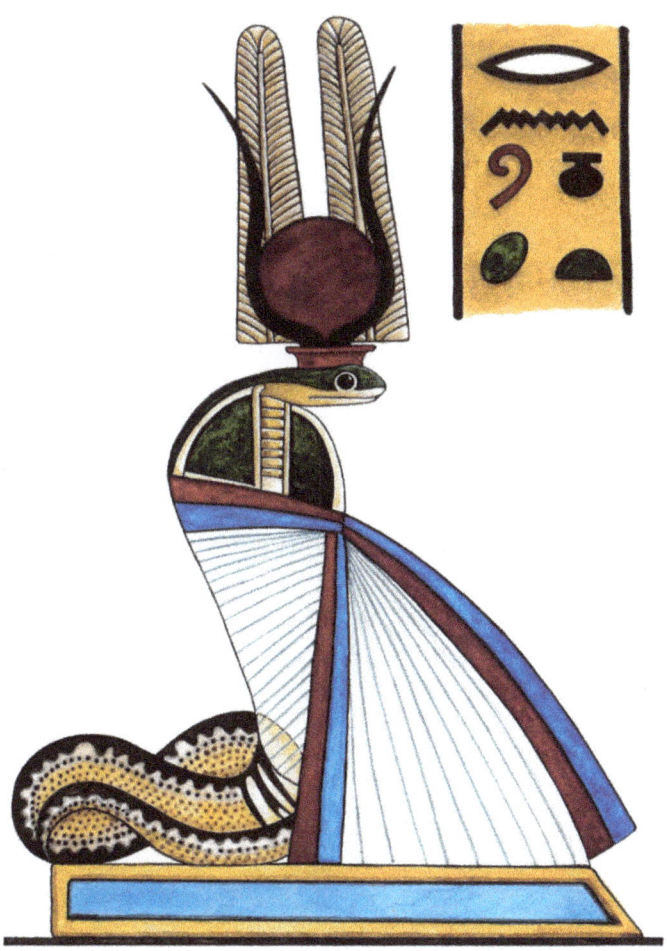

Renenutet

life. The Ribbon, magically, is also a version of the cord that holds an adept's life measure.

> Influential is this bread,
>> The ordaining words of the Great God,
>> When he exalts/refines his members.

The bread theme has many magical layers to it, and on the surface can be confusing. But looking through magical eyes, what these lines are saying is: this cooking process is powerful. Bread in this context is the final product of winnowing, grinding, kneading, and rising—turning the harvested wheat/barley into bread. In this process, the finished people are like wheat seeds that can be transformed into bread. This is the process of Osiris. This is the root of the ritual link between bread and a Divine body.

The wheat/barley, separated from the chaff by air, then goes through an alchemical process and is reconstructed to become 'risen'—the allegory of becoming Justified. Those who are "of the gods" have succeeded in this process. "The ordaining words of the Great God" refers to the alchemical process of the Utterance that becomes a living human being, that is then governed in death by judgement—*wDa mdw* in Egyptian, literally "separating the words." It is a step in the whole cycle of creation/destruction of physical manifestation.

Scene 3

Standing in the Desert, a staff with a ram's head, with two kneeling figures either side of it. Left of the staff, Duat; right of the staff, Desert.

The accompanying text reads:

> "My Akhet to you;
>> The ordinance of brightness to you who are foremost!"

> While *they* are dismembered for him,
>> *They* have been selected who exist on the Desert:[13]

> "I have hidden you from those atop Earth.
>> My breath to you.
>> Provided is the Ribbon for the Best!"

Say these, who are of the gods:

"This is Re; and are these not the ordaining words
    Of the Great God who raises/refines his members?"

Say these of those in the Desert to Re:

"O you who have hidden us,
    Come then to us,
    Re, from whom we came forth.

Oho! For who is in his sun-disc?
    It is the Great God, of myriad developments."

Their gifts are bread loaves,
    Their beers are strong ales,
    Their cold refreshment is water.[14]

Now, putting forth to this Desert,
    Rendering gifts to those in it,
    Means (being) one of those in it.[15]

Commentary

In the third scene, a main feature is the Ram's head of Re. On either side of the pole, two deities are kneeling. They are the essence of the spirits of the Duat/Underworld and the Zemit/Inner Desert. Re addresses these powers, and the Justified ones within the Desert, and more or less repeats what was said in the last scene: he is delivering the Finished Ones so that they can be guided to the First Gate of the Duat.

---

[13] Here, *they* refers to two different groups.

[14] Here is the next stage of the gifts theme: now three sorts of gifts are provided. For easy future reference, we will call this triplet the "offering list." The theme will deepen greatly, as will the meanings of the offerings, as we journey through the book.

[15] The first instance of another theme whose meaning will deepen as we journey through the book: the synthesis of one who "renders gifts to X" with X itself.

It stands upright, in contrast to the image above it of the Was sceptre, Power, also flanked by the powers of the Duat and the Zemit, but placed upside down or in opposition.

Though this scene mainly repeats the last scene's content, it still holds pertinent clues to the magician. In fact, quiet clues are scattered throughout the *Gates*.

We know the allegory of bread and beer—that the gods and Justified in the Desert have been alchemically reborn/remade—but what about "their cold refreshment is water"? This refers to a process that happens in the path of the adept through life.

Those who reach deeply into the Inner Mysteries—which today means adepts and mystics and in Ancient Egypt would have meant some kings/queens and some priests/priestesses—learn through experience and sound judgement to tame and tap into the *fire within*. This is a deep and profound power that burns within some people destined for magic. If they learn to tame it and work with it then it becomes a source of their magical power—*wAs*. The fire is cooled, tamed, and worked with: it becomes their "refreshment" so long as they do not deviate from their fulcrum of balance, in which case they burn once more.

If they do not learn how to tame it then it consumes them. This is the basis for the mental, emotional, or physical imbalances that can literally burn through a magician. It becomes the fire of madness, or the fire of inflammation that consumes and destroys. The taming of the fire is never finished; it is a constantly developing process of polishing, refining, and constant testing. The fire burns when the adept makes a wrong move. The fire is the root of the "adversary," a power in constant opposition to the magician, which grinds away at them to polish them through struggle throughout their lives. The experiences of these struggles, and the wisdom and perception they gain from them, become keys that help them navigate the *Gates*.

In ancient Egypt, this adversary was the power of Set, a destructive force of fire and heat, yet part of creation, destruction, and order. This power opposes creation to maintain balance: it is part of the process of Ma'at. Set was an adversary to Apep, the power of chaos which threatens everything.

The power of Set within Justified ones who serve has been tamed, and thus nourishes them. They can work with the power in coolness, and the Desert holds no threat to them.

So the first set of scenes of the First Hour establishes who the newly dead are. It also introduces who the assistants and guides of the Desert are that receive the Finished Ones, and introduces the power of the Desert, Zemit, and the power of the Underworld, Duat, who act together to create a threshold.

As an aside, the two powers of Duat and Zemit which act together are heavily linked to Aker, the two powers within one that constitute the Akhet (the horizon, or the threshold between one world and another) who is often depicted as two lions facing each other. Magically, when you are working in this system, it is important to pay attention to details and to understand fully the often mind-boggling series of connections and weaves between the powers. Understanding the connections between Aker and the two powers of Duat/Zemit will be helpful to magicians working this system.

This is one of the hieroglyphic names of Aker: notice Set and the bird? And remember that hieroglyphic words were not just sounds put together; they have many layers of meaning and interpretation.

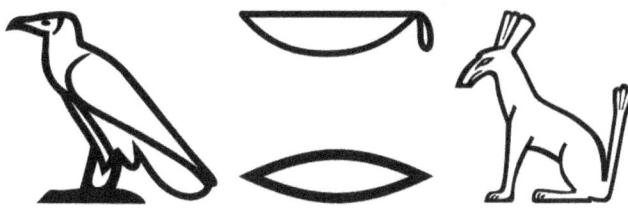

In the first hour you have the staff of Set, the Was staff, and the staff of Re, the Ram staff. Set—fire and air—is one of the main powers of the outer Desert and the Zemit, and Re is the power of the sun which lights up the Duat.

Aker is the threshold, and has a big presence in the Zemit and the Duat. In *The Coffin Texts* Aker becomes the ferryman of Re in the nocturnal barque, and in *The Book of the Dead* Aker carries Khepri's sarcophagus through the Underworld Caverns.

Aker is the past and future—yesterday and tomorrow—the threshold that allows the 'now' to exist, and he guards the east–west boundaries: life and death.

Magically, the power of the Zemit and the Duat are entwined. The Desert is the threshold between the living world and the Underworld. When you add Aker into that mix, and understand the presence of Aker in the Zemit and Duat, then you get some interesting power patterns.

The ones who are "of the gods," the Justified ones who work in service here, meet and greet the newly dead, and explain the processes they are about to undergo. If the dead king is successful, then he or she will become 'Osiris' i.e. as bread that is risen and/or reconstituted.

When an adept candidate undertakes this process while still in life and succeeds, then they become first an Osiris in life, a Finished One, and then Justified: of Just Voice. The meanings of those terms will become clearer to you as we go through the gates.

Scene 4

This scene is identical to Scene 1. On Seti I's coffin, it begins with "a hidden place for their selection," and ends with "for his Western Eye."

First Gate

A giant serpent:

> The Guardian of the Desert.

The accompanying text reads:

> He exists over this door;
>   He opens for Re.

Perception to the Guardian of the Desert:

"Open your portal for Re;
  Open your door for He of the Akhet.
The Hidden Region is in pregnant darkness
  Until the developments develop of this god."

Sealed is this door
  After this god enters.
Alas, then, for the ones in their Desert,
  Should they hear the shutting of this door.

First Hour

The First Gate on Seti I's sarcophagus.

Commentary

At the threshold of the First Gate, we meet the guardian of the Desert. Magically, this guardian prevents those who should not be there from getting any further and passing through the First Gate. The Inner Desert, or Zemit, is a boundary place that gives the magician access to lots of different realms that come together at this threshold. The guardian prevents the living from accessing deeper places inappropriately, and prevents the mundane, unbalanced dead from entering the process of the *Gates*.

At the beginning of the gate, Perception tells the guardian to open the gate. In some translations Perception is presented as Sia, the power of perception embodied in a deity, but this has led to a misunderstanding of exactly who is commanding the gate to open. It is not a deity who commands, but the candidate undergoing the gate's trials, be they dead or alive.

The command comes from the candidate's inner knowledge as they stand before the gate. Each gate tests, weighs, and measures within the person who stands before the gate. With the First Gate, the candidate declares that they know what they are asking for: access to the dangerous and powerful trials that lie ahead. They *know*, and they feel that they are ready.

The darkness is "pregnant," full of potential. It will not be birthed until the human spirit—the *Ba*, which Michael translates as "Presence"—has been fully through the process.

If they successfully complete the *Gates*, then they become an Akh, which Michael translates as "Radiant." Their inner consciousness becomes fully awakened and aware of the Mysteries and the powers of the Divine.

"He Who Is Of The Akhet" is the candidate for renewal through the *Gates*. The living magician seeks regeneration and Justification through surviving and successfully completing the *Gates*. The process for the dead and the living magician is the same.

The guardian of the First Gate is a powerful and often terrifying being. A magician for whom I have a great deal of respect once recounted to me the first time he tried to penetrate deep into the Inner Desert, to access a threshold there: he was painfully and unceremoniously bounced out of the vision and left to tend his bruises.

So for a living magician who wishes to traverse the *Gates* and attain Justification, the first test at the First Gate involves their inner senses, knowledge, perception, and their inner spirit: their developed ability to work in vision.

Second Hour

Scene 5

Twelve striding figures, who are the first half of a set of twenty-four figures (the second twelve being in Scene 6):

Those who are at peace, who adore Re...[16]

The accompanying text reads:

> They, having adored Re on Earth,
>   They, having ensorcelled Apep;
> They, having put forth their peace
>   Made a consecration for their godhoods:
>
> They are themselves after their peace.
>
> They come into power by means of their cold refreshment.[17]
>   They receive their gifts.
> They feed upon their peace
>   At the gate of he whose identity is hidden.
> Their gifts are at this gate;
>   Their peace is in the presence of who is in it.

---

[16]The second half of the title is in Scene 6.

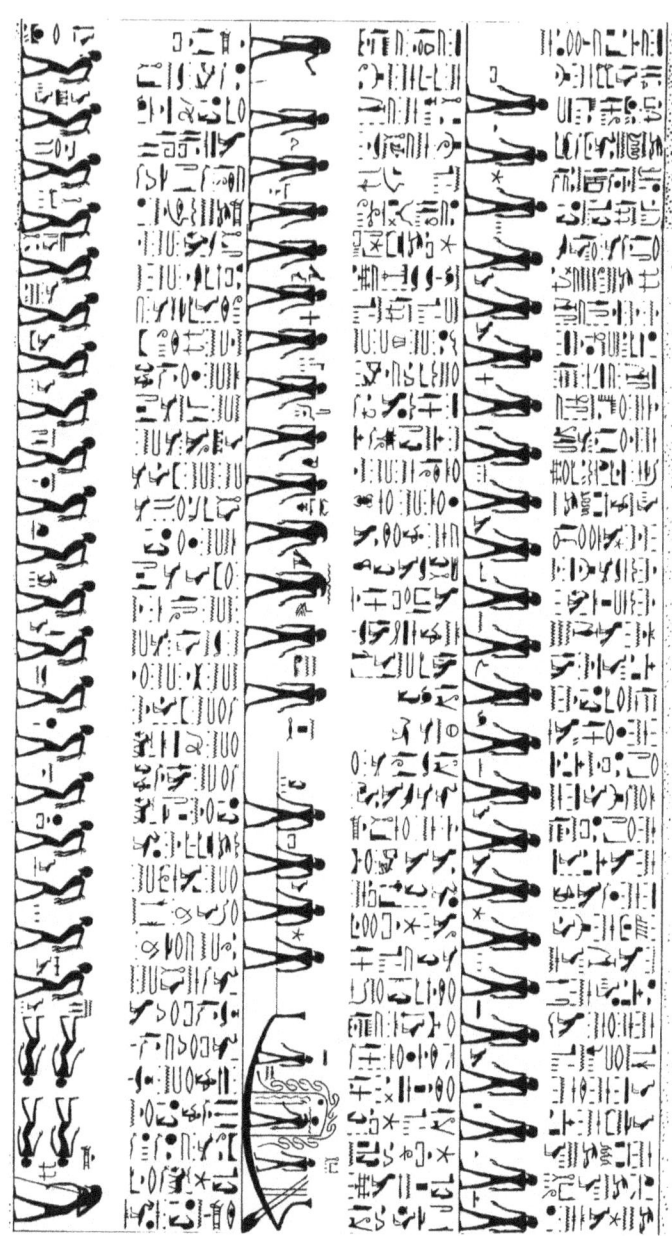

The Second Hour (Bonomi and Sharpe 1864)

Says to them Re:

"You are those who are in your peace.
  You come into power by means of your cold refreshment.
For are your Presences not selected?
  Would your gifts be wiped away?
You are those who adore me;
  Who rail, for me, against Apep."[18]

Commentary

As the second hour opens, we are introduced to qualities, workers, and candidates who are undertaking a passage through the Duat. This multilayered approach is a feature of each hour, and each layer must be understood in relation to the others.

Each hour deals with particular human qualities; this one deals particularly with "those who are at peace." This hour examines being at peace, and describes workers who have achieved this quality and who have chosen to stay in the Duat in service to aid the dead, living candidates of the Mysteries, and the progress of Re through the Duat.

As you progress through the gates, you will find that the previous hour's qualities often overlap with the next one's: each hour develops from, and builds on, the previous one.

The first part of the text speaks about workers in the Duat. They used their inner knowledge to suppress Apep, and their inner stillness, their peace, is declared. It states that their inner stillness is a product of how they lived their lives: "they are themselves after their peace." It speaks of the cooling of the inner fire, and their acceptance in life of the gifts that come to the candidate of Justification in life or death: the trials that grind and polish. Those trials and the inner stillness that comes from a magical, mystical, or spiritual life nourishes them, and gets them ready for the trials of the *Gates*.

---

[17]The association of "cold refreshment" with coming into power will be important later.

[18]These (hopefully rhetorical) questions set up the contrast between the selected/adorers of Re and the dismembered/adorers of Apep, which will be the main theme of this hour.

It also speaks to those possessing these qualities who are traversing the hours in death or in life. It says, "if you have these qualities, they are the key to safe passage through the gate." Those inner gifts and developments, that stillness, is then offered to the power of the gate. Stillness triggers stillness, and the peace radiates to the threshold keeper of the gate.

Then the candidates/workers are addressed by Re and told that they will not have their lifetime of experience taken away: their inner accomplishments stand. This is very similar to the Greek account of the death process and the drinking of water from Lethe, the river of forgetfulness, from which adepts of the Mysteries were warned not to drink. Re is warning them of a process that is coming, but also telling them that because of their 'gifts,' their lifetime achievements, or their service in the Duat, they will not have their 'remembering' taken from them.

Let's look briefly at the Greek version of the *Gates*: the passage through Hades.

If you look closely at the powers of the five rivers of Hades, and the mother and sisters of Lethe, then you will start to see parallels with the *Gates*.

The five rivers of Hades are:

Styx	boundary
Cocytus	lamentation
Acheron	sorrow
Lethe	forgetfulness
Phlegethon	fire

In Hesiod's *Theogony*, which was composed around 700 B.C., the mother and sisters of Lethe outline how habits acquired when alive can become traps in the Underworld. The mother of Lethe is Eris (Strife) and her sisters are Ponos (hardship), Limos (starvation), Algae (pains), Hysminai (battles), Makhai (wars), Phonoi (murders), Androktasiai (manslaughters), Neikea (quarrels), Pseudea (lies), Logoi (stories), Amphillogiai (disputes), Dysnomia (anarchy), Ate (ruin), and Horkos (oaths).[19]

As you can see, Hesiod's advice for mortals passing through the Underworld has more to do with mundane living, whereas the *Gates*, which is much older, is more concerned with a person's magical and mystical evolution. Nevertheless, it is interesting to compare the two texts, and you will see why this is pertinent as we progress through the early hours.

---

[19] Hesiod and Anon 1914, pp.96–97, l.226–232

Scene 6

Twelve more striding figures, the second half of the set of twenty-four figures (the first twelve being in Scene 5):

...are the Righteous in the Duat.

The accompanying text reads:

> They spoke Truth upon Earth.
>> They did not arise to railing speech.
>> They are called forth to this gate.
>
> Their lives are in Truth.
>> Their cold refreshment is in their lake.
>
> Says to them Re:
>
> "Truth is yours; it is of your life.
>> Your peace is yours; it is of Truth."
>
> They come into power by means of their cold refreshment.
>> Which watering is as fire
>> For sinners, companions of crookedness.
>
> These ones of the gods say to Re:
>
> "Established is Re with his sun-disc.
>> Powerful is the shrine, and he who is in it.
>> Spiral is for his guarding."
>
> The illumination of He of the Akhet investigates
>> Those in the Gate of the Place of the Mysteries.
> Now, rendering them gifts
>> Means being in the peace of a seat in their cavern.

Commentary

The Righteous—whether workers, dead, or living candidates—are identified in the second hour as people whose lives are lived according to Ma'at, in balance and truth. (The word Ma'at is rendered simply as "Truth" in this translation, though the English word does not do full justice to the Egyptian concept.) Ma'at is the underlying principle of order in the universe, and those who avoided manifesting disorder—"arising to railing speech"—are called to the gate.

In life, a magician, priest, priestess, or monarch, will be confronted by ever more difficult trials to test their Ma'at, their Sia, and their Heka. Sia, which is (Inner) Perception, and Heka, which is Magic, are both fed by and governed by the principle of Ma'at.

When a tide of destruction rolls through your life, how you deal with that tide, using your Perception and Magic while upholding Truth, is what determines the development of your skills, knowledge, and evolution. Remember, Perception guides the Sun Barque through the Underworld, while Magic moves the rudder...

The trials of the *Gates* are not new; they are echoes and tests of trials overcome in life. Each gate measures and confirms what the candidate already overcame in life.

Those who overcame those trials in life, through their Perception and Magic, while operating within Ma'at, lived their lives in Truth, and their cold refreshments are in their lake. They transformed their potentially destructive inner fire into something cool and nourishing.

It is not just dead and living candidates of the Mysteries who move forward through the hours according to their measure; as we go through this text you will also see how people working in service in the Duat are moved from one hour to the next.

> They come into power by means of their cold refreshment.
>   Which watering is as fire
>   For sinners, companions of crookedness.

This is another reference to the inner fire that can burn and destroy, the inner fire that for the 'ungodly,' i.e. those who did not transform and evolve, remains as fire.

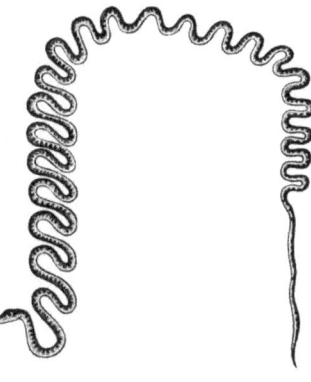

Mehen

"Established is Re with his sun-disc.
 Powerful is the shrine, and he who is in it.
 Spiral is for his guarding."

Mehen, rendered as **Spiral** in Michael's translation (see the Glossary entry), is a great serpent who protects both Re and the Righteous, and who directly opposes Apep.

The illumination of He of the Akhet investigates
Those in the Gate of the Place of the Mysteries.

When you work in vision, your **Presence**, which the Egyptians called your *Ba*, is at work in the realm you are visiting. Your Presence is your magical inner aspect. When a deity meets you in vision, they are meeting your Presence; you are, in vision, a Presence; a *Ba*.

Here, the light of "He of the Akhet," who may be the candidate, a magical worker, or the god Re, touches those who dwell in the far depths of the Duat with their brightness. The Ma'at that the candidate carries within them affects those in the depths, and the candidate briefly visits them, lighting up the space for them.

This is an interesting part of the *Gates*. In life, visionary adepts who work within this Egyptian system, and who work in service, go in vision to the depths of the Duat and visit the powers that dwell there. These powers, who present as deities and often as serpent powers, dwell by choice in the depths in darkness, as their power would be far too destructive in the physical world. By them staying where they are, the physical world, and order, is maintained.

The candidate visits these powers by bringing their brightness to the darkness, and gifts the deity in the depths with the candidate's emanation of inner peace and stillness.

In adept training, one of the things the adept is taught to do is to descend to these depths and visit with deep deity powers who have withdrawn from the world. Often the deity asks the adept for the gift of temporary brightness, which is done by the adept mediating the lights of the Milky Way into the deep cavern where the deity resides. This is an act of both compassion and veneration for the sacrifice these powers make by withdrawing themselves for the good of all living beings.

It also introduces us to another aspect of the hours, one you will come across quite a bit. Some of the dead can pause in their journey through the Duat, and rest in a cavern. This has many different magical connotations. Some of those resting are akin to Sleepers, ancestors who sleep within the Earth. Others are hibernating in the silence. Some are restricted to one area until they have undergone certain transformations. And others stay in certain caverns as an act of service.

Once through the first gate, the candidate casts their brightness into the depths of the second hour as an act of compassion, as does Re. He casts his light into the darkness before moving towards the second gate.

Scene 7

The Sun Barque, in the centre of which is the Meat of Re, with Spiral over him. In the front of the barque is Perception; by the oars, Magic. The barque is towed

by four Underworlders. Thirteen figures stride towards the Sun Barque, the first seven of whom each have a name:

    Grain

    Armless

    Presence

    Distant One

    Freed of Heart

    Union

    Child/Foster Child

The remaining six are named as a group:

    Gods who are entering

The accompanying text reads:

> The voyaging of this great god on the paths of the Duat.
>   The towing of this god by gods, by Underworlders.
>
> For making the divisions within the Earth.
>   For making the designs for the ones in it.
>   For separating the words in the West.
>
> For making a great one from a small one
>   Among the gods in the Duat.
>
> For putting the Radiant on their seats,
>   And the Mortal to their separation.[20]
>
> For causing destruction of what remains to be persecuted
>   Concerning what is criminal of a Presence.

---

[20] Remember the promise that *they* would be dismembered?

Says Re:

"O behold me: I provided the Ribbon.
   You came into power by me through the shrine in the Earth.

Perception and Magic united with me
   To formulate your business, and transform your forms."

He does not seal his breath from you.
   There is peace, which is in her[21] peace.
There is no entry for the Mortal at your threshing floor.
   Your portion is what belongs to gods.

Say these of the gods to Re:

"Pregnant darkness is on the paths of the Duat.
Open the sealed portals, you who part the Earth,
   Towed by the gods, creator of himself."

Their gifts are into offerings;
   Their beers are into their cold refreshment.[22]

The giving to them of gifts
   Is in the Silent Land, in the West."

---

[21]"Her" probably refers to the Hour which we are passing through (Hornung and Abt 2014, p. 42).

[22]*Awt.sn m <u>Hnkt, Hnqt.sn m qbHw.sn</u>* Pay attention to the wordplay here, for all is not as it seems. Superficially, this couplet reads: "their gifts are gifts (synonym), their beers are cold refreshment." This line replaces here the usual 'offering list': "their gifts are bread loaves, their beers are strong ales, their cold refreshment is water." Right away we should notice that something is going on here, because "their gifts are gifts" is a tautology, and "their beers are cold refreshment" implies pouring an ice-cold beer right over one's head, not drinking it. In the normal offering list, the "cold refreshment" is water—and there is nothing cooly refreshing about water-borne stomach bugs. The word for "cold refreshment" is usually used to describe libations, not beverages. The suggestion is to cool down by pouring water—or apparently in this case, a nice cold beer—all over yourself. This couplet is not satisfying when taken literally, which suggests that we might want to try *not* taking it literally. Deciphering this couplet provides us with the first clue in a classic grimoire-style word puzzle. Solving the puzzle will unlock the true meaning of the 'offering list.' *Hnkt* "gifts" and *Hnqt* "beers," the words at the centre of this unusual couplet, differ only by the placement—back or forwards in the throat—of one consonant: *q* versus *k*. And if we treat the *q* in *Hnqt* as a *k*, giving us

Commentary

The scene opens with a gathering of gods, workers, and so forth, who assist the passage of the Sun Barque through the gate. Mehen/Spiral protects the deity in the barque, and the powers of Magic and Perception guide the barque through the Duat towards the Hall of Judgement.

The purpose of this journey to the Judgement Hall is "making a great one from a small one," i.e. the Justification process. It distinguishes between those Justified in life who are now travelling through death, and those not Justified in life who are now in death and ready to face that process: "To put the Radiant on their seats, and the Mortal to their separation."

In the adept Justification process, a candidate who has successfully completed the trials is given a seat among the gods beyond the final gate. On death the Justified adept travels to their seat, and in life, visits and works with the gods in their sitting place. The monarch, if Justified in life, would be travelling towards that sitting place to take up their position as a god among the gods.

This opening scene also tells us that, as in all the other gates, there are destructive functions at work. Here "what is criminal of a Presence" is torn apart, and the Presence of the wicked is restricted or locked down: the second death.

One of the main features of the Underworld is the locking down of what should not surface. This also applies to mundane people who have got through the First Gate but who should not be there, as well as monarchs and adepts who became Justified in life but then failed to uphold their responsibilities.

The second part of the scene is a four line speech by Re, and a four line commentary about him. Re expresses his Justification: he has the Ribbon, and he has the shrine in the earth, and his Perception and Magic are skills within him. This is an interesting declaration from this god: "I have completed the process so that you too can complete it." It brings to mind the Christian concept of Jesus undergoing the Harrowing of Hell, his successful completion of which enables others to also be successful. Maybe that Christian concept has its roots in this Egyptian pattern?

---

two *Hnkt*s, then we get a couplet that describes a well-known magical and mystical dynamic: "Their gifts into their offerings; their offerings into their cold refreshment." To paraphrase: "First you must give, then you will receive." Substituting *k* for *q* will be important later on in solving the 'offering list' puzzle.

The commentary that follows states that "there is no entry for the Mortal at your threshing floor. Your portion is what belongs to gods." This is speaking about a threshold beyond which the Mortal, people unsuitable for the trial by scales, cannot pass. The Threshing Floor beyond that threshold is where the very best are harvested, and those who successfully undergo that trial become "of the gods," i.e. *as gods*.

This is the first clue that the *Gates* operates on a higher, more powerful octave than other funerary texts which include trial by scales, as its scales weigh the harvest of "those of the gods," as opposed to the more mundane scales in, for example, *The Book of the Dead*, which merely weigh good and evil, truth and untruth.

The candidate, dead or living, must move forward and journey deep into the Duat to be tested by the scales in the presence of the gods, a step in the process of Justification.

In the final part of this scene, those who are "of the gods" in this part of the Duat address Re. They talk about the "pregnant darkness," i.e. the darkness of gestation, from which Justified life—Osiris—can spring. They call on Re to open the gates due to his Divine presence, being the one who was self-begotten and self-winnowed. By his passage in the barque, as the solar deity passing through the Underworld, Re opens the gates—and this lets human candidates pass through them, providing they are fit to do so.

Scene 8

A figure leans on a staff:

> A Finished One

Before him lie four figures:

> The Idle

Second Hour

Before them stand twenty figures with their arms bound behind their backs:

Ones of the Desert, of the Forecourt of Re,
    Who were spiteful of Re on Earth.
Who made evocation, for evil, against the One In The Egg.
    Threshed are the Witnesses of those who have uttered noise
        against He of the Akhet!

The accompanying text reads:

Done by a Finished One for Re:

Becoming radiant, as a god,
    Adoring the Presence of him.[23]
    Repelling the evil of his adversaries:

"True of Voice is my father Re against you;
    True of Voice am *I* against you.
I, the son who came forth from his father;
    I, the father who came forth from his son.

You are bound.
    Your bonds are enduring lashes.
I have ordained for you your bindings;
    There will be no opening of your arms.

The radiance of Re is against you;
    Quick is his Presence against you.
The Power of my father is against you;
    The valour of his Presence is against you.
Your evil is upon you;
    Your carnage is against you.
Your spite is upon you.
    Your wages are according to your evil.

You have been scrutinized by Re.
    Threshed is your witness, which is yours, which is evil;
And your deep darkness, which is yours, which is wicked.
    You have been scrutinized in the presence of my father.

You are those who have done evil,
   Who have done carnage in the Great Forecourt.
Your remains are to be cut out;
   Your Presences are for nonexistence.
You shall not look upon Re in his forms
   As he voyages through the Place of the Mysteries.

Oho, Re!
   You are valiant, Re!
   And your enemies are for the Place of Destruction."

Commentary

This is the scene where those who have reached this far into the Duat, but should not be there, are dealt with. "Ones of the Desert" refers to those who belong in the Desert, who should not have passed beyond the first gate. The utterance of Re binds them, dismembers them, and beheads them: *Hsq*, **cut out**, also means "behead." Beheading is a specific action in the Duat, and part of the second death process.

This scene also brings up specific actions which express in the Mysteries as the "Harvest." You will have noticed a theme of winnowing, threshing, grinding, and making into bread. The threshing is a process that happens in the life of the initiate and adept, where the sum total of their actions are threshed, assessed, and weighed in the scales.

The weighing of the life harvest is the process that happens to the candidate in the Hall of Judgement; but in this scene, Re preempts that process for those who carry a 'bad' harvest:

> Threshed is your witness, which is yours, which is evil...You have been scrutinized in the presence of my father.

This preempting gets rid of the undesirables before they reach the Hall of Judgement, the destination for those Justified in life who are now dead, and also living candidates who are seeking Justification.

---
[23] Re.

Again, for a successful passage through the *Gates*, it is one's actions in life that matter, not how one behaves at the thresholds of the gates. This understanding seems to be lost or ignored in some versions of *The Book of Going Forth by Day* a.k.a. *The Book of the Dead*, a funerary text that became more widely used by anyone who could afford it. *The Book of Going Forth by Day* exists in many different versions, many of which contain spells to fool the guardians, and to force the heart to speak good things on behalf of the dead, regardless of how they behaved.

As we see in *The Book of Gates*, getting past one set of guardians does not mean safety: the undeserving dead are caught out by various traps along the way. This is most likely happening in this scene: the undeserving are bound up and torn apart by the threshing and utterance of Re.

Second Gate

The arrival by this god at this gate;
   The entry into this gate.

The gods in it worship this Great God.

Gate caption:

Quick-Thinking

Uraeus serpents caption:

She kindles for Re

Guardian captions:

Who Absorbs Corruption: he bends his arms for Re.

Who Swallows Blood: he bends his arms for Re.

Mummies caption:

The Second Nine:

"Open is the gate for He of the Akhet;
   Revealed is the door for One of the Skies.

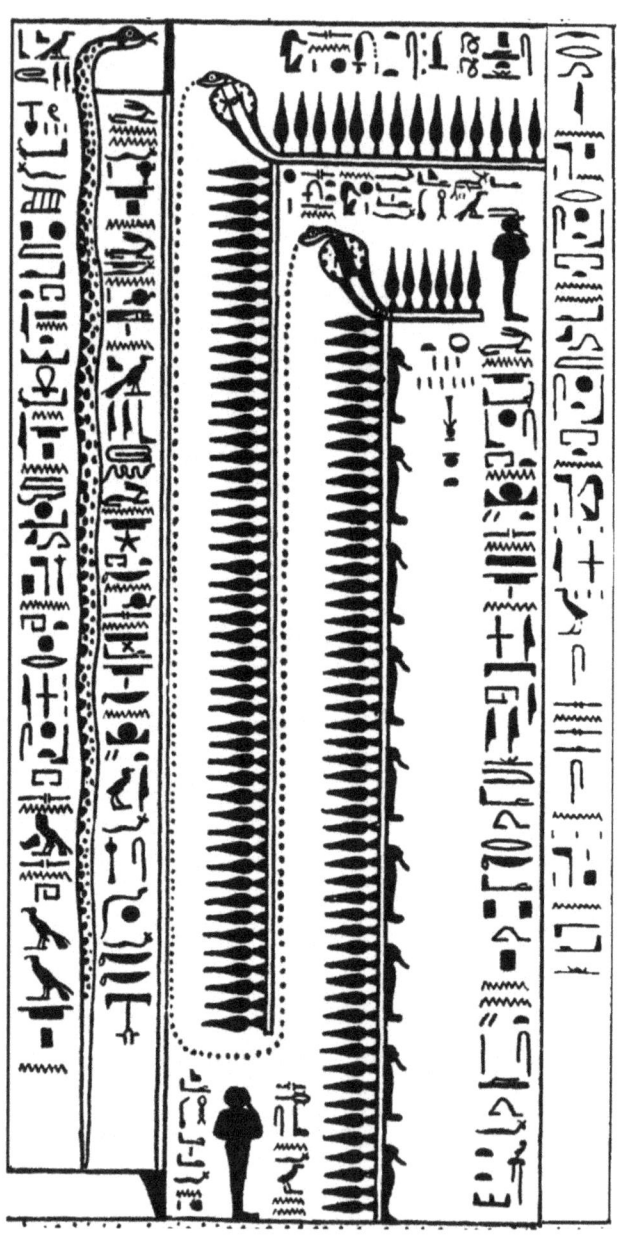

The Second Gate on Seti I's sarcophagus.

Oho! Come now, that one who is passing through, he who voyages the West!"

Doorway serpent caption:

Coiling One:

He exists over this door;
    He opens for Re.

Perception to Coiling One:

"Open your portal for Re;
    Reveal your door for He of the Akhet.
Now he makes bright the Original Darkness;
    He gives a lightening in/from the Hidden Region."

Sealed is this door
    After the entry of this Great God.
Alas, then, for the ones in their gate,
    Should they hear the shutting of this door.

Commentary

And now we arrive at the second gate. You will notice that each gate is a being within itself: it is named and has powers, and around it are guardians and assistants who either trap and attack, or allow the candidate through. As before, the passage of the brightness of Re through the gate opens it and lets the candidate proceed if it is appropriate.

This gate is pretty straightforward and should be understandable by now. Notice it is Sia—Perception, inner senses, inner knowledge—that speaks to the serpent at the gate. For candidates, it is their inner knowledge and magic that repeatedly moves them through the gates—their attained magical wisdom.

Also notice that the gate is then closed to those who should pass no further: "Alas, then, for the ones in their gate, should they hear the shutting of this door." They are plunged into darkness and must await the next passage of Re to light up the hour again for them. If they have then developed enough in that hour, then they will move forward with Re through the gate and into the next hour...and into their next stage of development.

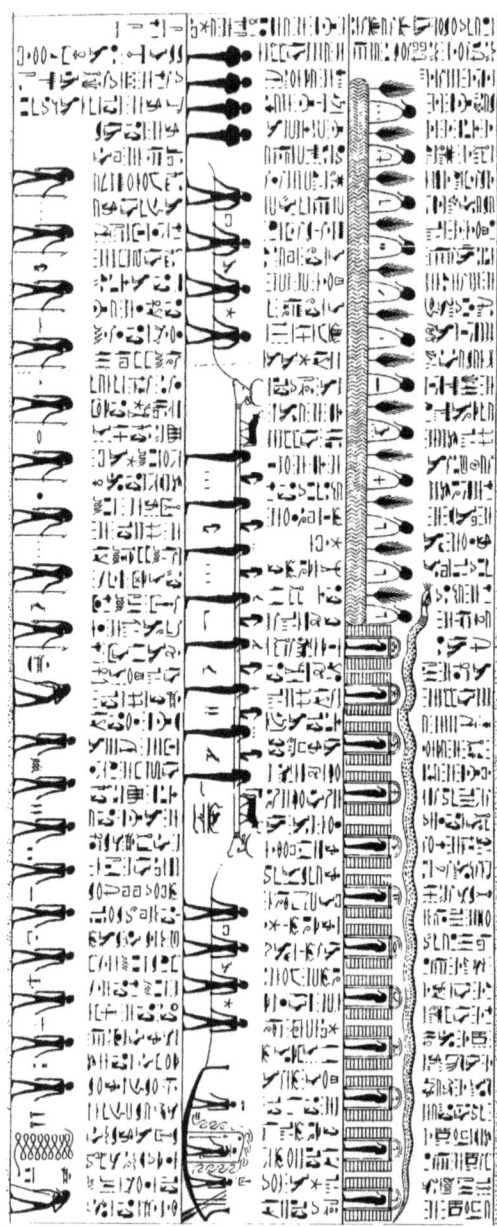

The Third Hour (Bonomi and Sharpe 1864).

Third Hour

Scene 9

Twelve shrines, their doors open, black mummies inside each. A great serpent, called Glister, lies over them.

The accompanying text reads:

    Gods, hallowed,[24] in the Duat;
        In their shrines, the flesh[25] of a god.
        Glister, he guards their shrines.

Says Re to them:

"Let there be opening for your shrines!
    My brightness shall enter upon your darkness/greed;[26]
For I have found you mourning,
    And your shrines sealed over you.
For a while I shall give breath to your nose,
    While I ordain as yours your abhorrence/overflow."[27]

Say they to Re:

"Oho, Re! Come then to us,
  Great God, who is ignorant of his wiping away;
One whom, those ones before him—his followers,
  His entourage—enquire about his distance.[28]
Twice joyful it is, when Re spreads across the Earth,
  And when the Great God passes through the Place of the
    Mysteries."

Their gifts are bread loaves,
  Their beers are strong ales,[29]
  Their cold refreshment is water.

Now, giving as them means living
  As they live: Glister being in them.

---

[24] *Dsryw*, "hallowed." This is the first time in the text that we have encountered this word. Usually it has a sense both of "holiness" and "set-apart-ness." However, these beings are not necessarily as holy as they seem...see the commentary. Also significant is the similarity between *Dsrw*, "hallowed," and *Dsrt*, "strong ale," an ingredient of the 'offering list' first encountered in Scene 3. (This, along with these "hallowed" beings who are not necessarily holy at all, is the second clue to unlocking the true meaning of the 'offering list.' Store it away in the back of your mind for later.)

[25] Usually *Haw* is translated **members**.

[26] *snkw* It is not clear from this word's odd spelling whether it means "greed" or "darkness." Like several words in this text, it possesses some odd features which seem to wave at the reader to pay careful attention. The question to be answered is: is this word "greed" or "darkness"? It is possible that the second *k* for *snkkw*, "darkness," has been omitted; but then why the sun determinative? The expected determinative for the word is N2, the sky with a broken *wAs* sceptre, not N5, the sun-disk (Gardiner 1957, p.485). In our opinion, the word evokes both concepts: darkness and greed together. The sun determinative is intended to direct our attention to the *things that shine* in the scene: Glister the serpent, the "flesh of the gods" in the shrines, and Re. For *snkw*, see Faulkner 1962, p.234.

[27] *baHw*, plural of *baH*, which can mean either "have abundance, be well-supplied, flood, inundate, fill up, overflow, be sated" or "be detested." We have already had one instance in this scene of a word serving double-duty; this is another. For *baH*, see Faulkner 1962, p.81. These "hallowed" beings are being revealed as anything but: they are dark and greedy, and have filled themselves to overflowing with *stuff*. The hieroglyph is also a visual pun on the Akh bird: instead of being a noble crested ibis (G25), they are represented as a heron on a perch (G31) (Gardiner 1957, p.470). The heron, when it is not on a perch, is the determinative used in the word *bnw* "Benu Bird/Phoenix." The problem with these people is that they *will not get off their perch*. The meaning of this will reveal itself when we deal with the Benu bird later.

Third Hour 63

> Sealed then are their doors upon them
>   After the passing of this god.
> Alas, then, for them, when they hear
>   The shutting of their doors upon them.

Commentary

The third hour opens with Re passing through the depths of the Underworld. For magicians who work in the Underworld, they will recognize the deities sealed and guarded here: these are synonymous with the ancient deities and beings sealed up in the caves of the Abyss.

Also found here are those who in life became *as gods* but who were unbalanced enough to require sealing up in the Underworld as they traversed death. If a human completes the stages of Justification in life, but seriously fails to uphold that balance, then they do not suffer the second death; they 'live' eternally, but become trapped in the Underworld. As Re passes through the depths, the brightness shines on them briefly, awakening them. They mourn his passing as they are once more cast into darkness.

---

[28] They are asking, in an exceptionally toadying way, "you who do not know what it is like to be destroyed, why are you so far apart from us?" They claim to be his followers…they may believe they are, but they are not…

[29] We are now in a position to apply the first two clues to this line: replacing *q* with *k*, and reading "hallowed" into *Dsrt* instead of *Dsrt* "strong ales." This gives us *Hnkt.sn m Dsrt*. We can make sense of this if we read *Hnkt.sn* as a *sDmtj.fj* form of *Hnk* "make offering (+ *m*) of," (Faulkner 1962, p.173), with the *j* not written because of the plural ending (see Allen 2014, p.394, 23.13.) This gives us: "…who will make offering of the hallowed things (vessels)". So at this stage, our 'offering list' now reads: "Their gifts are bread loaves, they who will make offering of hallowed vessels, their cold refreshment is water." Well, these beings may well want to offer their so-called 'hallowed vessels,' but you can decide for yourself whether Re is going to accept them. In fact, we could also read *awt.sn* "their gifts" as a *sDmtj.fj* form as well, which would give us "they who will extend." This will be important later.

Scene 10

Twelve mummies seated between ears of barley, above a lake that is sometimes painted red in copies of this book:

> Gods in the Lake of Exaction

The accompanying text reads:

> That lake exists in the Duat;
>   It is compassed by these ones of the gods.
> They are inside their cloths,
>   But/And their heads/best are/is exposed.[30]
>
> This lake is filled from the final reckonings;[31]
>   The lapping of the lake is cords.
> Strangers are the sons who look upon its water;
>   Blackened is their front, staring at what is in it.

Says to them Re:

> "Your portions, which are of the gods,
>   Are in the reckonings of your lake.
> There is a stripping/uncovering for your heads/best,
>   Mysteries for your selves,
>   And breath for your nose.
> Your peace is what is yours of the final reckonings;
>   The extension[32] is yours, which is of your lake.
> Its water, which is yours, has no hotness from/for you;
>   It has no fiery blast from/for your remains."

---

[30] Note that *hAy*, "exposed," can also mean "shine over, illuminate."

[31] This word is a pun on the word for "barley," ears of which stand between each of the seated mummies in this scene.

[32] The "final reckonings" which are in the lake are here stated as being "extensions." *Awt*, which we have until now translated as "gifts." The word can also mean "extend, stretch" when

Third Hour

Part of the Lake of Exaction as depicted in the Tomb of Seti I.

Say they to Re:

"Come then to us, he who is ferried in his barque.
    His eye kindles/begets for him a lamplight;[33]
    His Akhet makes bright the Duat.
Oho! You arise, having Radiance for us;
    The Great God, who kindles/begets out of his eye.

Their extension is in the bread of the final reckonings;[34]
    They will make offering of the final reckonings.
    Their cold refreshment is water.

Now, giving as them, extending,[35]
    Means being a master of a rod[36] from this lake.

---

paired with a papyrus scroll determinative. We had our curiosity piqued about this word in the previous scene, where we noticed that just as *Hnkt.sn* could be translated as "they will make offering," *Awt.sn* could be translated to mean "they will extend," which gave us the reading, "they will extend into bread." Now in this scene, the "final reckonings," which have been identified with ears of barley...grown to make bread...are then identified with "extensions." Indeed, this barley will "extend into bread." This unlocks the hidden meaning of the first line of the 'offering list.' We can now read: "They will extend into bread, they who will make offering of hallowed vessels, their cold refreshment is water." The meaning of this will become much clearer as we continue our journey through the book.

Commentary

Though slightly more dramatic, the Lake of Exaction is very similar to the river Lethe, the river of forgetfulness. It also brings back up the dynamic in the Second Gate which tells those who *know themselves* that their life experience will not be stripped from them.

It is a lake of fire that strips the knowledge of the life just lived from those who do not know how to avoid it. Their heads are bare: they do not wear the Ribbon; they do not *know*.

The river contains their life harvest mirrored back to them: their memories, actions, and self-image are all contained within the lake, which they peer into. Its waters, filled with the records of their life, is very alluring: they wish to dive back into that life.

But the job of the lake is to burn off those memories to release the soul from the life that no longer exists: "Strangers are the sons who look upon its water." Just as drinking the river Lethe removes all memories of the life lived, so the Lake of Exaction burns off one's self-identity to release one from the binds of memory and life: "Blackened is their front, staring at what is in it."

Justified candidates in life are trained from quite early on not to partake of the gifts of this lake: *do not drink from the river lest you forget*. The Justified retain the knowledge of their life so that they can be truly held to account, and also so that they can retain that learning and knowledge. This also brings up something inherent within esoteric training: "Man, know thyself."

In Initiate and Adept training, you are taught to self-reflect and 'look in the mirror.' To see yourself for who you really are, and your acts for what they truly are, is a vital part of the Mysteries. Being able both to recognize and to accept yourself, to see your weaknesses and faults, and work on them, obviates the trial of the lake of fire/forgetfulness. Instead the lake becomes a mirror in which you see yourself, and can say: "I Know You." This transforms

---

[33] This is an instance of an English word being used more to distinguish between various Egyptian types of "flame" than for precise meaning. Read "flame, taper," and see **lamplight** in the Glossary.

[34] *Awt.sn m tA-kmwTyw* And here is the confirmation, bringing together the "extensions," the "bread," and the "final reckonings," which is a pun on "barley." This version of the line is only in this scene: afterwards it goes back to its usual "their gifts/extensions are in bread."

[35] And again, a further departure from the usual form. It seems to say: "by giving as these beings give, you extend, and so become a Master of Renewal in this lake." This is again persuading us to reframe "gifts" as "extending."

[36] The word (see Glossary) can refer to a stalk (here of barley), a staff, and rays of light, and has connotations of renewal and transformation.

this aspect of the trials of the Duat into a simple act of recognition: the lake of fire is cooled by your coolness.

For the mundane however, the lake's fire burns away their harvest. The fire that burns the harvest is also the fire within the person in life that they never tamed, the fire that drives people to behave outside the balance of Ma'at. Such fire, if not worked with, prevents a person from knowing who they really are.

The fire of the lake is not a punishing fire, and the burning off of a person's self-identity is also not a punishment, but an act of compassion. It releases them from the bonds of their previous life so that they can go back into life and try again.

So, we have passed by the gods sleeping in the Underworld and are now passing the dead who do not seek Justification, but who are currently trapped in a glamour of their own making.

The second part of this scene is a speech by Re. Re tells the dead that what they harvested from life is in the lake: whatever comes from that harvest will uphold them in the passage through death and back to life. If the harvest is poor, then He allows their faces to be stripped and their self-identity destroyed, while giving breath to their nostrils: their identity goes, but their chance of life does not.

In the final part of the scene, the people in the lake offer up their harvest to Re as he passes by. Note the last line, an instruction of compassion for the Justified as they pass by this place: "Now, giving as them, extending, Means being a master of a rod from this lake." Those who pass by with a good harvest will move on to become Justified. Doing so also brings renewal to the Underworld. This phrase both reflects the Mysteries of the harvest, and reminds the candidate that their act of Justification and renewal benefits all beings, not just themselves—and as such is an act of compassion.

Scene 11

The Sun Barque, in the centre of which is Re, with Spiral over him. In the front of the barque is Perception; by the oars, Magic. The barque is towed by four Underworlders.

In front of the Sun Barque is a long object with bulls' heads at either end, and two bulls standing at either end:

    The Earth Barque

Eight mummies carry it:

    Bearers

A figure sits in each of the seven spaces between the mummies:

    Indwelling Gods

Four figures tow the Earth barque:

    Underworlders

The accompanying text reads:

> The towing of this great god by gods, by Underworlders;
>> The arrival of this great god at the Earth Barque, ship's mast
>>> of the gods.

> Says to them Re:

> "O gods who are subjects of the Earth Barque,
>> Bearing the ship's mast of the Duat:
>
> Ascent to your forms,

And sun-breeze to your ship's mast,
    For hallowed is that which is in it.
The Earth Barque, it returns to me;
    The ship's mast of the Duat, it lifts up/weighs my forms.
Behold me as I pass through the Place of the Mysteries
    To make the designs of those in it.
The Earth tremors,
    The Earth tremors:
Valiant is the Ram/Presence
    Because of the Two Bulls'/Sustainers' lowings.
At peace is a god in what he has created/winnowed."

Say these of the gods to Re:

"Valiant is Re, quick his Ram/Presence when with Earth;[37]
    Valiant are his gods for Re in his peace.
Joyful is the ship's mast of the Duat..."

    ...But surpassed is this barque.
Alas then, for them, after Re's passing over them;
    Yet their peace is the young/the plants/in making years.

Now, giving to them their peace
    Means hearing their voice.

Commentary

This is where the barque starts to descend deeper into the Underworld and its Mysteries below. Re announces that the Earth, the physical world, is left behind as he progresses deeper into the Underworld; and Re tells the bearers of the barque to work hard and support the ship.

    He speaks of the earth lamenting the loss of the sun, but by passing through the Underworld, he blesses and brings brightness to the darkness of the depths. His harvest/actions as a deity bring brightness and peace to the Underworld.

---

[37] Here Earth receives a god determinative. The "his" of the following line may refer either to Re or Earth.

Re

The last part of this scene mirrors one of the Mysteries revealed in the last scene: that those in this place, this part of the Underworld, are nourished by the passing of those with good harvest: "Yet their peace is the young." Those candidates and Justified dead who pass through this place are walking towards renewal and becoming *as gods*: through their success, their becoming whole, a fragment of the vessel is healed. This is one part of the deeper esoteric Mysteries, and will be understood by mystics and adept candidates.

Successfully traversing this stage of the Underworld, and filling this place with one's inner peace, mirrors Re's dispensing of brightness to the darkness. It is a deep and profound service that happens simply by the actions of the candidate doing what they should be doing. Walking in life and death on the path of Ma'at benefits everything and everyone around you.

Scene 12

Four standing wrapped figures with invisible arms.

The accompanying text reads:

> The towing of this great god, by Underworlders,
>   By the hallowed barque in the Earth.
>
> Ordaining words for the wrapped-up ones whose arms are hidden:
>
> "Your portion which is yours, wrapped-up ones of the Earth;
>   The roar: 'His Hind Leg Is Forward!'
> Stripping for your heads/best,
>   Hiding for your arms,
> Breath for your nose,
>   Unravelling for your wrappings.
> You come into power by means of your extending;
>   You are at peace in what I have created/winnowed."
>
> Their extension is in bread.
>   They will make offering of hallowed things.[38]
>   Their cold refreshment is water.
>
> Now, rendering as them their extensions
>   Means that they make their linen dazzle in the Duat.

---

[38] No W23 jar determinative here. This is another hint for us to pick up the meaning of *Dsrt* here as including a whiff of hallowedness.

Commentary

In this section, Re passes through a place where some are bound and waiting in the Underworld. The deity utters to them and triggers the process of the "unravelling for your wrappings."

"Your portion which is yours, wrapped-up ones of the Earth; The roar: 'His Hind Leg Is Forward!'"

The shrieking utterance, which Michael has translated as "the roar," is referred to a lot in Egyptian texts in relation to the voices of the deities. It is about the power/vibration of the utterance that brings change. More than speaking, it is a command that triggers action simply through its sound.

The wrapped-up ones are commanded: "Let His Hind Leg Be Forward!" This is a magical command to move towards the future or rebirth. In Egyptian magic, the actions of the legs are triggers for the pathways ahead. Movement forward is south, to the future. The left leg triggers the path into life and the right leg triggers the path into death; this can be seen reflected in statues and wall paintings. The magical directional attributes are:

South	Forward	Future
North	Behind	Past
East	Left	Into Life
West	Right	Into Death

By commanding the wrapped-up ones to put their hind legs forward, the unravelling process begins which allows them to move forward into a new life.

> Stripping for your heads/best,
>   Hiding for your arms,
> Breath for your nose,
>   Unravelling for your wrappings.

Here, a process is declared in which the dead first have their faces stripped (the lake) and their arms/actions are suppressed, but then they are released forward. It is stating a process of hibernation for want of a better word, for those dead who had their self-knowledge dissolved and were then bound to rest.

Once their resting is done, Re triggers a slow awakening from their hibernation, the "Unravelling for your wrappings," which brings them back to a conscious awareness to move forward into a new life, rather than progressing deeper into the Duat.

Scene 13

A figure leans on a staff...

    Finished One

...before a serpent with many coils:

    Apep

Behind the serpent are nine figures:

    Assembly opposing Apep

The accompanying text reads:

    Done by a finished one for Re:
    Becoming radiant, as a god,
        Forcing into place the Trespasser:[39]

    "You are turned about: you cannot arise;
        You are ensorcelled: you cannot find yourself.
    True of Voice is my father against you;
        True of Voice am *I* against you.
    I resist you for/by Re;
        I blot you out for/by He of the Akhet."

They say, Nine of their Re,
    When they oppose Apep upon Re:

"The severing of your head, Apep;
    The severing of your coils.
You cannot displace the barque of Re;
    You cannot fall upon the god's yardarms.
There comes forth a fiery blast against you
    Belonging to the Place of the Mysteries.
For now we have scrutinized you,
    You are destroyed."

They live by the extension of Re,
    In the peace of the Foremost of Westerners.

Now, putting forth what is theirs on Earth,
    Sucking in what is theirs—cold refreshment,
    Means being a master of the extension bestowed by Re.

Commentary

In this scene Apep is neutralized by a Finished One: "Done by a finished one for Re." This character is normally viewed as being the god Atum; however this is not necessarily the case, especially since there is no god determinative here. (In this translation we nearly always translate god names literally rather than simply transliterating them into English. This greatly clarifies the meaning of the text, regardless of whether the god names actually refer to gods.)

Magically, a Finished One is someone who has gone through the whole process of Justification and is working towards finally becoming *as a god*: a Finished One has the power akin to Atum.

    "You are turned about: you cannot arise;
        You are ensorcelled: you cannot find yourself."

---

[39] Compare this with the similar formula in Scene 8.

Third Hour 75

The Finished One, as well as the Nine of their Re, use magic to vanquish Apep and subdue him. The Finished One is working in service. Apep cannot be destroyed—he is part of creation, just as Re is—but he can be subdued and rendered harmless so that the barque can pass through safely. The spell used, turning Apep upside down, preventing him from rising, and making him unable to find himself, temporarily pulls the plug on Apep. To be upside down in the Duat is to be without power. To be unable to rise is to be without power. To be unable to find yourself is to have one's power neutralized.

If you read the last part of this scene carefully, and look at it magically, then, drawing on what you have discovered so far, you will see that the Nine of their Re are living or dead adepts/priests who work in the Underworld in service, who can pass unhindered between the worlds:

> They live by the extension of Re,
>   In the peace of the Foremost of Westerners.

Scene 14

A figure leans on a staff...

> Finished One

...before nine figures carrying ankhs behind them and dominion-staffs before them:

> Masters of what was bestowed

The accompanying text reads:

> Says a/the Finished One[40] to these who are of the gods:
>
> "O gods, who possess life and dominion,
>   Who brood upon their sceptres/fine gold:
> Oppose the Trespasser upon He of the Akhet;

Put to slaughter the meat of evil's mould."

They say, these of their gods, when they ensorcel Apep:

"The opening of the Earth to Re;
    The sealing of the Earth for Apep.
Underworlders of the Foremost of Westerners,
    Who are in the Place of the Mysteries:
Adore Re; resist his adversaries.
    Save what is great from the arm of evil's meat.
Oho! Cast down for Re the adversary of Re!"

They live by the extension of Re
    In the peace of the Foremost of Westerners.
Who puts forth for/as them upon Earth,
    Who sucks in, for/as them, cold refreshment,
Is True of Voice in the West,
    Hallowed and Equalled by their hidden seat.

Alas for them who are for Re,
    They mourn for the Great God
    After he passes over them.
He travels on, they are covered by pregnant darkness,
    And sealed are their caverns over them.

Commentary

"These who are of the gods" are described as carrying the Was sceptre, which Michael translates literally as "dominion-staff." This gives them power over adversaries in the Underworld. They also hold the *ankh*: they carry the power of life through the gates of death. They are instructed to protect the candidate against the power of Apep: "Oppose the Trespasser upon He of the Akhet."

The distinction made to the candidate as they pass through the Underworld increases and refines. In this scene they are referred to as "True of Voice in the West," i.e. Justified of Voice in the passage of death. Each scene

---

[40] Here receives a god determinative; however, so does "these who are of the gods"! So it may be Atum, or not.

ending adds something to the candidate's status and understanding. Here, for the first time, their status is explicitly defined as connected to being True of Voice, and the effect this has on those in stasis in this place, as they pass through this chamber.

Third Gate

>The arrival by this Great God at this gate;
>>The entry into this gate.
>
>The gods in it worship this Great God.

Gate caption:

>Mistress of Endowing

Uraeus serpents caption:

>She kindles for Re

Guardian captions:

>Tremors the Earth: he bends his arms for Re.
>
>Trembles the Earth: he bends his arms for Re.

Mummies caption:

>The Third Nine of the Great God inside (the gate):
>
>"Open to you is the Earth;
>>Opened up for you is the Duat.
>
>One of the heavens, you strip away our obscurity.
>>Oho! Re! Come then to us!"

Doorway serpent caption:

>Inciting one:
>
>He exists over this door,
>>He opens for Re.

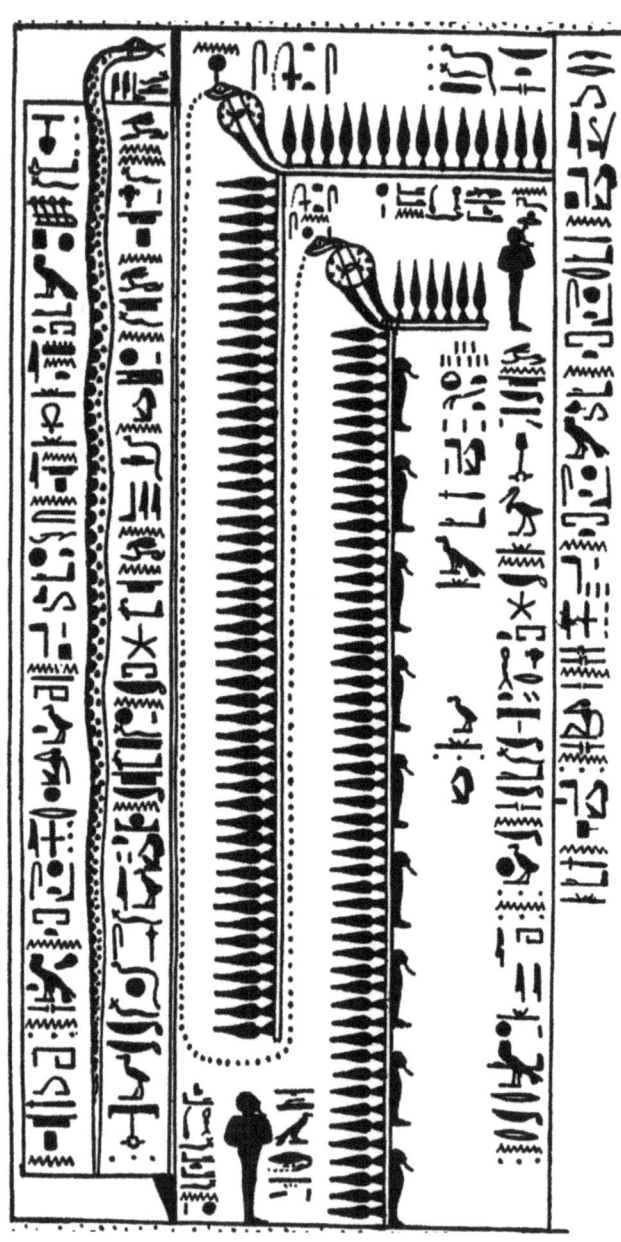

The Third Gate on Seti I's sarcophagus.

Third Hour

Perception to Inciting One:

"Open your portal for Re;
  Reveal your door for He of the Akhet.
Now he makes bright the Original Darkness;
  He gives a lightening in/from the Hidden Region."

Sealed is this door
  After the entry of this Great God.
Alas, then, for the ones in their gate,
  Should they hear the shutting of this door.

Commentary

The name of the Gate leads me to suspect that the deity power of this gate is a form of Renenutet, the cobra goddess of the harvest who appears not only in the living world, but also in the Underworld. For magical adepts who work with visionary magic in the Underworld, she often appears as a cobra goddess deep in the Underworld, but connected to the Ished tree by its roots (Egyptian sacred Tree of Life). The names of the Justified risen have their names written on the leaves of the Ished tree.

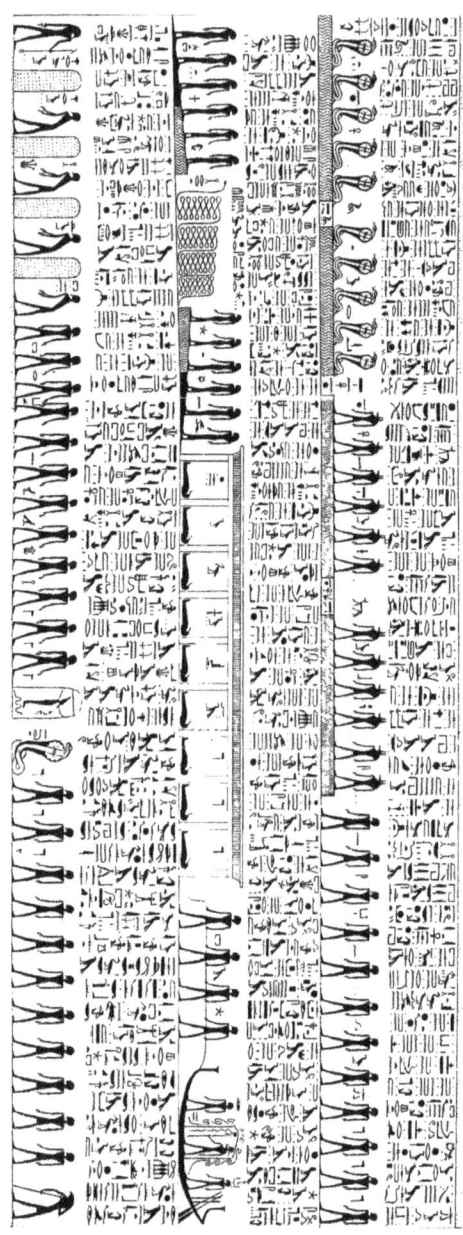

The Fourth Hour (Bonomi and Sharpe 1864).

Fourth Hour

Scene 15

Twelve striding figures:

> Gods conducted to their sustenance

The accompanying text reads:

> Being conducted to their sustenance:
>   The purifications through the provision of devotion,[41]
> The selections/dismemberments[42] during their lifespans,
>   The steering of peace to its seat.

Says to them Re:

"Your portions are yours, gods who are in your peace;
  You steer your sustenance to you, and you are at peace.
Your adversaries, who are destroyed, they do not exist;
  You Radiant Ones are at your seats, Rams/Presences at what
    is sealed."

Say they to Re:

"Praise to you, Re,

> He of the Akhet;
> Hail to you, a Presence
> >   Quick in the Earth;
> Hail to you, who eternally recurs,
> >   Master of the years;
> Who is eternally the same,
> >   Who cannot be extinguished."
>
> They extend into their peace.
> >   Their cold refreshment is water.
>
>
> Alas, then, for them, should they hear
> >   The shutting of their doors upon them.
> Who gives to/as them their extending,
> >   Is one who tows what is held fast by Presences.[43]

Commentary

These 'gods' are humans who became *as gods* in their lifetimes. They are purified (priestly) ones lifted up while they were alive, "selected during their lifespans," who have opted to work in the Duat in service.

In this scene we see how their Presences are not held here by force, but are operating in service. These Akhs—Radiant Ones—are where they should be, at their seats and working in service; and they are present in this sealed place to work.

They greet Re and proclaim that his presence is able to reach deep into the Earth, and can affect all areas of the Earth.

> Who gives to/as them their extending,
> >   Is one who tows what is held fast by Presences.

If you have not spotted it yet, the final couplet, which repeats with variations, speaks about the dynamics of this part of the hour. It tells of the effect

---

[41] This phrase, *sDfA-tryt*, generally means making an oath of allegiance.

[42] Here with the wounded man determinative which in the previous scene was our indicator to translate "dismemberment" rather than "selected." Here we ignore this determinative, viewing it as a likely blind.

[43] i.e. the Solar Barque.

that Re has on those contained in each section. The candidate, as he or she passes through, mirrors the actions of Re.

The power of Re as a deity, as he passes through each gate and section, reconfirms and reawakens each place's dynamics and actions. The same thing happens when the candidate passes through...

This speaks to a deeper dynamic in magic. By being as you should be, and doing what you should do, you trigger action around you. You *are* magic; you do not need to *do* magic. That is the difference between one who is Justified or is a candidate for Justification, and one who simply does magic: being present is enough.

It also subtly highlights an aspect of the Mysteries that is important when working with powers and deities. The greatest gift you can offer a deity is your work, your life, and your actions within that life, not a cookie or a glass of wine.

So as Re passes through an area, he enlivens whatever function that area has. And the candidate, as they pass through *as Re*, also enlivens the function of the area and its beings, if they are carrying and dispensing their harvest.

Scene 16

A lake…

> Lake of life

…over which stride twelve figures with jackal heads:

> Jackals in the lake of life

The accompanying text reads:

> They are in the circumference of this lake:
>   The Presences of mortals cannot penetrate it
>   For the hallowing that is in it.

Says to them Re:

"Your portions are yours, gods, in this lake;
   You guard your life in your lake.
You are at peace because of the guarding jackals;
   Who are themselves at peace, and the limit of your lake."

Say they to Re:

"You are purified, Re, in your hallowed lake;
   You purify gods in it.
The Presences of mortals cannot penetrate it,
   As you yourself have ordained, He of the Akhet."

Their extension is in bread.
   They make offering of hallowed vessels;
   Their water is wine.

Alas, then, for them, should they hear
   The shutting of their doors upon them.
Now, rendering what is theirs—their extension,
   Means being a master of the surplus inside them,
   Which is inside the circumference of this lake.

Commentary

In Hornung's translation, the second line in the offering list is rendered as "their beer is Djeseret." [44] *Dsrt* has strong connotations to do with the scales, the celestial Hall of Judgement, and the weighing of the harvest.

   If you think about the magical process that the soul of the king, Justified one, or candidate is going through, which is the Mysteries of Osiris, then you will start to see how tightly that Osirian process is woven into these stages of the Duat. The bread is the body of Osiris, the beer or wine is the blood of Osiris, and the water is the lymph of Osiris.

---

[44] Hornung and Abt 2014, p.109

In this text there are layers upon layers of these harvest motifs connected with the process of Justification (to become an Osiris is a major stage of Justification), and also with the magical Mysteries, in which inner cause and outer bodily effect are tightly interlaced. How the adept tames and works the powers determines how their physical body will respond to power (the cooling of the fire, the cool water, the lymph of Osiris...) and how that alchemical process is then translated into the descent through the Duat. "They make offering of hallowed vessels." Their 'blood' is judged, or has been judged.

The lymph of Osiris is the fluid of life, the last element poured into Osiris to trigger life and renewal. "Their water is wine." This also relates to the process of the Heb Sed, the regeneration of the king.

However, the *Gates* is not only about becoming the risen Osiris; it is also about being *as Re*: awakening and enlivening the stages of the Underworld so that others can do their jobs. The candidate, or the dead who are walking in Justification, can confirm their life acts of service by mirroring them in the Duat. So it is more complex than a lot of funerary texts, and has more to do with becoming "one who is of the gods" than simply surviving being processed through the gates.

I struggled for a little while to understand the function of the jackals in the purified lake, until I had to take a ritual bath. Then it struck me that this lake is a mirror of the waters of purification in adept life. In fact, everything in the *Gates* is a mirror of the adept life, and the process of Justification. As above, so below. Just as when an adept, or adept candidate, goes through various stages of training and experiences, and sometimes purifies themselves in a consecrated bath, so the candidates in death must purify themselves from the remnants of the descending gates before they tread forward to ascend out of the depths: "You are purified, Re, in your hallowed lake; You purify gods in it."

Scene 17

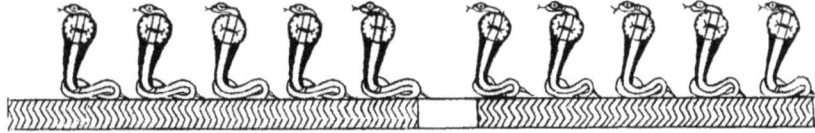

A lake...

    Lake of Risen Ones

...above which are ten Uraei:

Risen Ones; living ones

The accompanying text reads:

Their speech is what they say
  After Re arrives at/in them.
Presences return;[45] shadows are destroyed,
  At hearing the voice of the Risen Ones.

Says to them Re:

"Your portions are yours, Risen Ones,
  In the lake which you guard;
Your flames are a fiery blast in my adversaries,
  You are a fire in those who are evil to me;
Oho! to you,
  Risen Ones."

Say they to Re:

"Come then to us, who spreads across the Exulting Earth;
  Come then to us, who saves him by himself:
Thou, that art[46] what is Radiant of the Duat;
  Great God, in the Place of the Mysteries."

Alas, then, for those whom Re has passed over.

Commentary

This is a turning point in the passage through the Underworld. Now the candidate prepares to ascend to a different level of the Underworld. The lakes of this hour cleanse and prepare the candidate for what is to come.

---

[45] Here perhaps read "turn back."
[46] The start of this sentence is written archaically in Egyptian, so I have done the same in English.

It also introduces the candidate to the Mysteries of serpents who give prophesy, who utter out of the depths to those on the surface. This layer of being is connected with the mythologies to do with pre-Apollonian Delphi and other places where serpents and prophecy are connected.

Here we also see the dynamic of protective cobras that spit fire at the enemies of Re, and they protect this lake from the enemies of Re.

Scene 18

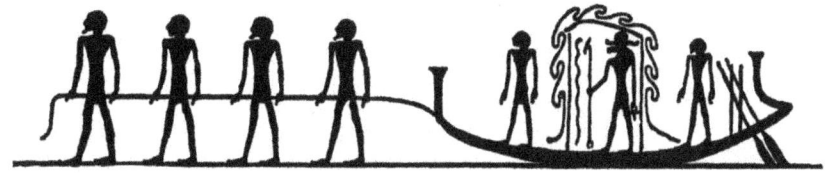

The Sun Barque, in the centre of which is the Meat of Re, with Spiral over him. In the front of the barque is Perception; by the oars, Magic. The barque is towed by four Underworlders.

The accompanying text reads:

> The towing of this Great God by gods, by Underworlders;
>   The voyaging in the Place of the Mysteries;
>   The formulation of the business of those in it.
>
> "Tow you me, Underworlders whom I have looked upon;
>   I, who made you.[47]
> Put out your arms: tow you me by/with them:
>   Return you to the East of the skies,
> To a seat that lifts up its maker,
>   That mountain which is a Mystery.
> This dazzling belongs to the circumference of gods:[48]
>   They receive me; I come forth from/into/though this.
> From/into the Place of the Mysteries you have towed:
>   I formulate your business at a gate held secret by Under-
>   worlders."

---

[47] A possible other reading: "I, your **companion**." There are in fact many alternative readings here, because of the large number of connotations the verb *jrj* has: please see **make**.

[48] As in aureola.

Commentary

Here we see again the turning point of the passage of Re through the Underworld: "Return you to the East of the skies." The Underworld workers pulling the bark start the long journey towards the east, dawn, birth, brightness, ascension from the Underworld, and the beginning of a new life, or ascent to the heavens.

"That mountain which is a Mystery" is part of the death Mysteries, knowledge of which has survived in magical training to this day. It is a trial which must be overcome to step into the stars or Justification. Notice again the brightness, the blinding light that is the aura or 'gold' of the gods and ones who are of the gods.

Full Quareia adepts should recognize "the seat which uplifts its maker" and understand what Re is referring to, which is the final destination of the barque and the candidates.

Scene 19

Nine mummified figures lying in shrines:

> Gods of the threshing floor[49] of Seat-of-the-Eye in their hollows.

The accompanying text reads:

> Says to them Re:
>
> "I looked upon gods,
>   I winnowed those in their hollows:

---

[49] *xtyw* "of the threshing floor" could also be *xtw* "followers." I have rendered this as "threshing floor" due to the placement of the *st* throne immediately after the word, the beginning of the word "Osiris," (**Seat-of-the-Eye**) which is very suggestive of the determinative for "threshing floor/platform." See Faulkner 1962, pp.198–199.

Fourth Hour

>   You are raised up; you are beaten down, gods.
>
> (Now I shall ordain for you your designs,
>   You who are in the front of your hollows.
> You are those who guard the Presences:
>   Live you through their putrefying,
>   Breathe you through their corruption.)
>
> You are raised up, belonging to my sun-disc:
>   You are steered to my dawning.
> Your portions are yours in the Duat,
>   That is, those things which I have ordained as yours."
>
> Their extending is in meat.
>   They will make offering of hallowed vessels.
>   Their cold refreshment is water.
>
> Alas, then, for them after, should they hear
>   The shutting of their doors upon them.

Commentary

Here Re passes over the Presences of gods, humans, and/or powers contained within the Underworld, and over certain beings who feed on them. He awakens them and tells them they have purpose, and reminds them of that: "Now I shall ordain for you your designs, You who are in the front of your hollows..."

Everything has purpose, and the Underworld houses forces that bring destruction or breaking down to maintain balance.

Scene 20

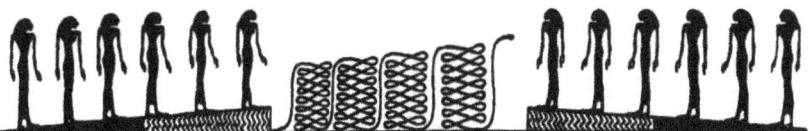

Twelve female figures:

>   Hours in the Duat

Six standing each side of a great serpent:

> Rope, she births twelve serpents;
> > Being destroyed upon her, she (re)absorbs (them):
> > Such are Hours.

The accompanying text reads:

> They attend to their lake;
> > They steer Re over their banks.
>
> Says to them Re:
>
> "Hours have heard what was called out to you:
> > You made what you are in.
> You are in the peace of your gates,
> > Your prow in pregnant darkness,
> > Your stern in brightness.
> Your lifespan is Rope,
> > Your living in what comes forth from her,
> > Your portions in the Duat.
> You absorb the births of Rope;
> > You cause the destruction of what comes forth from her.
> You shall govern me, I, whom you birth/who births you:
> > Beget for me that there be salvation upon me,
> > And for your own peace, my Hours."
>
> Their extension is in bread.
> > They will make offering of hallowed vessels.
> > Their cold refreshment is water.
>
> Rendering what is theirs, their extension,
> > Means coming forth foremost of the Radiant.

Commentary

Here we are introduced to the serpent power of time and measurement, the Rope: the measure that defines birth, life and death, beginning, middle, and end. This power of the Rope is equivalent to Morta (Parcae) or Atropos

(Moirai) the cutter of fate, the serpent power that defines the end of the measure:

> Your prow in pregnant darkness,
>   Your stern in brightness.

Just as in life the first of the three powers of fate is Clotho (Moirai) or Nona (Parcae), so in the Underworld and in death, the first of the three powers is death, or the cutter of time.

> You absorb the births of Rope;
>   You cause the destruction of what comes forth from her.

This tells of the power of Rope to absorb time and life. She takes what was born by Rope. As life and time is created, so she absorbs that life and time. The candidate is told to submit to this power, to cast their gifts before Rope. In doing so, they step further towards Justification:

> Rendering what is theirs, their extension,
>   Means coming forth foremost of the Radiant.

The time let go of is the time and fate of the life that has been lived. This must be cut and composted before the new time and fate can be created.

This is a major step of initiation in life for the adept candidate. (As in death so in life; as above, so below.) Before the adept candidate can move forward, they must submit to destruction and let go of their hold on life. They must submit to their fate, and let go of their fear of death. Their lifespan is in the hands of the gods, and the candidate must drop all sense of control over life and death. This also mirrors the first step taken by the magical apprentice: they learn the dynamic of *giving before taking*.

As a magician, you start to see the deep parallels in the steps of initiation and learning towards adepthood, and the passage of the dead moving towards judgement and Justification. It is not, as is commonly perceived, a matter of practising in life in order to traverse death as a candidate. It is far more complex than that. It is more that the adept Justification in life and the adept Justification in death are two sides of the same coin. One cannot happen without the other, and they run parallel to each other, out of time, as a holism of action. Think of the image of the Ouroboros.

Scene 21

An unnamed figure with a falcon head, leaning on a staff, stands at the back of eleven figures facing the shrine:

Gods pertaining to the Ribbon

Between these figures and the shrine is a Uraeus:

Balm

Figure in the shrine:

Foremost of Westerners

Behind the shrine stand twelve more figures:

Gods; the increase of the shrine

The accompanying text reads:

Distant One garners for his father,
    Making him Radiant, providing for him the Ribbon.

"Sailing south is my heart in the presence of my father;
    True is my heart, my father.
I save you from the arm of those who work against you;
    I make you Radiant by means of your bestowals.
Coming into power is yours, Seat-of-the-Eye;
    Eminence is yours, Foremost of Westerners.
Your portions are yours, ruler of the Duat,
    Towering of form in the Place of the Mysteries.
The Radiant have respect for you;
    The Mortal have awe for you.
The Provision of your Ribbon

>   Is by me, by your son Distant One;
>   Now I shall reckon up what is wrong inside."

Say these of the gods of Foremost of Westerners:

> "One is towering, Underworlder;
>   One is valiant, Foremost of Westerners.
> Your son Distant One, he provides your Ribbon;
>   He makes you Radiant, he persecutes your adversaries.
> Springing-up to you, and being-joyful in your arms,
>   Seat-of-the-Eye, Foremost of Westerners."

Says Foremost of Westerners:

> "Come then to me, my son Distant One:
>   You save me from the arm of those who work against me.
> You ordain them for the one who oversees destruction:
>   He, who guards the traps."

Says Distant One to these of the gods, the increase of the shrine:

> "You are the reckoning up by/from me,
>   Gods who are among the followers of Foremost of Westerners.
> You stand erect;
>   You do not backslide;[50]
>   You come into power.
> Come you, and make offering,[51]
>   Namely the bread of the Utterance; namely, the beer[52] of Truth.
> Your lives are as what my father lives on;
>   Your portions are in the Place of the Mysteries.
> You exist as the increase of the shrine,
>   Within the ordaining of Re.
> Though I call upon you,
>   It is he who formulates your business."

Their extension is into bread,

Their scale-pans are hallowed,
Their cold refreshment is water.
Now, giving what is theirs, their extension,
Means being a companion of the breakfast in the shrine.

Commentary

In this scene, a falcon-headed figure appears with a staff. This is a different 'worker' presentation from the previous appearance, the Finished One, and reflects how different workers who express deity powers operate in various sections of the Duat. This worker expressed the power of Horus, whose name is translated literally in this text as **Distant One**. You will better understand these different workers/deities once you have looked at the seventh hour.

Distant One speaks to Re and makes reference to his heart spirit: his heart speaks truth. Remember, in the process of Judgement and Justification, the heart spirit speaks of the life of the person, and informs the scales about whether the person truly lived in the ways of Ma'at.

Distant One garners for his father,
Making him Radiant, providing for him the Ribbon.

This talks about Horus, and the actions of Horus/the Distant One moves them towards the likeness of Osiris. This is a bit of a riddle, and its meaning becomes a lot clearer once you study the Seventh Hour, and then reflect back on this scene.

---

[50] *Hmw*, usually translated "return," but here in its sense of "retire, retreat." See **return**.

[51] Here not *Hnk* but *drp* "offer to (god), offer (things), feed (someone), present (dues), make offering, grant." See **cater for**.

[52] This is the next stage of the offering list puzzle. We have already been translating *Hnqt.sn* "their beer" as *Hnkt.sn* "they will make offering" (reading *q* as *k*). The previous line, "come you, and make offering," using *drp* instead of *Hnk*, should remind us of this substitution and reassure us that we are indeed looking at a word puzzle. Now we are invited to consider how Truth (Ma'at) might be related to *Hnqt* or *Hnkt*. And indeed, if we look up *Hnkt*, we discover the very similar word *Hnkw*, "scale-pan of balance." At the time of this text's composition, the consonant *t* was disappearing from the ends of words: words like *Hnkt* and *Hnkw* could have sounded very similar. If we read *Hnqt* in this line as *Hnkw* "scale-pan," substituting *k* for *q* and dropping the final *t*, then we get: "Namely the bread of the Utterance in the scale-pan of Truth." If we read *Hnqt* as "scale-pan" in the offering list, then we get...well, see the end of this scene. The idea is that those whose "extensions" will become bread also have 'hallowed' scale-pans...

Fourth Hour

Foremost of Westerners in his shrine, from the Tomb of Ramses I.

Remember, the Ribbon is a serpent power, and reflects the threshing of the harvest and the overcoming of the death/rebirth cycle, becoming as forever living—Justified. Through the service and progress of Horus/the Distant One, the Ribbon of Justification and deification is repaired.

Also in this scene, Distant One encourages workers and gods not to fall into the sleep of the Duat, but to stay awake and energized. Through their work, Re succeeds, and through Re succeeding, the workers and deities of this place can continue to function. It is really a scene of cheerleading and encouragement. Behind that is hidden a layer of Mystery regarding the soporific nature of the Duat: to fall asleep or to lie down is to go into hibernation and become trapped in that place.

This is highly relevant for adepts working in vision in the Duat: it is very important to not fall asleep when working in vision in this place, as to do so can fragment you.

Scene 22

Four flaming traps, attended by four figures:

>Overseeing their traps

A figure by the traps holds an ankh behind them and a dominion-staff in front:

>Overseeing destruction

The accompanying text reads:

>Says Distant One to these of the gods:

>"Hold fast for yourselves the adversaries of my father

Who are sucked by you into your traps
Because of the calamities they have worked
   Against what is great—which, being found, births me.
Your portions are yours in the Duat:
   Guard the traps, and the heat,
   As Re has ordained.
Though I call to you,
   It is he who formulates your business."

It is this god who, standing erect,
   Has authority over these of the traps.

Commentary

This brief scene shows us beings that work in the Underworld and who trap and contain powers of destruction that would threaten Re or the candidates as they pass through. The containment also stops these powers rising to the surface and bringing destruction to the day/life.

Fourth Gate

The arrival by this Great God at this gate;
   The entry into this gate.

The worship of this Great God by the gods in it.

Gate caption:

She Who Keeps

Uraeus serpents caption:

She kindles for Re

Guardian captions:

Absorber: he bends his arms for Re.

Approacher: he bends his arms for Re.

The Fourth Gate in the tomb of Seti I.

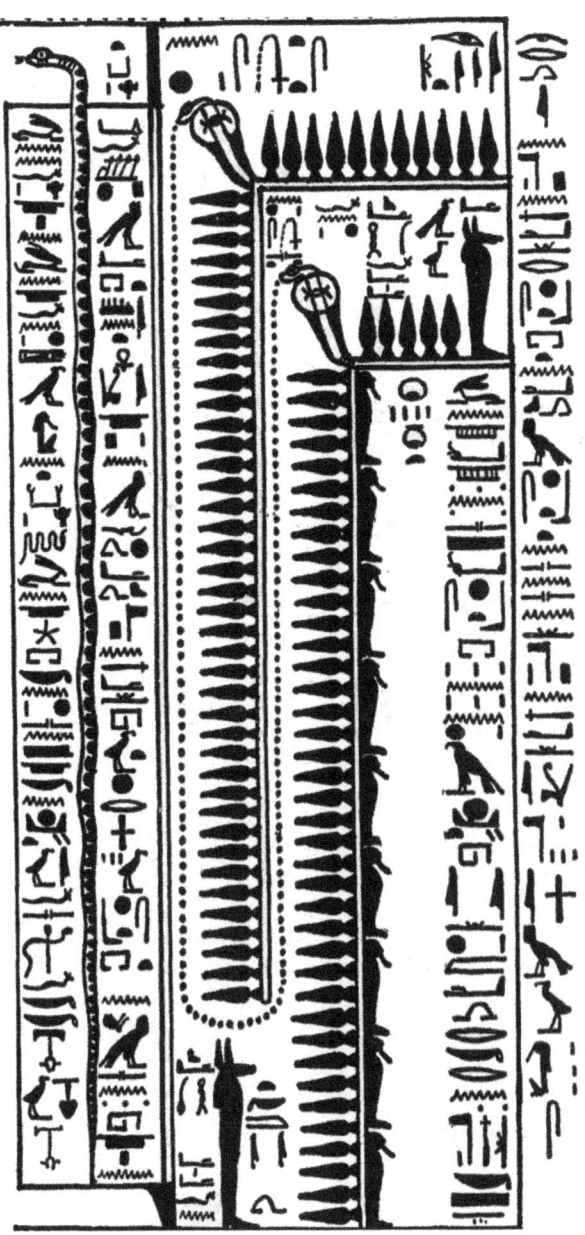

The Fourth Gate on Seti I's sarcophagus.

Mummies caption:

The Fourth Nine:

"Open are our doors; revealed are our gates
  For Re, Distant One, He of the Akhet.[53]
Oho! Re! Come then to us,
  Great God, Master of the Mysteries."

Doorway serpent caption:

Face of Lamplight:

He exists over this door,
  He opens for Re.

Perception to Face of Lamplight:

"Open your portal for Re;
  Reveal your door for He of the Akhet.
Now he makes bright the Original Darkness,
  He gives a lightening in/from the Hidden Region."

Sealed is this door
  After the entry of this Great God.
Alas, then, for the ones in their gate,
  Should they hear the shutting of this door.

Commentary

The name of the Gate, *jryt*, "She Who Keeps," puns on *jryt* "milch cow."[54] This connects the gate's name to Hathor, making it a hidden title for this goddess who appears in both life and death. This gate is the power of Hathor in the Duat, welcoming the dead, Re, and candidates to the threshold of Judgement. She is mother, tender, guardian, and one who make sure that only those of Ma'at pass by her.

---

[53] Or: Re-Horakhty. It is, however, possible to read this as three separate beings.
[54] Faulkner 1962, p.28

Fifth Hour

Scene 23

Twelve figures with hands outstretched downwards:

> Praising in the Duat

The accompanying text reads:

> They make praise for Re in the West,
>   They make towering the Distant One of the Akhet;
> Being wise of Re upon Earth,
>   And their putting forth to him their peace in their seats,
>   Their Radiances are at a hallowed[55] place of the West.

Say they to Re:

> "Come in, Re: you arise in the Duat;
>   Praise to you: you enter a hallowed (area) in Spiral."

Says to them Re:

> "Peace to you, who are at peace;
>   I was at peace in your works for me.
> While I shine in the East of the skies;

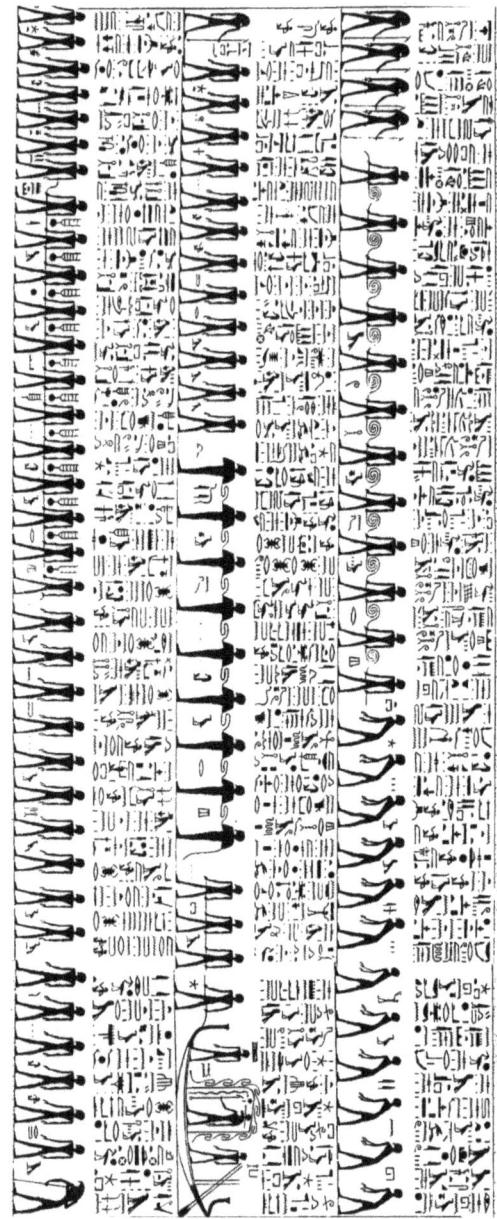

The Fifth Hour (Bonomi and Sharpe 1864).

> While I am at peace in the chamber/stone vessel/excess of my Eye."[56]

> Their extension is in the peace of Re.
> Their scale-pans are in his hallowed (area).
> Their cold refreshment is the water.

> Now, putting forth what is theirs on Earth
> Means praising in the presence of Re in the West.

Commentary

Once more we meet powers/Justified that 'knew' Re on Earth. The refrain used in magic with powers, "I know you," here translated as "being wise of X," is an important one. It speaks to having a deep understanding and living experience of the deity power, and being *as one with* the power flow of the deity. This is often misunderstood in magic, and has devolved down into a parody of the deep Mystery: the magician thinks he knows a deity because he knows the name, action, colour, day, hour, crystal, picture, etc. of the deity. This simple but devastating mistake has led to many generations of magicians being locked out of the deeper elements of the Mysteries.

Those who are praising in the Duat are ones who truly 'know' Re, because they have been *as* Re in their magical lives, regardless of whether they are/were human, animal, spirit, or deity. It also brings us full circle back to the threshold of the Inner Desert: "Their Radiances are at the hallowed Desert of the West." They work at the threshold between the worlds, having a radiant presence both in the Inner Desert and in the Duat. This tells us that they are no longer in life (not in living service) but are what magicians call 'inner contacts' or humans out of life who operate in service.

---

[55] See **hallowed**. Here it receives the N25 determinative, "sandy hill-country over edge of green cultivation," generally indicating words such as "hill country, foreign land, *desert*, necropolis, upland tomb, East," etc. (Gardiner 1957, p.488) One could read this word specifically as "hallowed Desert" rather than just "hallowed place."

[56] *aAyt* with house determinative. There are three words layered on top of each other here, I think: (1) *aAy*, "excess." (see previous scene) (2) *aAt* "stone vessel." (3) *at* "chamber." There is a sense of a vessel containing *what remains* which is also a chamber in the Underworld. Sort of a harvest cup.

Remember that Mehen, which Michael has translated as **Spiral**, is a serpent power deep in the Duat that protects the Justified, upholds the Justified, and apposes Apep.

Re's speech strengthens the understanding of the 'Peaceful Ones' and the mirroring of the deity in their own lives: "I was at peace in your works for me."

The next line tells of Re's work rising in the east as the sun each day, then descending down into the depths at night. But that is only the most superficial layer of the understanding, and beneath it hides a deeper Mystery.

> While I shine in the East of the skies;
> While I am at peace in the chamber/stone vessel/excess of my
>   Eye.

This talks about the deep Cave of the Mysteries, the cave at the centre of the Underworld, which houses the deified life until it is ready to wake and ascend back to the living world, bringing with it renewal and Justification. This is mirrored in many of the Western Mysteries as the vault or chamber of Osiris, or in some of the Mysteries as the Cave of the Four Winds or the Cave of Atum.

The "chamber/stone vessel/excess of my Eye" refers to the magical vessel, and each of these words adds to that understanding. These three words are meanings that all stem from the hieroglyphs, and instead of choosing one the closest to the meaning, we thought it best to list all three, as they each add a fragment to the translation, fragments that all point to specific aspects of the Mysteries of creation and destruction.

Re outputs creation from his eye or mouth, and the vessel that receives that outputting is the planet, womb, and so forth. This polarized dynamic is a major aspect of magic: giving/outputting, receiving/vessel. The stone cup or cavern is the cauldron in which the alchemical changes occur, and is the root of the use of the cup in magic. The alchemical change in its most powerful form is evolution through life and death.

Fifth Hour

Scene 24

Twelve figures carry a rope with coils between each of them:

> Possessing[57] the rope in the marsh[58] of the West.

The accompanying text reads:

> Possessing the rope in the West,
> > Governing[59] meadows for the Radiant.
> Receive for yourselves the rope:
> > Hold fast for yourselves an aroura[60] of the marshes of Westerners.
> Their Radiances to your bases,
> > Gods to your seats.[61]
> The Radiant of/and the Magic Cord[62] are in peace:
> > The marsh of a Radiant one, an oipe,[63] is what is in the rope.
>
> True you are for the things that are;
> > Not true you are for things that are not.[64]
>
> Say they to Re:
>
> "True is the rope in the West;
> > At peace is Re in one who tows.
> Your portions to you, gods;
> > Your allotments[65] to you, the Radiant.
> Behold Re as he makes your meadows:
> > He ordains to you a fen to be in.
> Oho! Voyager, He of the Akhet,
> > Behold the gods at peace in/through their portions,

---

[57] Alternatively: portions, apportioners.
[58] See **marsh**. Note that a phonetically identical word means "offering loaves," recalling the bread in Ma'at's scale-pan in an earlier scene.

The Radiant at peace in/through their allotments."[66]

Their extension is in the Marsh of Rushes;
Their peace in what comes forth from in it.

Now, putting forth what is theirs on Earth
Means being in this meadow of the Marsh of Rushes.

Commentary

This is an interesting scene for magicians, and one that Quareia adept students in particular should recognize: the rope of measuring. The rope is used for measuring land, life, and structure. In the Duat it is a power that is used to apportion the lifespan. For those living ones who are traversing the gates, the old life was cut, and now the new life, and the path that new life will walk, is being measured out.

As is the case with all Egyptian funerary texts, every word has a few different meanings that connect into the surface layer of meaning, so that the Mysteries behind a word can be understood: one obvious and more hidden. The word *nwH*, cord or rope—for measuring—is related to the word *nwt* "yarn (for weaving)."[67] This is about the weaving of the new life, of the new

---

[59] *sSm* also has a sense of measuring out here. See for instance the related word *sSmt*, "working out proof (mathematical)." (Faulkner 1962, p.247)

[60] *stAt*, here written *styA(t)*. Aroura, a land measure equal to about two thirds of an acre. There is punning at work here, for *sTA* is tow. All that towing has now turned into a smallholding in the Duat.

[61] More punning here: *nTrw* "gods" with *nTr(y)w* "magic cord." (Faulkner 1962, p.143)

[62] Even more punning: *nTry* + god determinative can mean both "Magic Cord" (as a deity), or "a divine one," an epithet of Osiris. (Hornung and Abt 2014, p.153)

[63] A grain-measure equal to four hekats, or about twenty litres. (Gardiner 1957, pp.197–198, §266) But don't let the technical term distract you from the important equivalences made in this line.

[64] Dividing everything imaginable into two groups: what is, and what is not, and pointing out that the rope registers truthfully for the former, and falsely for the latter. (For the division of everything imaginable into "what is" and "what is not," see the phrase *ntt jwtt*, Allen 2014, p.356, §22.8.)

[65] **allotment** This word with a scroll determinative means "part, division." With a different determinative it means "reed mat/carpet." It's a pun which perhaps may emphasize that the akhs are not necessarily getting actual arable land here: they are getting portions of the reed marsh.

[66] Note the equivalence made here between **portions** and **allotments**.

[67] Faulkner 1962, p.127

allotment of the path that life will take: the yarn of the fate weaver in magic. In Egyptian magic this is connected to Neith as the weaver of life, and to Clotho (Greek) and Nona (Roman), who spins the fate of a person, place, or nation.

When this cord is worked with in magic, the cord itself has its own consciousness, and is connected to serpent powers that work in time, measurement, and fate. In this part of the fifth hour, the candidate, who previously let go of their old fate when the power of fate ended the old 'weave,' now has a new fate measured and created.

This is deepened with the line "The marsh of a Radiant one, an oipe, is what is in the rope." This talks about the grain measure, the harvest of the soul, be it a deity or human, and how its time is allotted within the rope.

The marsh is the womb; the cord/rope contains the lifespan of the grain and weaves it in a fate. The rope also holds sound, as visionary magicians and Quareia adept candidates will know. The sound/vibration creates and weaves an interface for the spirit to come into life: this is the serpent power of prophecy and utterance into being. This is depicted in some tomb images as heads that rise out of the rope when it is straightened (for measuring).

Before we go any further, it would be useful to point out that the fourth gate, in its deeper aspects, is Hathor. Hathor is known among other titles in the Duat as Mistress of Reeds. This pertains to the marshes where the river Nile meets the land: the threshold between water and earth, the place where the reeds grow. Until the building of the Aswan High Dam, when the Nile flooded, it created a temporary marshland where its waters covered the earth. When its waters receded, they left a rich black silt which nourished the land and created new topsoil within which crops could be grown. This was the beginning of new growth, the preparation of the land ready to receive the seed. Thus the marshes are the point where the land is prepared by the river for the seed to be planted and spring to life.

These marshes had small islands of reeds that rose out of the muddy waters which were reminiscent of the Benben, the primordial mound in the Egyptian creation myths which rose out of the waters, and was the first 'island of life.'

Mehet-Weret,[68] the great cow who carried Re between her horns, who lifted him out of the waters and onto the land, is connected with Hathor (and Neith). As such she was the mother of Re (and Horus): she was the threshold and bridge between the water and earth. Now you should start to

---

[68] *mHt-wrt* "the great flood-waters." (Wilkinson 2003, p.174)

see her importance at the fourth gate. You should also start to realize that in the fifth hour, when you see the word 'marshes,' it contains all these complex interwoven meanings.

> Your portions to you, gods;
>   Your allotments to you, the Radiant.
> Behold Re as he makes your meadows:
>   He ordains to you a fen to be in.

Here you start to see the weave of a new fate in action. This is the allocation of a new womb/mother. We are looking at a section in the Duat that deals with reincarnation. Remember, the passage through the Duat is not a straight path from A to B; it has many different qualities and areas. At any point in the journey, if you look closely, you will see options presented for reincarnation, options for resting and sleeping, options for stopping and working in a specific area, or options to follow Re through the Duat and up to the heavens.

Scene 25

Four figures carrying ankhs behind them and dominion-staffs before them:

> Overseeing the rope in the West

Fifth Hour

The accompanying text reads:

Says to them Re:

"Hallowing is yours, boundary-beings,
   Overseeing the rope in the West.
O establish the meadows given to gods,
   To the Radiant, companions of towing in the Marsh of Reeds."

They place the meadows, the fens
   For the gods, the Radiant, who are in the Duat.

Their extension is in the Marsh of Reeds,
   Their peace in what comes forth from in it.

Commentary

In this scene, ones who are "overseeing the rope in the West," ones who work with the Rope, are told to make fast the land given to the gods. This is where the lengthening or tightening of the Rope is commanded for the creation of fate to occur. This is worked with in the Quareia training, in Adept Module X Lesson 3, where the adept candidate learns to wield the Rope for the measurement of their inner allotment. This is a very old part of magic, and not only triggers the adept's new allotment of fate, but also teaches them how to "oversee the Rope in the West," to work in the Duat in service.

Scene 26

The Sun Barque, in the centre of which is the Meat of Re, with Spiral over him. In the front of the barque is Perception; by the oars, Magic. The barque is towed by four Underworlders.

The towing of this Great God by gods, by Underworlders,
  Voyaging in the Place of the Mysteries.

The accompanying text reads:

"Tow you for me, Underworlders;
  Praise you for me, foremost of the stars.
Enduring be your ropes,
  Those by which you tow me;
Established be your arms
  And the swiftness of your strides;
Radiance to your Presences,
  Valour to your hearts.
Open you the beautiful path
  To the caverns of the Mysteries' bestowals."

Commentary

This scene returns to addressing those who were praising in Scene 23, workers who partake of the Jubilation of Re, and thus also of themselves. This hints towards an element of the Justification process, in which the candidate is starting to move towards their 'Jubilation,' their regeneration. This was something done by the monarch at the end of thirty years of rule, to Justify them again and to regenerate them. It was known as the Sed, or Heb Sed—the Jubilation or 'celebration' of renewal and rebirth as one of the gods.

The Heb Sed Jubilation was done when the monarch was exhausted and at the end of their reserves of vital force, Perception, and Magic, and was used to magically renew the monarch with vital force. It was a form of rebirth.

This is mirrored in the passage of Re through the Duat. The fourth and fifth hour speaks to the end of descent and the preparation for renewal and regeneration brought by ascent out of the Underworld and up into the heavens. The passage of death and renewal in the Duat are dynamics that also appear in the life dynamics of the Egyptian pattern.

Those holding the rope are instructed to be **established** in their arms and in the swiftness of their strides. This refers to the power of measurement, the power of Djehuty, who brings containment, measure, and boundary. The power of Djehuty is knowledge, and on the surface this can be understood as learning, books, and wisdom. But at a deeper level it is containment, measure,

Fifth Hour

and boundary: the creation of limitation that allows experience, which brings wisdom from direct experience.

The rope holders are commanded to walk as Djehuty, to measure equally and consistently. Djehuty places a major role in the passage of the dead, as well as Ma'at, the goddess of truth and balance.

Scene 27

Nine figures with concealed arms, carrying a serpent:

> Possessing the Perverter

The accompanying text reads:

> They are in this design: possessing this serpent,
>   Holding (it) fast at the arrival of Re to them
>   That he may be at peace with the Lifespan Mistress.
> This serpent is always hurrying at her,
>   And cannot ever meddle with her.

> Says to them Re:

> "Hold fast for yourselves the Perverter:
>   Do not you give to him the path,
>   That I may pass through you.
> Making-Mysterious for your arms;
>   Destruction for whom you guard.
> You guard the developing of my developments;
>   Your bonds are for the developing of my Radiance."

> Their extension is in hearing the voice of this god.

> Now, putting forth what is theirs
>   Means hearing the voice of Re in the Duat.

Commentary

Here we see the mirror opposite of the Rope, the serpent power of the life measure, in the form of the Perverter. This serpent, Perverter, is an adversary power that works in opposition to limit or 'pervert' the intended newly created life measure. This is also an example, as is the opposing powers of Mehen and Apep, of Ma'at in action. Everything has its counterbalance: creation versus destruction, limitation versus expansion.

Ma'at is more of a power than a personality, and we see the presence of Ma'at throughout the gates in the power of balance and opposition. The candidate for Justification, be they human or deity, must have a balance of powers to become the fulcrum of the opposing powers, if they are to step forward into Justification. This is true in life as well as in death, hence the constant references in the previous gates to one's life actions defining one's harvest in death.

In this scene, the carriers of the serpent are commanded to hold fast the Perverter, so that it cannot impede the progress of Re or those *like him*, such as candidates ready to step forward into the Hall of Judgement.

Scene 28

Twelve figures:

    Presences of humans in the Duat

The accompanying text reads:

    Their having spoken Truth upon Earth;
        Their having been dedicated to the forms of the god.

    Says to them Re:

    "Valour to your Presences,
        Breath for your nose.

>Cuttings[69] are yours from the Marsh of Rushes,
>> For indeed you are those who are Righteous.
>> Your bases are yours at the corner-place:[70]
>>> The ordaining words of those in whom I am are there." [71]

>Their extension is bread,
>> Their scale-pans are hallowed vessels,
>> Their cold refreshment is water.

>Now, putting forth what is theirs on Earth
>> Means being a Peaceful One of their daily bread.[72]

Commentary

This scene asserts the importance of the candidate living by the rule of Ma'at.

This scene shows us a group of Egyptians who have been waiting in the Duat to develop towards being judged. They are listed literally as **humans**, which in this context means Egyptians. You will see in the thirtieth scene why that should be.

The judgement they await is not in the Hall of Judgement, as they have not developed enough towards the Justification process, but they are suitable for judgement at the porch, which Michael translates as "corner-place."

As in life in Egypt, so in death. While most cases of civil judgement in Egypt were done at the scene of a crime or the house of a person, important cases were held on the porch of the Temple, and the court was usually presided over by scribes, priests/priestesses, and high officials.

Telling these dead humans that their bases are at the porch of Judgement is telling them that they can have the lesser judgement before moving forward in their future life, which will then be spun for them.

---

[69] A pun on *Saw*, which can mean "cuttings" or "fens," but here, due to the knife determinative, it should be rendered as "cuttings." There is also a visual pun, as *Saw* is rendered with the top of the Djed pillar here, directing our attention to some of the qualities of the *mAatyw* **Righteous**. "Cuttings" also picks up the 'reed mat' adumbration from a previous scene.

[70] The literal translation; it means "Magistrate's Court." See **corner place**.

[71] "Those in whom I am" receives a god determinative.

[72] *mjnt* can refer to a kind of land, or ones daily fare. See **daily bread**. Notice the equivalence being made, again, between the land given the Righteous in the Duat, and bread.

Scene 29

Figure facing the figures from the previous scene, holding a dominion-staff before him:

>Overseeing his corner-place

The accompanying text reads:

>Says Re to this god:
>
>"Call upon what is great, overseeing his corner-place,
>>Concerning the Presences of these of the Righteous.
>
>Give them peace on their bases
>>At the corner-place of those in whom am I, myself."

Commentary

In the twenty-ninth scene, we are introduced to the Overseer of the Porch, the overseer for the Hall of Judgement, and the porch outside the hall for lesser judgement.

In the last line, Re says that the porch is the Porch of the Temple: "the corner-place of those in whom am I, myself." i.e. the porch of the deities and godly ones—the Temple.

Scene 30

A hawk-headed figure leans on a staff...

> Distant One

...at the back of a queue of figures, labelled, in fours:

> Humans
>
> Asiatics
>
> Nubians
>
> Libyans

The accompanying text reads:

> Says Distant One to these of the flock of Re
> > In the Duat, the Black Land, and the Red Land:
>
> "Radiance to you who are of the flock of Re,
> > Developing in what is great, the foremost of the skies.
> Breath to your nose,
> > Unravelling to your wrappings.
> You are tears of my Akhet
> > In your identity as humans.[73]
> Then, being great of the water that causes development,[74]
> > You are said to be in your identity as Asiatics;[75]
> And there should develop for them Power,[76]
> > As it is she who can save their Presences,
> > From which you are those whom I have threshed.
> Then, being of my peace in Infinity,[77] which comes forth from
> > in me,
> > You are in your identity as Nubians;[78]
> And there should develop for them what is of the Distant One,

As it is he who can save their Presences.
Then, as it was the seeking of my Eye which ended in your development,
There is your identity as Libyans;⁷⁹
And there should develop for them Power,
As it is she who can save their Presences."⁸⁰

Commentary

In this scene, the most famous one in *The Book of Gates*, Horus addresses "different races." In Ancient Egypt, their neighbours from the Near East, North Africa to the west of Egypt, and Africa below Egypt, were more or less it as far as the Egyptians were concerned in terms of who was part of their order of creation.

Note that the Egyptians considered themselves human but assigned race to the others. This is not what we in the modern world would perceive as being racist; the Egyptians were anything but racist. Rather it is, I suspect, a remnant of the distant past where tribal groups would each refer to themselves as "the people," i.e. the humans. We see aspects of this today in various tribal societies where the name the tribe assigns for itself often means "the people," or "the humans." For example, the Navajo call themselves "Dine," which simply means "the people."

This scene tells us that the Egyptians considered the Duat to be a place for all peoples, not just the Egyptians. It was there for anyone who lived by

---

⁷³Punning *rmTw* **humans** with *rmwt* **tears**.

⁷⁴*sxpr*, causative of *xpr*, **develop**.

⁷⁵Punning *aAmw* "Asiatics" with *aA mw* "great of the water." File this pun away in your mind, as it is the next hint in the unravelling of the offering list, that will eventually explain the meaning of "their cold refreshment is water."

⁷⁶Here with a seated woman determinative: read as the goddess Sekhmet.

⁷⁷Potential second meaning: "among the masses," i.e. the general population.

⁷⁸Playing on the prominence of *H* in *HH* **millions** and *nHsyw* **Nubians**.

⁷⁹I think punning **TmHw** "Libyans" with *tm HHjw* "complete of searching." This, and the *sDm.n.f* form of "which was your development," seems to locate Libyans at the end of this developmental process.

⁸⁰This is also a scene about various stages of mystical development, each stage associated with the image of a particular foreign stereotype, like different loci in a memory palace. Revisit this scene after you have worked your way through the text, and the meaning should reveal itself pretty plainly. Also note the hidden directional attributes. Look at a map if it isn't obvious, and assume that Egypt is the centre.

Fifth Hour

Ma'at. It also refers to the protective deities and the tribal groups familiar with those deities—warrior lion goddesses were also known in the near East and along North Africa, hence, I guess, the reference to Sekhmet, translated literally by Michael as **Power**, as being the protector of those groups. A sort of "oh yes, we have her, we call her X" sort of situation.

Scene 31

Twelve figures carrying a serpent, with the hieroglyphs P6 ("mast") atop O50 ("threshing floor") between them:

> Possessing *a* lifespan in the West

The accompanying text reads:

> They who establish a lifespan, and make the days stand erect,[81]
>   Of Presences in the West ordained for the Place of Destruction/Preparation.[82]

> Says to them Re:

> "O gods of the outer chamber of the Duat:
>   When possessing *two* tapes[83] in the towing out of a lifespan,
> Holding fast for yourselves the two tapes,
>   Tow you out the lifespan that runs through[84] it
> Which belongs to Presences in the West
>   Ordained for the Place of Destruction.
> You destroy the Presences of my adversaries
>   That you ordain for the Place of Destruction:
>   They shall not look upon the Place of the Mysteries."

> It is the Assembly which destroys adversaries.

Their extension is from being True of Voice.

Now, putting forth what is theirs on Earth
Means being True of Voice (and) in their presence.

Commentary

This is a very interesting scene in that we see the two threads or cords spun to make a lifespan. The Presences in the West in this section are "ordained for the Place of Destruction/Preparation," which is to say that they are marked to go back in life, and will not move forward to the Hall Judgement to be confirmed as Justified/ready for ascent. They were judged at the porch, and will partake of a new lifespan.

Translating Egyptian hieroglyphs can be a bit of a nightmare at times, because there are often puns on words, images, and meanings, and one word can have many nuances. When Michael looked a lot more closely at the actual hieroglyphs on the coffin of Seti I and on the tomb walls, and added to the magical knowledge we know of this place, something interesting started to emerge.

An apparent misspelling in this scene of the word *Htmyt*, "Place of Destruction," when read literally, spells *sAyt*, **Place of Preparation**, as in preparing for new life—as will become clear later in the text. And indeed, some of the other nuances of *Htm* **destroy** are "liquidation" and "payment (of debts)."

Htm, **destroy**, is also the Egyptian word for galena. Galena is ore of lead, and sometimes contains traces of silver. In magical alchemy, lead (the planetary influence of Saturn) is connected to the weight of a mundane life, and its connections to Saturn are that of the struggles of life.

The Egyptians loved playing around with words, and often stacked up multiple layers of meanings in a word or sentence. So here we have a place denoted by words that can mean rebirth, copulation, releasing (liquidating), and lead. I suspect we are looking at the very early formation of connec-

---

[81] *saHa* "make stand erect," causative of *aHa* **stand erect**.

[82] Depending on how the word is read, it could be *(H)tmyt* or, reading exactly what is there, *sAyt*. See **Place of Preparation**.

[83] *mtwy* dual of *mt* **tape**, as in "strip of cloth." Punning on *mtw* the **Mortal**, and *mtry* **Witness**, the sense is that the lifespan is twisted up with something extraneous to it, something that oughtn't to be there.

[84] *Hr*, literally "is through."

Fifth Hour

tions in mystical alchemy between the metals and the progress of the spirit: lead/mundane, silver/evolving, gold/a godly one.

So at this point of the *Gates*, those who have got this far but who are insufficiently polished, as a result of their life harvest, to face the trials of the Hall of Judgement, are enmeshed in the double rope of life and death. They are marked for return into the trials of life and death...the cycle of mortality.

Scene 32

Eight (sometimes nine) figures:

>Assembly which is in the Duat

The accompanying text reads:

>It is they who ordain destruction
>>As/Of writing(s)[85] from the lifespan of Presences, of the outer chamber of the Duat.
>
>"Your destruction to my adversaries,
>>Who you write down for the Place of Destruction.
>
>I have come in here to scrutinize my remains,
>>To put the evils onto my adversaries."[86]
>
>Their extension is bread,
>>Their scale-pans are hallowed vessels,
>>Their cold refreshment is water.
>
>Now, putting forth what is theirs on Earth,
>>He cannot enter into the Place of Destruction/Preparation.

Commentary

Those who have been ordained for going back into the cycle of life/death are dispatched. Those who got this far into the hours of the Duat know that rebirth is not an easy option at all, and that it will mean trials and suffering. However, it also gives them an opportunity for development, so that hopefully, next time, they will move beyond this stage.

There is also a little hint about service: "Now, putting forth what is theirs on Earth, He cannot enter into the Place of Destruction/Preparation." It means that those who work in service while in life for the souls of the place, they will not return here.

If you had not already noticed, this is a good example of how these ending lines can refer to those who serve in vision in life in a section of the Duat. By working in service in an aspect of the Duat, they come to know it well, and to learn its lessons while still in life. By doing that, they avoid having to undergo, yet again, the trials of that particular aspect of the Duat in death.

Fifth Gate

> The arrival by this god at this gate;
> The entry into this gate.
>
> The worshipping of this Great God by its indwelling gods.

Gate caption:

> Lifespan Mistress

Uraeus serpents caption:

> She kindles for Re

---

[85] Note that they could be writing down things to do with the lifespan, or they could be documents *contained within* the lifespan.

[86] i.e. to return evil encrustations back to whom dealt them, and/or to state who dunnit.

Fifth Hour

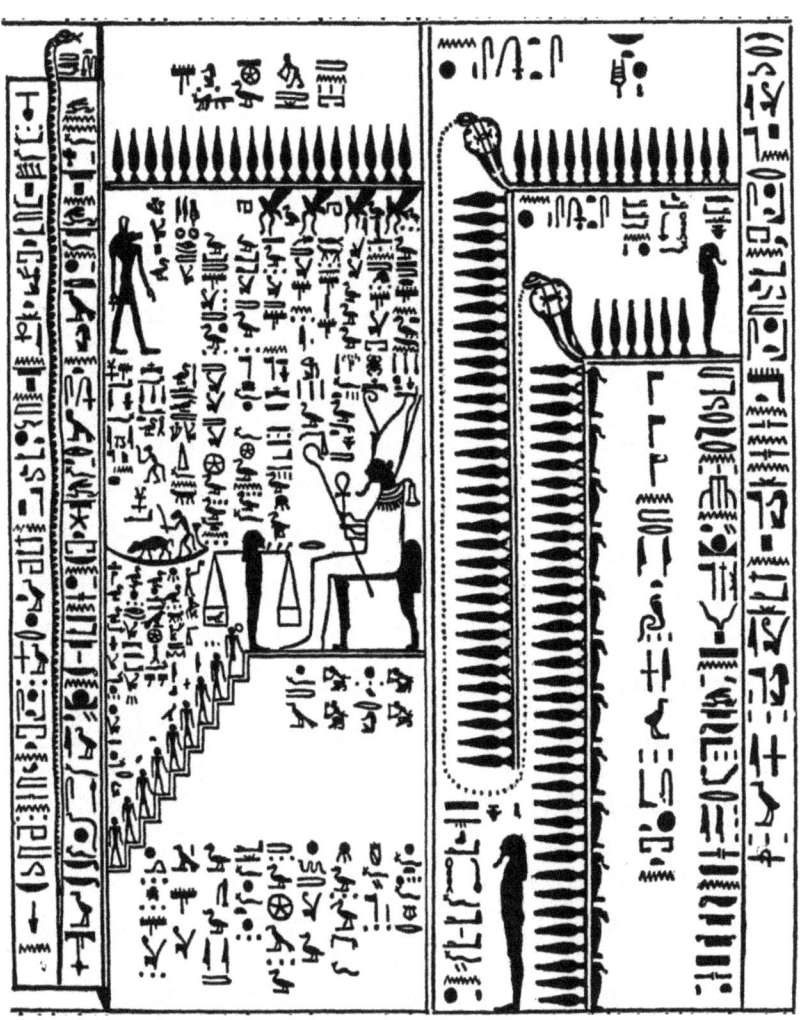

The Fifth Gate, the Judgement Scene, and the Fifth Gate concluded, on Seti I's sarcophagus.

Guardian captions:

> True-heart: he bends his arms for Re.
>
> Mystery-heart: he bends his arms for Re.

Mummies caption:

> Gods and goddesses[87] in this gate:
>
> "Come then to us, foremost of the Akhet,
>   Great God, parter of the Mysteries;
> Open for you are the hallowed gates,
>   Revealed for you are the Mysteries' doors!"

Commentary

And here we come to the Hall of Judgement, where the progress of Re, living candidates, and dead ones who were Justified in life, is now checked to see if it truly *measures up* to the path ahead of them; the path of true Justification in death as well as life, and of seeing if they can indeed become one "who is of the gods."

This also means never having to go through this test again, even if they *do* go back into life, or into the physical world while not actually being alive (such as being a sleeping monarch). But more commonly, those who pass this test go on to serve in the inner realms in some way.

Scene 33

Title:

> The covering of the gods who are among the Underworlders;[88]
>   The bread-measure[89] of the threshing floor.

---

[87] Note the phonetic spelling: see **goddess** for other phonetically identical words.

[88] The Judgement Scene, which is mainly written cryptographically, was translated with reference to Manassa 2006.

[89] Bread pun: this is specifically a measure for loaves of bread.

Antelope heads:

Roarers:

They guard the weight of the Radiant,
    Issuing instructions for those who are scrutinized:
It is they who are exulted,
    And, by those in the Earth, who keep safe from the Place of Destruction.
It is they whose heads/best come forth from/through the Mystery:
    They appear in glory in (their) governance/manifestation.[90]

Anubis figure:

The lifespan of the human
    Belongs to the Royal Child:
He who inlays/overlays/absorbs[91] his father.

About the boat with the monkeys:

The word of the Righteous is exulted:
    He separates the words, the winnowed kernels,[92] that are of the bread.

The monkey in the boat:

The monkey/other:
    This god
        Is the appearance in glory
        Of what is absorbed:
            He gives (out) the fluid.[93]

---

[90] This could refer both to the antelopes and the people they guard.

[91] *sam*, causative of *am*, **absorb**. See **inlay** for definition. The word can mean all these things: the Royal Child is interpenetrating and absorbing his 'father,' the 'human.' Do you remember how the last stage in the process of becoming Radiant described in Scene 7 is "the Child"? Recall the lines, in Scene 8, "I, the son who came forth from his father; I, the father who came forth from his son." The human being's lifespan now belongs to the Royal Child, the adept who "came forth from his father" and is therefore the father's son, but who is in another sense linked with *the* father.

[92] See **winnowed kernels**. This puns on Djehuty.

The pig:

What is absorbed.[94]

Explanation of what is going on with the monkeys:

The god, his appearance in glory, the eye [being his authority],[95]
Underworlders are of his guarding.
"You have been exulted, Underworlders, because of your (own) governance."[96]

Caption for the figure superimposed on the scales:

One holding the god,[97] borne by/bearing the Scales,
Is (also) the plummet which keeps pure the Scales.

Explanation of the figure superimposed on the scales:

The god rendering the weighing of the temple bread,
    The cakes/documents,[98] namely the Radiant;
Bearing the words/ashlars/ones-to-be-installed-as-gods[99] in the Scales.
(The Evil, the Mortal, are finished developing.)
Weighing the words/ashlars/ones-to-be-installed-as-gods
    Is protecting the Eye.

Figures on the staircase:

Nine who are in the Seat-of-the-Eye.

The Radiant who are in the West.

---

[93] Superficially, he spits. But the notion of a holy fluid has run through this text.

[94] The pig, an *unclean animal*, has been absorbed, and what comes out is "fluid."

[95] Missing on Seti I's coffin: a blank space has been left here. Filled in from alternate versions given by Manassa (2006, p.124).

[96] i.e. You ascended as a result of your conduct.

[97] The sign is literally a little man holding a *nTr* sign.

[98] The bread theme intersects with the law-court theme here: this word is written *Sawt* "documents," but the determinative is what you would expect for *Saywt*, "cakes."

[99] The signs here can be read as *mdw* or *wdnw*. (Manassa 2006, p.128). *wdn* is used to mean "install (as god or king)" in the Pyramid Texts. (Faulkner 1962, p.73)

Fifth Hour

Text above these figures:

> Now what/who is Radiant of Re is at peace in the Duat;
>> He opens up the Original Darkness to be rejuvenated into life.
>
> At peace is the god through what he has ordained,
>> When he appears through his Eye.

The four figures with axes against their heads:

> Adversaries of Seat-of-the-Eye.

Text beneath the threshing floor/staircase:

> His adversaries are under the stairway;
>> Gods, the Radiant, are before him/in his phallus/in his measure-of-capacity.[100]
>
> He cultivates the differences in the Underworlders;
>> (But) he ordains for his adversaries the Place of Destruction:
>
> Their presences, he works their slaughtering.

Commentary

Title: This tells us what is about to happen: the person will be clothed as a godly one, if their harvest measures up.

Antelope heads: These beings overlook the harvest of those to be scrutinized. They are an inherent part of the pattern of this Mystery, and they emerge and shine in their brightness as the candidate approaches Osiris.

Anubis figure: An alternate reading of the caption is:

> The standing-place of Re,
>> having become beautiful in redness.[101]

Having become beautiful in redness is saying that the person has been recognized in the (Inner) Desert as being 'bright,' and is the mortal who

---

[100] A triple pun on *m-bAH* **before him**: see Faulkner 1962, pp.77–78.
[101] Manassa 2006, p.130

awakens to the Divine within. It is also the redness of the sun as it prepares to rise, and the redness of the ribbon of Justification.

About the boat with the monkeys: The apes/monkeys/baboons in the Duat are often aspects of Djehuty/Thoth, who is heavily connected with the process of Judgement, along with Ma'at. Here we have the heart spirit of those being judged, speaking truth of the harvest. In most Egyptian funerary texts, the heart spirit speaks on behalf of the person, as the heart is the seat of Ma'at and cannot lie. The power of Djehuty, depicted as the "apes in the boat," listens to the voice of truth, and judges the words of those who have made it this far.

The monkey in the boat: Again this is a sideways reference to the presence of the power of Djehuty, the one who measures. One of the aspects of Djehuty that connects him to measurement is his baboon form. In ancient Egypt it was believed that the Baboon urinated on the hour every hour for twelve hours a day, hence the connection between the baboon and Djehuty/Thoth: "He puts out the fluid."[102]

The pig: The pig is often ignored in this text, as it appears so cryptic. However magicians should easily recognize the Egyptian version of the scapegoat here. In Egyptian society, the pig often took the role that the goat can in Jewish mythology: remnants of 'sins' are cast into the creature which is then driven out of the hall.

An aspect of the pig in its role as scapegoat can be seen hidden in the story of the Black Pig.[103] As the candidate or dead reach the hall, any possible scapegoated sins cast magically against the candidate are projected onto the pig which is then driven away from the hall.

This is talking about situations like false witness, or magically chaining false crimes to the soul of a person—a particularly nasty and well-known aspect of unbalanced magic that still appears occasionally in Near Eastern cultures. It is used as a form of cursing, with the intention that the person on death would be falsely judged and their soul destroyed. The monkey, however, Djehuty, is an upholder of Ma'at, and spots false judgement in his measuring. He casts it into the pig, which is then driven out of the hall.

Explanation of what is going on with the monkeys: Here people traversing the Underworld, living and dead, are told that by reaching this point of the *Gates*, they no longer have to go through the trials of birth and death.

---

[102] Clagett 1995, p.148
[103] Murray 1913, pp.56–58

Fifth Hour

Caption for the figure superimposed on the scales: This is showing how the person is the fulcrum of the scales. They are not judged by the scales, which is a lesser version of this dynamic; rather they are being weighed to ascertain if they have yet reached the point in their development at which they have truly become the fulcrum of the scales. It is a higher octave of the judgement by scales. Their harvest is not weighed by the scales, their harvest is to *become* the scales, the fulcrum of balance, a Justified one of true voice—one with Ma'at, one who is of the gods.

Explanation of the figure superimposed on the scales: This verse explains a little more about the nature of the Justified One being the scales. "The cakes/documents, namely the Radiant" refers to what has been made of their harvest. What was threshed has been transformed into cakes. Alchemy of the soul. The documents refers to the evidence of the heart spirit rendered unto the power of Djehuty.

It also points out that those who were not right for stepping into the role of the scales are "finished developing." That is to say that they will go no further. They are the ones outside the Hall, preparing to go back into life/rebirth.

So instead of stepping *before* the scales, they step *into* the scales. They are weighed and tested by their ability to become the scales and be truly balanced. This is a process known in Kabbalah as *Tikkun Olam*, the repair of the cracked vessel, or completion for eternity.

Figures on the staircase: The figures on the staircase are ones who are Justified and can take their place before Osiris and become the scales. Through becoming the scales, they become Osiris.

Text beneath the threshing floor/staircase: These are the ones with no place before Osiris, who cannot become the scales, and who are therefore destroyed.

Fifth Gate concluded

Doorway serpent caption:

> Kindling with his Eye:
>   He exists over this door,
>   He opens for Re.

> Perception to Kindling with his Eye:

> "Open your portal for Re,
>   Reveal your door for He of the Akhet.
> Now he makes bright the Original Darkness,
>   He gives a lightening in/from the Hidden Region."

> Sealed is this door
>   After the entry of this Great God.
> Alas, then, for the ones in their gate,
>   Should they hear the shutting of this door.

Commentary

Once the candidate has successfully become one with the scales, they can pass through the Fifth Gate. They and Re (they are as one, alike and of each other) illuminate the original darkness, and bring brightness to this place. This is a mirror of the first act of creation: *let there be light*.

Sixth Hour

The sixth hour was not included on Seti I's sarcophagus. Instead it was reproduced in full on his tomb walls.

Scene 34

Twelve figures carrying forked sticks: [104]

> Ones possessing mortal-grapples

The accompanying text reads:

> Says to them Re:
>
> "Receive for yourselves your mortal-grapples
>   Which you hold fast for yourselves in your arms.
> Oho! What is yours is in the Absorbing One;
>   Oho! Dispute you what should be in him,
>   That what is best in him[105] may come forth, and he retire."

---

[104] The sixth hour, missing from Seti I's coffin, has been translated using primarily the sixth hour as written in Seti I's tomb. Photographs of the whole hour are available in Hornung 1991, pp.128–133.

Say they to Re:

"Now our mortal-grapples, Re, are in the Absorbing One;
    We dispute with an evil serpent.
O Re, behold what is best as it comes forth
    From this part of the coils of a retiring serpent."

These gods are in the barque,
    Opposing Apep in Nut
    When they are passing through the Duat.
They, opposing Apep when he is upon Re in the West,
    Are Underworlders steering this god.

Their extension is in bread,
    Their scale-pans are hallowed vessels,
    Their cold refreshment is water.

Now, putting forth what is theirs on Earth
    Means opposing the Trespasser when he is upon Re in the
    West.

Commentary

These are powers that keep the destructive serpent power under control in the Underworld and the stars/sky. The forked staffs are snake catchers, similar to the bottom of the Was sceptre, which is also forked as it has power over serpents. These snake catcher sticks are still in use today in Egypt: the forked end is placed on the neck of the snake to pin it down. These powers guard Re and the candidates as they pass through the Underworld and as they traverse the stars.

---

[105] Again, the head/best pun: *tpw jm.f.* "What is best in him," and/or "the heads in him."

Scene 35

Twelve figures carrying a serpent which has a head between each god, and another head on the serpent's own head:

>The possession of the Absorber;
>>The coming forth of the heads/best in his coils.

The accompanying text reads:

>With their persecution of what is evil of zeal,[106]
>>They force into place adversaries of Re.
>They are who hold fast the Trespasser,
>>Rendering the coming-forth of the heads/best in him.

Says to them Re:

"You have returned the Trespasser;
>You have retired Apep.

The heads/best in him come forth at his wiping away;
>I call upon them, and he is destroyed.

O heads/best, absorbing for yourselves that which absorbed you,

>Consume you him from whom you have come forth."

Re calls upon them, they come forth:
>Thus they may absorb their coils, that he might pass through them;
>And thus the heads/best might (re)enter into their coils afterwards.

Eyeless is this serpent,
>Noseless and earless;
He breathes by his roars,
>He lives by calling upon himself.

Their extension is in being at peace upon[107] Earth,
   In accordance with Re at his coming forth from/into the Duat.

Now, putting forth what is theirs
   Means being one who stands erect,[108] in the possession of grace.

Commentary

An interesting thing pops up here (literally!): the heads in the serpent. This dynamic occurs in serpents of destruction, measure, protection, and prophecy. It represents attendant or integrated beings within the serpent that act as eyes, ears, or mouths for the serpents, and/or consciousnesses that the serpent has taken into itself and trapped.

As Re and the candidates start the long journey of ascent out of the Duat, they encounter many different serpent beings, some helpful but most dangerous. Attendants and workers in each hour are called to suppress the dangerous serpents through pinning, separating them from their powers, and so forth. The powers of destruction, which are an integral part of the Duat, have to be overcome for creation to rise out from the Duat.

Scene 36

---

[106] *Hr* "zeal" punning on *Hr* "face," amplifying the head/best theme. Please note that zeal, as used in this text, means only "intense (sometimes fanatical) enthusiasm; activity arising from warm support or enthusiasm; strong feeling, such as love, anger, etc., or passionate ardour." (Schwarz 1991, p.1252) It does not relate to the Zealots, the militant Jewish sect who vigorously opposed the Roman domination of Palestine until the ruin of Jerusalem in 70 A.D..

[107] *tp* again, so this could be read as "Their extension is being at peace, being the best of Earth."

[108] *aHa* + god determinative.

Heads from Scene 35 in the tomb of Seti I.

Twelve figures hold a rope twined round itself…

> Possessing what is in the twice-twisted one.[109]
> Come forth the hours from in it.

…its middle passing round, or through, the neck of a mummiform figure:

> Entering-Into[110]

The accompanying text reads:

> "Hold fast for yourselves what is in the twice-twisted one,
>   Which you have withdrawn from the mouth of Entering-Into.
> The coming-forth of your hours
>   Is your becoming Radiant from yourselves, through them;
> The peace of the hours has to do with your portions

---

[109] *(j)m(j)-ann.wy* "what is in the twice-twisted one," i.e. the rope doubled round itself. Do not confuse this with the "two tapes" in Scene 31, which are *mtwy*. Different things.

[110] *aqn* with god determinative. From *aq n* "enter into (a state)" (Faulkner 1962, p.49). Usually just transliterated as "Aqen," this intriguing character also appears in Spell 99 of *The Book of the Dead* (Faulkner 1985 [1972], pp.90–97). Possibly "one to whom entry belongs."

As the twice-twisted one (re)enters the mouth of Entering-
   Into."

Comes forth a coil, develops an hour;
   With Re's calling, she is in the peace of her seat:[111]
   Thus Entering-Into absorbs the twice-twisted one.

Say they to Re:

"Now the twice-twisted one belongs to Entering-Into;
   Now the hours belong to the Great God.
Your Radiance, Re, is your sunshine;
   Your peace is your remains, whose bestowals are hidden."

Their extension is in bread,
   Their scale-pans are hallowed vessels,
   Their cold refreshment is water.

Now, putting forth what is theirs on Earth
   Means what pertains to a coil in the twice-twisted one.

Commentary

This scene brings to the fore those of the double rope, i.e. those destined to be reborn back into the cycle of life and death, i.e. time, and "given hours." Entering-Into, Aqen, also known as "the mouth of time" is one who swallows down those of the double rope, for time to be formed.

Whereas the single rope/serpent power measures time and place, the double rope combines opposing powers: nothing can manifest without the polar opposites of positive and negative—the rule of Ma'at—so whereas a single rope measures, this double rope creates time by nature of its duality.

---

[111] Hours are later depicted as female figures, so the feminine gender of the original has been retained.

Scene 37

The Sun Barque, in the centre of which is the Meat of Re, with Spiral over him. In the front of the barque is Perception; by the oars, Magic. The barque is towed by four Underworlders:

> The towing of this Great God by gods, by Underworlders.

The accompanying text reads:

> Say they to Re:
>
> "The towing is for you, Great God,
>   Master of Hours, who formulates the business of Earth.
> The living of gods *is* his forms;
>   The Radiant are those who look upon his developments."
>
> Says to them Re:
>
> "Radiance to you, towing ones,
>   Hallowing to you, towing ones,
>   Smoothing my way through the requirements[112] of the Duat.
>
> Tow you me to the Place of Establishing Designs;
>   Stand you erect at that Mountain which is the Mystery of
>   the Akhet."

Commentary

Re instructs those who tow him to take him to the Place of Establishing Designs, the staging area of life. Life is limitation of expression—birth, life,

---

[112] *Xrt*, usually **portion**.

death—which flows through a fate pattern, which also limits it to some extent. Re then says to those towing him: "Stand you erect at that Mountain which is the Mystery of the Akhet." This is directly related to the Mountain within the Western Death Mysteries.

In the esoteric Western Mysteries, after the dead have gone through their various stages of dissolution, they climb a great mountain, and if they reach the top then they traverse down the other side into life, or they step off the mountain into an inner realm to exist as an inner contact.

The peak of the mountain is the end of the dissolution phase of death, and the cusp of the journey back into life. It also refers to the upward climb back into life, or the continuing climb beyond life into the stars, a dynamic known in Western Magic as the *Ladder of Ascent*. It is also the steps climbed out of the Cave of Osiris towards the Inner Temple in the stars, a dynamic known in certain aspects of Western Magic.

The mountains of ascent in the Western Mysteries are depicted in various artworks connected to the Mysteries, as well as mentioned in stories, texts, and poetry, and they are depicted in the background of the Judgement card in the Rider-Waite Tarot deck.

Scene 38

Twelve figures with hidden arms:

> Hidden-armed ones, subjects of the Mysteries.

The accompanying text reads:

> They exist under that which is made Mysterious of this Great God:
> It cannot be looked upon by ones in the Duat.
> It *can* be seen by the Mortal,
> When they are burning up at the Benben Enclosure

Sixth Hour

At the place in the possession of the remains of this god.[113]

Says to them Re:

"Receive for yourselves my governance;
  Embrace for yourselves your Mysteries.
You shall be at peace at the Benben Enclosure,
  Near the place in the possession of my remains, which I am in.
What is made Mysterious, which belongs to what you are in,
  Is what is made Mysterious of the Duat, which is held secret by your arm."

Say they to Re:

"Your Presence/Ram is for the skies, Foremost of the Akhet;
  It is your shadow that passes through the Place of the Mysteries.
  Your remains are for the Earth, (with you) belonging in the heavens.
We shall place Re (back) there,
  As you are estranged from it, Re.
You should breathe: you are in the peace
  Of your remains, which are in the Duat."

Their extension is the contentment[114] of being remobilized:
  At peace are the Presences with this.

Now, putting forth what is theirs on Earth
  Means searching out brightness in the Duat.

---

[113] These armless people are Mortal, i.e. those who are going back into life. They "burn on the Benben stone" like the phoenix, and rise from the ashes. This scene describes the rebirth of those Mortals into new lives. Note that Re says to *them*, and to no one else, "you shall be at peace in the Benben Enclosure."

[114] *Htpw*, usually translated **peace**.

Commentary

"The Benben Enclosure" means the deep place in the earth from which all life springs, the realm of Tatenen, an ancient Underworld god from whom creation rises. The Benben stone/mound harks back to the creation myth of a mound rising out of the chaotic waters, the first land that brought life.

The remains of the honoured/royal dead in Old Kingdom Egypt were placed in burial mounds that mimicked the Benben, mounds that eventually morphed into pyramids. From these Benben burials the soul would rise again for rebirth. Their Mysteries, which are unseen by those in the Duat, are those of the vital spark of the life Mystery: the Brightness.

The arms of the figures to whom Re speaks hold a secret—inaction or concealed action—and the bright spark is hidden within. This is a place where the fragments of the form are brought back together again, "Near the place in the possession of my remains, which I am in." The people with their arms hidden and their brightness hidden are ones who hold that spark of life, the trigger that starts the life formation process. They stay in this place in peace, keeping a presence here that radiates out and affects everything around them. They uphold the sacred Mystery of the conceiving of a life, in a place where scattered parts are brought back together—the process of Osiris.

Their speech outlines the active duty of the ones whose arms are concealed. They are instrumental in the process of renewal and ascent for Re (and all others passing through).

They declare their function to be the act of reuniting estranged parts and putting Re back into the heavens; and through their service, they develop. "Their extension is the contentment of being remobilized: At peace are the Presences with this." Through their service, new life can form and the deepest Mystery of life, which they guard, is triggered in those who are going through the 'reunion' phase. They assist in the rebirth of humans, and of Re.

The way that service is done is not only though holding the Mystery, but also through partaking of that Mystery, and rising out of the Benben in renewal.

Scene 39

Eight figures:

> Gods belonging to enclosure

The accompanying text reads:

> They exist outside the Benben Enclosure,
>   They look upon what Re is looking upon;
> They enter into his governance of the Mystery of living on:
>   They are those who are sent out as conformists.[115]

Said to them:

> "My extension is your extension;
>   Now my breathing is your breathing.
> You are those who are in my Mysteries;
>   While I exist at the backs of my Mysteries
>   Which are in the Benben Enclosure.
> Oho! to you:
>   Live shall your Presences!"

Their extension: the extension of He of the Akhet.[116]

Commentary

This scene introduces gods and godly ones involved in the rebirth process. They act as guardians, midwives, and assistants at the very beginning of the rebirth process. Re then speaks to those at the Benben: "Live shall your Presences!" This is the preparation for rebirth.

---

[115] i.e. as little images of his Mysteries, sent back into the manifest world.

[116] They are extending back into life, just as Re does when he rises over the horizon.

Scene 40

A figure leans on a staff…

    The Duat's

    …looking at twelve mummies on tables shaped like the Nehep serpent:

    Ones in the following of Seat-of-the-Eye,
        Dreamers who are in a torpor.

The accompanying text reads:

    Says The Duat's to them:

    "O gods, tenants[117] of the Duat,
        Who are in the rule of the West,
    Who are Upright, (though) upon their sides,
        Spending the night upon their supports:
    Raising for you of your meat,[118]
        Putting-together for you of your frames,
    Embracing for you of your limbs,
        Remobilizing for you of your meat;
    Breath that is delightful to your noses,
        Unravelling for your wrappings,
    Uncovering for your veils,
        Exposure for your divine ones:[119]
    You shall see the brightness by them.
    Standing-erect for you, namely you faint ones,
        That you may receive for yourselves your meadows
        At the marsh (which is) the Mistress of Peace.
    Meadows are yours of this marsh,
        Her waters are yours; your peace is in me,
        And the meadows in the Mistress of Peace."

    Their cold refreshment is water.

Now Care, he guards their remains,
   (But) their Presences pass through to the Marsh of Rushes,
Coming into power by means of their cold refreshment.[120]

Treading out[121] the earth, they reckon up their meat.

Their extension is bread,
   Their scale-pans are hallowed vessels,
   Their cold refreshment is water.

Now, putting forth what is theirs on Earth
   Means being an ennobled one at peace upon his support.

Commentary

This verse talks to those undergoing the Osiris process: their parts are reunified. They are called to rise, wake, and to receive their land allotted to them. All the parts that make up a living person are torn apart at death and separated out. As the eternal part of the person traverses the Duat, if it is appropriate, those parts are drawn back together and reawakened, ready for renewal in eternal life.

In the previous scenes we were shown the vital spark of life preparing to rise from the Benben. Here the form of the human is brought back together for the vital force to have a vessel. This hour is very much about awakening and assembling all the parts: the process of the Osirian Mysteries where what was torn apart is once again made whole.

---

[117] Also a potential connotation of "southern-sailing ones."

[118] i.e. human flesh.

[119] With eye determinative: less literally, "your divine eyes."

[120] Another two clues about the meaning of "cold refreshment" here: the water is defined as belonging to the "Mistress of Peace," and partaking of it is required in order for Presences to "come into power."

[121] See **tread out** for grain reference.

Scene 41

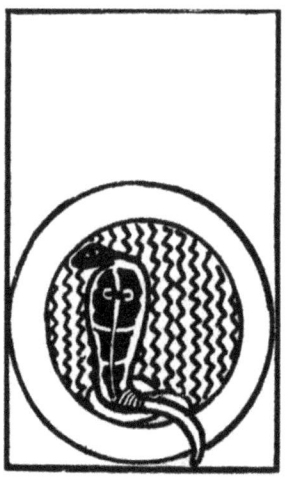

Twelve bowing figures...

> Gods who are in the Quarry Place of the Earth

...before a circle containing a Uraeus, bookended by two mummies:

> Glow-face
>
> Kindle-face

The accompanying text reads:

> They exist in the circumference of this Quarry Place,
>> There exists a Risen One who is alive in this Quarry Place,
>> The water of the Quarry Place exists as fire.
>
> Gods of Earth, Presences of Earth, cannot drop into this Quarry Place,
>> Which is in the arm of the flame of this Risen One.
>
> Breathes this Great God, who is of the outer[122] chamber of the Duat,
>> By the hallowed water of this Quarry Place.

Says to them Re:

"So Oho!, Gods who guard the hallowed Quarry Place,
    Rendering water to the outer chamber of the Silent Land.
Now the water of the Quarry Pit belongs to Seat-of-the-Eye,
    And your cold refreshment[123] to the Foremost of the Duat.
Now the balm of your fiery blast, which is your lickings,
    Is at the Presences of those who arise to disobey Seat-of-the-Eye.
Not lacking is the screech of the Quarry Place; none is like you,

And there is no coming-into-power from its waters for the gods who guard it."

Their extension is bread,
    Their scale-pans are hallowed vessels,
    Their cold refreshment is water.

Now, putting forth what is theirs on Earth
    Means being a hallowed one[124] in the West.

Commentary

The Quarry Place is where raw materials are excavated and shaped in form ready to be used in construction. So the same applies in the Duat: the raw materials for the life form are quarried and shaped in form ready for the construction of form for the Ascending One. It is both a place and a power.

Re's speech defines this as the Quarry Place for Osiris and the Osirian process. It also brings back mention of the coolness of water, which is the power balanced and transformed, and how that water can be fire that burns and attacks imbalance.

In the Egyptian pattern, this place speaks of the cave/chamber from which Osiris rises, and to Western magicians it also speaks of the magical

---

[122] Potentially *southern/forward* chamber, i.e. the bit of the Duat that is past the Judgement scene.

[123] Note here how the "cold refreshment" so essential for progress is here defined as coming from the water in this pit; and how it is linked to the venom of the Risen One, which can be both a cure and a poison: the "balm of your fiery blast, which is your lickings."

[124] *Dsry* + god determinative.

Abyss. For Quareia adepts, think of the Abyss and the cave/chamber with its access upwards to be states that run parallel to each other. For the Egyptians they were perceived as interwoven. This tells us that this is the last deep point of the passage through the Duat before the power shifts. It is also the end of the sixth hour and the threshold of the sixth gate, the middle of the twelve hours.

It is also the deep point where the voice of creation echoes down and across the Abyss in an act of creation or destruction: "Not lacking is the screech of the Quarry Place; none is like you." Quareia adepts should recognize what that means.

Sixth Gate

> The arrival by this god at the gate;
>   The entry into this gate.
>
> The worship of this Great God by the gods in her.

Gate caption:

> Expert of Her Master

Uraeus serpents caption:

> She kindles for Re

Guardian captions:

> Remobilizing: he bends his arms for Re.
>
> Standing erect: he bends his arms for Re.

Mummies caption:

> The Sixth Nine: m [125]

"Come then to us, Foremost of the Akhet,
  Great God who is parting the Mysteries.
Open to you are the hallowed gates,
  Revealed to you are the doors of the Mysteries."

Sixth Hour

Doorway serpent caption:

Walking Off Through His Eye:

He exists over this door,
    He opens for Re.

Perception to Walking Off Through His Eye:

"Open your portal for Re,
    Reveal your door for He of the Akhet."

Now he makes bright the Original Darkness;
    He gives a lightening in/from the Hidden Region.

Sealed is this door
    After the entry of this Great God.
Alas, then, for Presences in this gate,
    Should they hear the shutting of this door.

Commentary

Most of this you should understand now from your reading of the previous gates. Note the lines: "Now he makes bright the Original Darkness; He gives a lightening in/from the Hidden Region." This speaks not only of Re, but of the candidate and Justified dead passing through the gate. They have the knowledge of the brightness and can illuminate the original darkness—remember, *let there be light*. This action is repeated at each gate, bringing life and illumination to wake up the gate. Once the retinue passes, the gate falls into darkness and stillness again.

---

[125] The *m* is odd here: possibly it may have crept in from the beginning of the accompanying text, *my rk r.n* "come then to us," or it may indicate the halfway mark, *m* being the ideogram for "half, side" (Gardiner 1957, p.542).

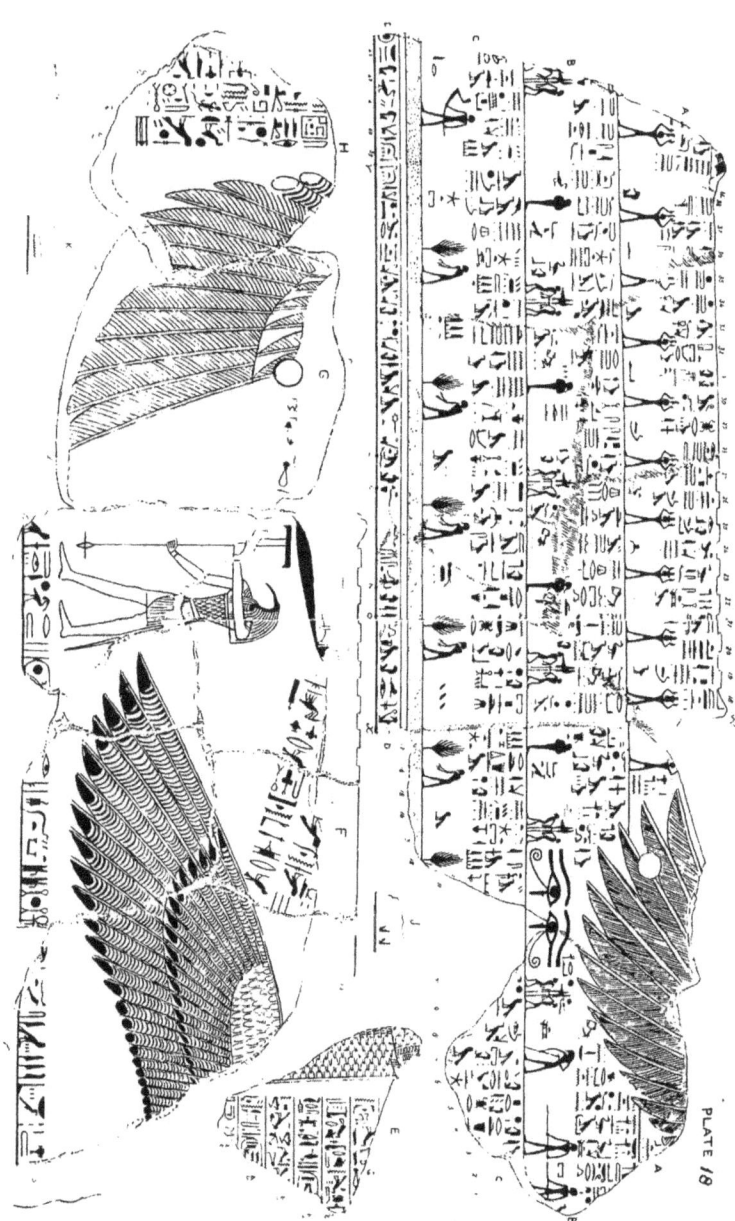

Fragments from the Seventh Hour (Bonomi and Sharpe 1864).

Seventh Hour

Scene 42

Twelve figures carrying breadbaskets on their heads:

    Those who are at peace; the development of the extension.[126]

The accompanying text reads:

    The begetters of consecrations of their gods,[127]
        Purifying their sustenances
    So as not to unbalance what is radiant upon his breathing,
        From/Or what is mortal upon his cold refreshment.
    They are those who are at peace in their extension;
        They have arrived at their godhoods, their sustenances.
    Their arms are theirs at their entering their loaves,
        At the gate which caters for her gods.

    Says to them Seat-of-the-Eye:

    "Your bread is yours, (being) your expressions,
        Ones who are at peace, developing extensions.
    You have come into power through your pairs of feet,

---

[126]Their extension is bread...

> You are at peace in/through your hearts.
> The arm/bun is yours which is of your godhoods;
> Your loaves are of your sustenances."

Their extension is bread,
  Their scale-pans are hallowed vessels,
  Their cold refreshment is water.[128]

Now, putting forth what is theirs on Earth
  Means being a master of peace in the West.

Commentary

Now we are back to the near Justified ones, who carry in baskets that which they made from their harvest: their bread. This is the products of their actions, deeds, learning, etc. They have survived the trials so far, and have come to the point in the hours of Osiris where things are put back together. Remember the connection between Osiris and the bread: they are moving towards becoming Osiris.

> Your bread is yours, (being) your expressions.

This is a very important line, and a deep part of the adept Mysteries. The bread is the product of the life actions and most importantly, evolution, of the person/soul. **Expression**, *tpy-r*, is in Egyptian literally "what is atop the mouth." Michael translated this phrase with a more general noun because the phrase itself has several different pertinent connotations that can all be approximated with the English word "expression": see the glossary entry.

However, **expression**'s most literal translation as "the utterance of your mouth" refers to a particular magical dynamic of creation. Everything is uttered into action, into life, and into being. The bread is the evolved measure of their utterances, which has been winnowed, harvested, threshed, baked,

---

[127] See Scene 5.

[128] We are now in a position to understand each line of this offering list: the extension into bread relates to the assumption of powers that come from Divinity. The scale-pans are hallowed vessels because the adepts have purified their sustenances, keeping clear of stimuli/nourishment that could unbalance them. For the identification of the adept with the scale-pan, see the Judgement Scene (Scene 33). The cold waters are a requirement for the above, and come from the Mistress of Silence whose venom is the waters of the Silent Land.

Seventh Hour

and so forth. What they did in life has come to fruition in death, or through the living passage through the *Gates*. They have become Osiris.

Scene 43

Twelve figures with Ma'at feathers on their heads:

The Righteous: subjects of Truth.

The accompanying text reads:

Workers of Truth:
   When they are on Earth,
   They are striving for their godhoods.
They are those who are summoned to a post of the Earth,
   To the enclosure (called) Living In Truth.
Scrutinized for them is their Truth,
   Before the Great God who causes the destruction of sin.

Says to them Seat-of-the-Eye:

"Truth is yours, the Righteous,
   You are at peace through your works,
Through developing into one of my followers,
   Who are tenants of an enclosure which is hallowed of his
        Presence.
You live as they live,
   You breathe in what they breathe in.
I have ordained for you an existence to its limit,
   Subject to Truth, without the exposure of sin to it."

Their extension is with the Truth,
   Their scale-pans are with the wine,[129]

> Their cold refreshment is with the water.
>
> Now, putting forth what is theirs on Earth
> > Means being a Righteous One of their lake.[130]

Commentary

Again this scene is about near Justified ones, and this time it looks at their Truth, their Ma'at, as is it measured. It also introduces the "post" of development, the understanding of which will open out further in the Seventh Hour.

The near Justified, living and dead, are likened to Osiris's "followers," i.e. those who will ascend with Re to become ones who are of the gods. Their being "tenants of an enclosure which is hallowed of his Presence" relates them to the Inner Temple, which is a reflection of the outer temple. It is a place where the Justified who are priests or priestesses serve. It also, more superficially, talks of those Finished Ones who work in service in this part of the Duat, which is steeped in the process of developing. This process is about becoming a Finished One and serving as a Finished One while developing for the next stage.

> I have ordained for you an existence to its limit,
> > Subject to Truth, without the exposure of sin to it.

This talks about the life measures of existence for Finished Ones, and their protection by deities/powers from destructive powers that strike when someone is not within Ma'at.

The developing comes from the coolness of their "lake," which again refers back to their ability in life to transform the inner fire into a coolness that nourishes: living within Ma'at.

Those who have been Justified in life must defend that Justification in death. If they are successful in defending/proving their harvest/bread, and can develop beyond the stage of the Finished One, then they become one who "shines for a million years." This is not literally million years; really it means "until the end of time." They are to become *as gods*.

---

[129] See Scene 16.

[130] Again, recalling Scene 16. Note that *S* could also be translated "garden." (Faulkner 1962, p.260)

Most of this hour in the Duat is about the various stages of development for the Justified One, what those stages are, and, as you will see, how one achieves them.

Scene 44

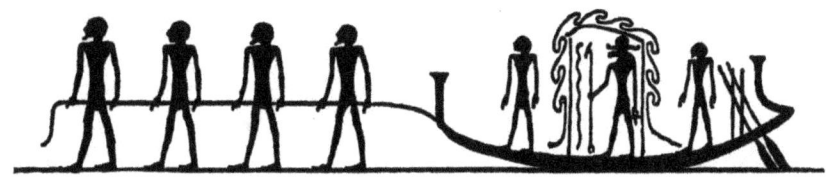

The Sun Barque, in the centre of which is the Meat of Re, with Spiral over him. In the front of the barque is Perception; by the oars, Magic. The barque is towed by four Underworlders:

The towing of this Great God by gods, by Underworlders

The accompanying text reads:

Say they when they tow Re:

"Towering is the sun-disc, which is the foremost one of Spiral;[131]
Shining is the head/best of one who is in his shrine.
You shall look, foremost ones of the Duat:
Your two eyes are yours, gods.
Behold Re, coming into power in the Silent Land;
The Great God, he ordains your designs."

---

[131] In one respect, Re is the foremost one of the serpent *mHn*, "Spiral," because he is the most basic force and being that goes through the spiral process. The spiral is the result of *Dt*, linear continuity, plus *nHH*, cyclical continuity. See Scene 15: "Hail to you, who eternally recurs, Master of the years; Who is eternally the same, Who cannot be extinguished." See also **eternal recurrence** and **eternal sameness**. Others also go through the spiral process—for instance, reincarnating humans—but Re is the most basic force that does this and is the model and ancestor of all smaller manifestations of this dynamic. If you look at how *mHn* "Spiral" is drawn, then you see the spiral quite clearly rendered, though it is not rendered as we who are used to perspective might expect. To an Egyptian, our method of rendering a

Scene 45

Seven jackal-headed influence-staffs,[132] *two enemies bound to each, plus one mummified figure attended by two figures leaning on staffs.*

First staff-leaning figure:

A Finished One

First influence-staff:

Bound beings: Adversaries of Re
Mummy: Holding fast

Second influence-staff:

Bound beings: Adversaries of a Finished One
Mummy: Being a brewer

Third influence-staff:

Bound beings: Adversaries of a Developing One
Mummy: Being empty of infiltration[133]

Fourth influence-staff:

Bound beings: Adversaries of an Empty One
Mummy: Respectfulness

Fifth influence-staff:

2d spiral, as a sort of series of almost-circles nearly on top of each other, would suggest that the spiral *goes back on itself*, which it doesn't: it always goes forward into the future. Apep's spirals, on the other hand, *are* rendered as going back on themselves, perhaps because it is a chaotic force and goes all over the place. Perversely, this makes Apep look more spirally to our eyes than Mehen! Further, note that in some respects, Re's "shrine," his holy home, could be conceived of as Spiral itself. Re's spiralling journey *is* his home.

[132]The poles themselves are instances of the hieroglyph *wsr*, influence.

[133]Reading *Sw dfy(t)*

>   *Bound beings:* Adversaries of Overflowing
>   *Mummy:* Being straight
>
> *Sixth influence-staff:*
>
>   *Bound beings:* Adversaries of Seat-of-the-Eye/a Wealthy One
>   *Mummy:* Threshing by foot
>
> *Seventh influence-staff:*
>
>   *Bound beings:* Adversaries of a Distant One
>   *Mummy:* Honour of zeal
>
> *Final staff-leaning figure:*
>
>   A Molten/Golden One[134] of the Gods

The accompanying text reads:

> The arrival by this Great God at the necks[135] of Geb.
>
> Adversaries have been scrutinized at them
>   As a result of ordaining words in the West.
>
> Says Perception to this god,
>   At his arrival at the necks of Geb:
>
> "Consider, Re, Great God:
>   Behold: you arrive at the necks of Geb."
>
> Says the Finished One to the necks:
>
> "Guard for yourselves the adversaries;
>   Hold fast for yourselves those being persecuted,
> O gods who are followers of the necks,
>   Who are in the following of Geb, the heir.[136]
> Hold fast for yourselves the adversaries;
>   Guard for yourselves those being persecuted.

---

[134] *nbw*: could refer to a "Golden One," or an abbreviated spelling of "Molten One," i.e. one at the beginning of the path, not yet formed, still hot, etc.

Neither let them come forth under your arms,
   Nor let them wobble under your fingers.
O adversaries, you are deigned[137] cut out:
   So much did Re ordain for you
By his founding of the Silent Land for his remains,
   And his creation of the Duat for his founding.
He entrusts you to your carnage;
   He scrutinizes you for what you did
   in the Great Forecourt of Re.
Like gods when they mourn the Sound Eye,[138]
   He places a Golden/Molten One of the gods for your guard.
Scrutinized are the adversaries, those being persecuted, those
      in the Duat—
   —those who are for these necks."

Commentary

In other translations the figure leaning on the staff is translated as the deity Atum, but there is no god determinative here. What is indicated is "this is like Atum," or the same power as Atum. This happens a lot in the Gates, and particularly in this section: the words sometimes point to powers and dynamics as opposed to specific deities. This is a common method used in the Mysteries, both Egyptian and Greek, and allows aspects of the Mysteries to be hidden in plain sight.

Atum is the beginning and end, the Beginning One, and the Finished One, and also Perfection. He repels and exposes adversaries, and provides protection. So the Finished One who oversees this scene is one with the Atum qualities and dynamics, and works in service to oversee the events and powers that unfold in this scene.

The text then introduces the *Geb Posts*, which are powers of influence to do with the land: *wsr* staffs of Geb. Superficially it appears that two adversaries of Re have been tied to each post and are guarded by beings within the

---

[135] *wsrt* is the word meaning "neck," which here refers to the staffs that are instances of the *wsr* **influence** sign. The word also recalls the phrase *wsr t tn* or *wsrt tn*, "influential is this bread," or "this neck," from Scene 2.

[136] "heir" receives a god determinative.

[137] *sjpt(w).Tn*, normally translated in this text as **scrutinized**.

[138] The Sound Eye is the source of notation of measures of capacity, and fractions (proportions).

Duat—the mummies. However, Michael spent a lot of time combining his knowledge of the Justification process with a very close look at the language and imagery used, and discovered a much deeper layer of teaching and advice to those treading the candidate process. Like a lot of the texts and scenes of the Gates, they hold multiple meanings.

One layer talks to the dead on the path of the Distant One, i.e. those striving to become as Re. It outlines the stages of developing through the Duat, and shows the qualities and conscious actions the dead can adopt to avoid being caught in a trap of their own making as they progress through the stages of the *Gates*.

The mummies who counter the adversaries are not Underworld demons who punish, as is often assumed—and that is a very Christian viewpoint, by the way. Rather they are Justified ones serving in the Duat for the advancement of others. Each one acts as a reflection and advisor to a soul who has found themselves challenged because of a weakness within them; but it is also a scene of advice for evolution of any soul seeking ascension.

The Geb posts are the key to the whole of the *Gates*, how they function, and why they function as they do. Once you understand the Geb posts, you are much closer to understanding the whole process of progressing through the hours in death and in life. It is no coincidence that the posts are located in the seventh hour, nor that there are seven of them.

The posts outline the stages of development for a living candidate, and advise them about how to respond to various adversities. Each post shows a deepening stage of evolution in the soul's progress. But there is a twist: it works in reverse! The influence posts mark the progression of the path of Osiris rising from the Underworld to his union with Re: becoming one who is of the gods.

The Geb posts also interlock with each other. As each phase is mastered and the candidate moves on to the next, deeper layers of the previous stage surface for reexamination and understanding. They create layer on layer of foundational understanding and skill that moves the magician towards evolution and ascent, so that by the time the magician reaches the stage of development of becoming a Finished One, they are learning to deploy in harmony all the skill sets they developed on the path.

At the end of this scene of the posts, we will look a bit more closely at the nature of the posts, and their importance to living magicians.

The magical progression of the posts starts at post seven and works backwards to one, but they are presented in the Gates with the last post listed first. Michael's translation shows the posts in their order as presented in the *Gates*; in my commentary, we will go in the order that a candidate would encounter them, i.e. the other way round.

Seventh Influence Staff:

> **Bound beings:** Adversaries of a Distant One
> **Mummy:** Honour of zeal

The seventh post shows the powers that threatens the Distant/Upward One, i.e. one who seeks to evolve and ascend. The power that counters the adversary is "honourable resolve," which is to say, being focused, honourable, and walking in Ma'at with the intention of not giving up no matter what. This prepares the soul to survive the trials of the Duat and to be reborn.

This post is connected to Horus, the son, the Distant One who rises towards the sun, and who was connected with the identity of the Pharaoh. In the Duat, on death, this is the stage where the soul seeks to move upwards to the sun, to become as Re, and one with Re. This separates such a soul from those who seek to return to life as quickly as possible, or who seek an easy heavenly afterlife—i.e. the mundane path.

Sixth Influence Staff:

> **Bound beings:** Adversaries of Seat-of-the-Eye/a Wealthy One
> **Mummy:** Threshing by foot

The sixth post shows the powers that threaten the Wealthy One, i.e. one who has been restored of their parts to become whole: Osiris. The power that counters the adversary is that of the Threshing Floor. By constantly threshing and weighing one's actions, and constantly improving the harvest in life, the power cannot tear apart that which has been made whole.

It also speaks to the wisdom that you evolve by developing your harvest as opposed to having others do it for you. This is reflected in the fifth hour, where the soul stands before Osiris in the Hall of Judgement, and becomes the scales: they become the fulcrum of the scales and thus weigh for themselves.

Quareia adepts should also recognize "threshing by foot" i.e. the Threshing Floor, a specific dynamic in the magical Mysteries.

Fifth Influence Staff:

>**Bound beings:** Adversaries of Overflowing
>**Mummy:** Being straight

The fifth post threatens the Overflowing One, one who has become filled with creativity. The power that counters the adversary of the Overflowing one is the *Plain Path*, or being **straight**. Through simplicity, necessity, and Ma'at, the dangers of, and to, the Overflowing One are neutralized. The plainer you make the path, the less obstacles you will encounter, and the more you will begin to recognize what those obstacles or adversaries are. It also points to learning how quality, not quantity, is what matters in the evolution process.

Fourth Influence Staff:

>**Bound beings:** Adversaries of an Empty One
>**Mummy:** Respectfulness

The fourth post shows the power that threatens the one who exists in peace and stillness. The countering power is "respect," which means understanding that everything has purpose and place, and to have no fear of a threatening power, but to respect its power, not react, and not let it influence you.

Third Influence Staff:

>**Bound beings:** Adversaries of a Developing One
>**Mummy:** Being empty of infiltration

The third post shows the power that threatens one who is still developing towards being Finished. The countering power to the threat is to be at peace, and not to respond to attacks, adversity, or malign influences. "Empty of Penetration" means being nonreactive, still, and silent, and not taking in that which can reach inside and disturb you.

This is a lesson that comes from being within the previous stage of consciousness. It is a precursor to self-restriction, a practising phase.

As you go through the stages of the Geb posts, you will begin to see how each stage overlaps and integrates the previous one: they are all interwoven and build as one complex weave of development.

Second Influence Staff:

> **Bound beings:** Adversaries of a Finished One
> **Mummy:** Being a brewer

The second post shows the power that threatens the Finished One, or fully Justified one. The countering power to that is *brewing*, meaning transformation, the alchemy of the soul, and continuing the process of development. In other words, the adept overcomes adversaries by working on their path and their own evolution, while also working as a "brewer" for others, by assisting and triggering their evolution and alchemical transformation. The two work together: as you help others in service, so you evolve to become as Atum: Finished.

First Influence Staff:

> **Bound beings:** Adversaries of Re
> **Mummy:** Holding fast

The first post shows powers that directly threaten Re, or those undergoing the development of the ones who are of the gods. The countering power to that threat is *restriction*, **holding fast**. If your imbalance is a direct threat to the Divine order and the progression of the Divine order, then it will be restricted.

It also speaks to the dynamic that to become one who is of the gods—to step out of the life/death cycle and move towards ascent to the heavens—one must cease to be part of living creation. One must restrict one's life expression by nature of one's being, and become 'immortal.' The ability to self-restrict is what negates the adversaries of ones who are of the gods, and it is something done by choice as opposed to by force.

Decoding the seven posts

The scene of the Geb posts is very clever and intriguing, as it shows very clearly from a magical perspective that the system of the *Gates* was as much a living path through the Mysteries as a path for the dead. And that is how it should be, as the true Mysteries reflect in death as well as in life, and whoever wishes to walk the Mysteries must walk them in life as much as in death.

It also displays very clearly how clever the Egyptians of this time were in hiding the keys of the Mysteries by embedding them in texts that are often flipped around. Things can be read backwards and well as forwards, and everything has multiple meanings.

The seven power posts of Geb should be recognized by any serious magician or hermeticist as having to do with the magical pattern of *seven* in the development of a magician on the path. The first post is in fact the last, and the seventh post is the first: they have been flipped around to hide them. It starts with the Distant/Upward One, the aspirant who wishes to climb the Ladder, and ends with Re, the Sun. Anyone who has studied and worked with the magical process of ascent should recognize this.

Each major step on the Ladder triggers traps and adversaries in life and/or death to challenge them, and this is what triggers development. Sometimes the adversary power emerges from within us and our own actions; sometimes it comes at us from life events. Where the adversary comes from is irrelevant; how we deal with it what is important.

And once you have overcome and learned from one stage, it is not left behind; rather it is added into the next phase of development. The constant polishing of the magician comes from the adversities that give opportunities for the steps to be forged in the ladder. The dynamic of *overcoming the adversary* creates a layer within the magician that matures and evolves them. Those layers add up as each phase is understood and overcome. The Finished magician, then, has a collection of knowledge and skills that helps them navigate on their path, skills which can be deployed when needed.

The mummies in this scene are there to advise those who are on their ascent how to tackle and process the adversarial powers of each stage. This scene displays a breathtaking depth of knowledge of the Mysteries, and demonstrates quite well how the magical patterns of ascent that we see in the Jewish, Hermetic, and Persian Mysteries have their roots in this older Egyptian pattern. Whether the Egyptians discovered it from another culture or developed it for themselves, I have no idea.

So this scene can be used by the living candidate for advice, and it also advises the dead Justified/candidate working their way through the Death Mysteries about how to deal with the adversaries from within, adversaries which could trap them.

Beneath this is a much deeper layer of meaning, which again works in reverse. As with all powerful Mysteries, once you peel off one layer, you find another underneath. The deeper layer speaks to the stages of birth and rebirth in respect of a candidate of the Mysteries who seeks to become *as a god* through cycles of rebirth.

If you follow the posts back from the seventh one, you first have *upward*, the first stepping forward with intent. Then you have *wealthy*, where the candidate manages to not get locked down in the Duat at death, and becomes "wealthy of lives," i.e. they become an Osiris and are reborn. Then we get to *overflowing*, where the spirit tries to live many lives to achieve things, which is a trap. Instead they are advised to walk the Plain Path, i.e. to aim for quality, not quantity. Then we have *empty*, where the spirit withdraws for a while from birth and rebirth, and stays in the stillness and silence. You passed many of these people sleeping in the Duat as we travelled through the Hours.

Then we get to *developing*, the true candidate process where everything in life and death is geared towards learning and evolving within the Mysteries. Finally we reach *Finished*, where the candidate has finished with the cycle of birth and rebirth, and serves as an inner being. This then leads to the completion step of being *as a god*, like Re (the sun), at the pinnacle of ascent, at the top of the Ladder.

The direct connection to the Mysteries displayed in this scene only emerged thanks to the long and careful work of Michael Sheppard, the translator, who took the time to take the actual hieroglyphs apart, and with what he knows of the magical process, was able to tease out the meanings hidden in the text.

Final staff-leaning figure

The Golden One of the Gods refers to a person who has become *as a god*. When one completes the Mysteries of life and death, and moves beyond being finished to being *as Re*, one becomes clothed in the skin of gold: one becomes as a *golden godly one*. This watcher oversees the process of this scene, and the text that follows instructs the dead and living candidates how to act/react around these posts and the adversaries tied to them. Its advice pertains as much to the Mysteries of Life as to the Mysteries of Death.

The Finished One's advice

Here the role of the posts becomes a little more clear, and all is not quite as it seems. The depictions of the posts, as we saw earlier, is a *wsr* staff of **influence**, identified in the text as a pole of Geb, the land. The poles are also connected to the candidate, as a child of the land. The pole and the candidate are resonances of each other, but this is not made obvious. A clue comes in the line, "O gods who are followers of the necks, Who are in the following of Geb, the heir." The line of hieroglyphs addresses both gods and students/lesser ones.[139]

The posts are both powers and echoes: what is addressed to the post is also addressed to the student/candidate. The students are told that it is their responsibility to understand the adversaries within and around themselves, and to engage the qualities/dynamics that neutralize the adversaries:

> Hold fast for yourselves the adversaries;
> Guard for yourselves those being persecuted.
> Neither let them come forth under your arms,
> Nor let them wobble under your fingers.

Here the candidate is warned to really "sort yourself out, and mind what you do." Your actions trigger the adversaries, and by adhering to Ma'at, and the wisdoms of the advisors at the posts, the candidate can sidestep and mature beyond the issues that arise as adversities.

At this point, both dead and living candidates are in a position where they should be aware, watchful, and wise. Those who have come this far in the Mysteries do not need babysitting; here they are instructed to take responsibility for themselves and their actions.

Scene 46

A figure leans on a staff…

> A master who is extended of heart

…before twelve figures, each holding an ear of barley:

> Making a pouring-forth, which is barley of the inundation in
> the marshes of the Duat.

---

[139]The influence-staffs being referred to as "necks" is a pun which plays on the near-identical spellings of "neck" and "influence" in Egyptian, and is satisfying for the imagery it provokes to do with utterance, grabbing things by the neck, and a tight passage through which air and sustenance passes.

The accompanying text reads:

> Their making a pouring-forth[140] *is* barley:
> > They seek out the Grain[141] of the Throat.
> Radiant is their barley in the Earth,
> > Comparable even to the Radiance of Re at his coming forth.
>
> At his passing over them,
> > Says to them a master who is extended of heart:
>
> "Radiance to your barley;
> > Flourishing for your emmer!
> Your peace is for Re;
> > Your loaves for the Foremost of the Duat.
> Your extension is for you yourselves;
> > You are at peace by means of what is in your arms.[142]
> These pastures, *which are in you,*
> > Are for Seat-of-the-Eye, that he be at peace with what is in him."
>
> Says to them Re:
>
> "Grows the Grain, (and so) develops Seat-of-the-Eye;
> > Breathe the Underworlders by his beholding,
> > The Radiant by smelling his odour.
> Radiance is for you, Seat-of-the-Eye;
> > Eminence is for you, Grain of the Throat;
> > Quickness is for you, who are Foremost of the West.
> It is he who is in the Marshes of the Duat
> > At their joining with their barley."
>
> Say they to Re:
>
> "Grow the grain-rations in the marshes of the Duat
> > At Re's shining over the members of Seat-of-the-Eye.
> At your rising, the plants develop,
> > Great God, who created the Egg."
>
> Their extension is the barley,
> > Their scale-pans are hallowed vessels,

Their cold refreshment is water.

Now, putting forth what is theirs on Earth
Means barley in the marshes of the Duat.

Commentary

The overseer of this scene is true of heart, and also in happiness. He is overseeing a process that brings joy.

> Making a pouring-forth, which is barley of the inundation in the marshes of the Duat.

Read this carefully, keeping in mind what you know about the post progressions, and the meanings of those progressions for those working through the death process to evolve and ascend. Also remember the powers connected to the marshes, and that they are a threshold place.

Remember the overflowing life? Keep this in mind when you read this scene, which addresses those going through the *overflowing* stage of the birth/rebirth process.

You will discover how many levels this scene has, and how it connects with what learned at the posts about "overflowing ones." Read the next scene similarly, and compare it to Geb posts five and six, and to the processes you have already discovered that are connected with the marshes and the harvest.

Scene 47

Seven figures carrying sickles:

> Keepers of sickles

---

[140] See **pour forth**: it is a *verbal* pouring-forth.
[141] Receives a god determinative: the god Nepri.
[142] i.e. the barley ears.

The accompanying text reads:

They exist in the possession of their sickles
   That they may reap the barley in their marshes.[143]

Says to them Re:

"Receive for/to yourselves your sickles;
   Reap you your barley;
   Place what is yours in your enclosures.
Cause Seat-of-the-Eye to be at peace, who is Foremost of the
      Cavern which is Mysterious of forms.
   Oho! to you, reapers!"

Their extension is bread,
   Their scale-pans are hallowed vessels,
   Their cold refreshment is water.

Now, putting forth what is theirs on Earth
   Means being of those in the possession of sickles in the
      marshes of the Duat.

Seventh Gate

The arrival at this gate by this Great God;
   The entry into this gate.

The worship of this Great God by the gods in her.

Gate caption:

Shiner

Uraeus serpents caption:

She kindles for Re

---

[143] Note that they hold their sickles against themselves: remember from the previous scene that the pastures can be read as being *in them*.

Guardian captions:

　Taken: he bends his arms for Re.

　Escaped: he bends his arms for Re.

Mummies caption:

　The Seventh Nine:

　"Come then to us, Foremost of the Akhet,
　　Great God, who is parting the Mysteries,
　Open to you are the hallowed gates,
　　Revealed to you are the doors of the Mysteries."

Doorway serpent caption:

　One Whose Eye Has Flown Away:

　He exists over this door,
　　He opens for Re.

　Perception to One Whose Eye Has Flown Away:

　"Open your portal for Re,
　　Reveal your door for He of the Akhet."

　Now he makes bright the Original Darkness;
　　He gives a lightening in/from the Hidden Region.

Sealed is this door
　After the entry of this Great God.
Alas, then, for the Radiant in this gate,
　Should they hear the shutting of this door.

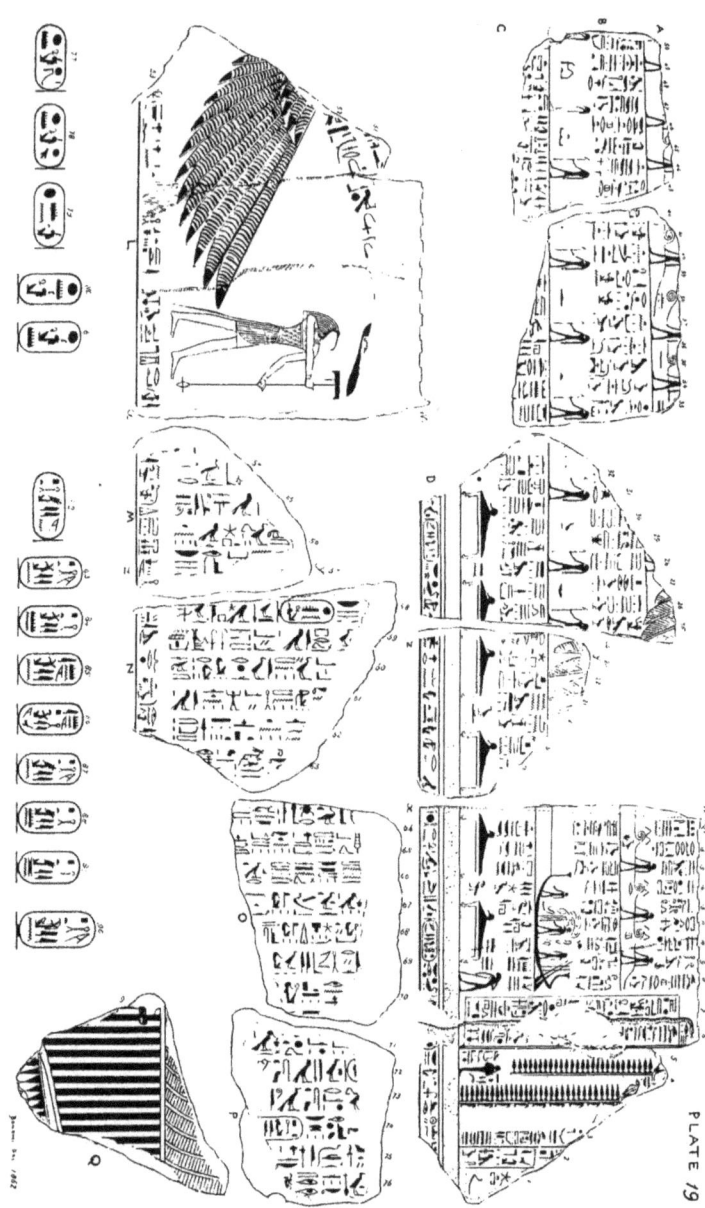

Fragments from the Eighth Hour (Bonomi and Sharpe 1864).

Eighth Hour

Scene 48

Twelve figures carrying a rope with four human heads, four falcon heads, and four signs meaning "remobilize": [144]

> Subjects of a rope which is birthing the Mysteries

The accompanying text reads:

> They exist in the possession of a rope which they bear.
>> Re appears in glory, and the heads/best in the rope comes forth.
>
> They tow Re to their gate:
>> They are returning to the home of the Nu.
>
> They are scrutinized, for they are Underworlders:
>> Let the adjudications come forth: straight is the rope.
>
> "Exposed are my own Mysteries
>> At the coming forth of the zealous/faces [145] from their coils.

---

[144] *dmD*, **remobilize**. The word can also mean "accumulate (grain)": see the Glossary. Stuart's illustration is the surviving portion of this scene on Seti I's sarcophagus, hence only five figures.

Exposed are those born whom I have birthed,
> At the coming forth of the heads/best, in whom is Seat-of-the-Eye.

Open[146] are those who tow
> When his rope is straight.

Tow you for me, subjects of the rope:
> Return you to the cavern of the Nu."

Their extension is bread,
> Their scale-pans are hallowed vessels,
> Their cold refreshment is water.

Now, putting forth as them on Earth
> Means tying a rope onto the barque.

Commentary

As you saw previously in the *Gates*, there are serpent ropes where heads (consciousness/power) appear. In the previous sections of the *Gates*, this serpent appeared as one who repelled Apep, and who measured boundaries. In this scene the Rope/serpent power brings together the harvest of the soul and the measuring of the future boundary: their next place/time/life.

> Re appears in glory, and the heads/best in the rope comes forth.
>
> ...
>
> Let the adjudications come forth: straight is the rope.

This tells us that when the rope is pulled straight, the heads appear and become active. The rope is part of the process making boundaries in the future existence of those who have reached this hour. The text also points out that those carrying the rope partake of its measurements: by working in service, they also get the benefit from the rope. They are subject to the Rope they carry.

> Exposed are those born whom I have birthed

---

[145] Another head-based pun: *Hr* can mean both "face" and "zeal," as well as "upon."

[146] *wn* **open** may also have the connotation of "initiated" here: see the Glossary.

Here we see those who are **exposed**, who facilitate the passage of Re through this section of the Underworld. Remember, those who are 'Justified,' dead or alive, not only have their boundaries—life pattern—measured, but they are also part of the regeneration process as a whole: they are released for regeneration, but they are also the releasers.

This speaks to a deep part of the Mysteries where time and process do not follow linear patterns; and by this phase of the passage through the Duat, the candidate is not only being worked on, but they are also the workers. Think back to the stages of passing through the hour with the Geb posts, and the descriptions of the phases of development, where those who *brew* are also being brewed. The two processes are entwined. By working, they are worked on; by being worked on, they are also working.

This also speaks to part of the living magical Mysteries: you do not evolve and grow by working on yourself; you evolve and grow by working in service for whatever and whoever needs it, in true necessity.

It also speaks to the process of the Finished ones at the Geb posts. The soul in the process of becoming a Finished One is advised to be the brewer as well as the brewed. Here we see that those in that stage of development, who have overcome their adversary as presented in the seventh hour, are now preparing to move forward.

"The coming forth of the heads/best, in whom is Seat-of-the-Eye" relates to the people holding the rope who have gone through the stage of being put back together. By towing Re with the rope, they partake of Re's development, and thus *their* development.

And once we get into this ascent section of the Duat, you will notice that in each hour the quality of the rope differs slightly. Through the development of the rope (as a being/serpent of time, boundary, utterance, and so forth) and its interactions with the various carriers of the rope, we see the process of passage through the Duat as being a holism.

Everything comes together and achieves many different functions at once, so that Re, the workers, candidates, and beings of the Duat, all come to fruition through their collaborative and interactive process. This echoes the complexity of fate patterns in life (as below, so above) and how fate patterns are often heavily entwined to achieve many different things for as many beings, people, and events as possible. Efficiency and recycling is key!

Scene 49

Twelve figures carry a serpent. A star is above each coil between the figures. A figure at the front of the serpent faces them.

    Subjects of the Absorbing One, who births the Hours.

The accompanying text reads:

    They exist in the possession of the Absorbing One;
        They hold fast (for) Re at his passing.

    Perception to these who are of the gods:

    "Tell the Absorbing One, ones who are in the Duat,
        That you behold Re as he reckons up his hours."

    They say, these who are of the gods,

    "Open your coil, and your Mysteries shall emerge."

    And the Great God is standing erect until he is equipped with
        his hours
        By every one of these who are of the gods.
    An hour must come forth from a coil,
        Must be at peace on a base.

    Says to them Re:

    "Give up for yourselves the Absorbing One;
        Hold fast for yourselves the Coiling One.[147]
    For bread is yours, it is in your hours,
        For water is yours, it comes forth from the Silent Place.
    For you come into power over whom you guard,
        Whom The Aged One Who Is Another One (also) guards,
    The Aged One Who Is Another One being the guardian…
        The Aged One Who Is Another One being the guardian…"

    Their extension is bread,

Their scale-pans are hallowed vessels,
Their cold refreshment is water.

Now, putting forth what is theirs on Earth
Means being the Radiant One of his hour.

Commentary

Here we start to see more of the Living Mysteries of creation appearing in the text. The godly ones are told by Sia, Perception, to utter to the Absorbing One to instruct that power and trigger the formation of time. Uttering is the first act of creation, and the candidate uses their inner senses, or perception, to realize that this is the stage of development of the *Gates* where the first utterance to trigger time into the life pattern needs to happen.

In this scene we are also introduced to The Aged One Who Is Another One, an ancient ancestral deity, and first ancestor to Egypt. This verse tells us that the Aged One guards and watches over the rope serpent power that births time (the hours): the past is guarding the future. The Aged One may also be the same power/figure as Kek, the ancient power in the deep darkness that supports and raises the birth of the dawn/light/day.

Kek and his female counterpart, Kauket, were early creation deities.[148] In this scene, the rope and barque passes over Kek/the Aged One, and the upward action of Kek protects the rope of time as it passes by. By the Aged One triggering in the presence of the rope of time, the uplifting action brings the future dawn into gestation: time meets light potential.

---

[147] i.e. you are not going to return to the beginning again, but you are still going to be subject to time. You do not have to start afresh because you have made bread and bathed in cool water.

[148] Pinch 2002, pp.175–176

Scene 50

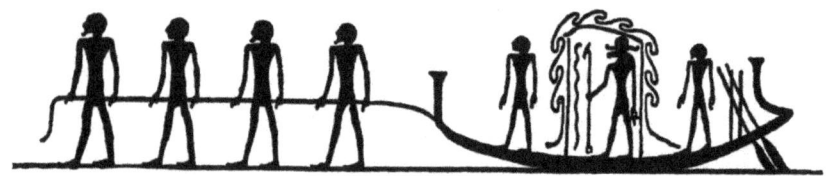

The Sun Barque, in the centre of which is the Meat of Re, with Spiral over him. In the front of the barque is Perception; by the oars, Magic. The barque is towed by four Underworlders:

>The towing of this Great God by gods, by Underworlders

The accompanying text reads:

>Say they, at their towing of Re:
>
>"Make praise, tenants of the Duat,
>   For Re who is in his Mysteries.
>Behold him: as he separates your words,
>   He causes the destruction for you of your adversaries.
>Behold him: as he ordains for you peace,
>   He steers to you your bases.
>Render you to him adoration in your forms,
>   For *thou art that* who begat your forms;
>Render you to him praise in your developings,
>   For *thou art that* who develops your developings.
>Worship you him, Underworlders!"
>
>These are the Assembly, which is in the Duat,
>   Who separate words for He of the Akhet.

Commentary

Those towing the barque declare to those in this hour, who are undergoing their developing, that the development of Re is also their developing. Their status in the Duat is confirmed: "he ordains for you peace, He steers to you your bases."

Eighth Hour

Scene 51

Twelve figures carrying Life and Dominion in their hands:

Masters of what is bestowed in the West

The accompanying text reads:

Says to them Re:

"O Assembly, who are in the Duat,
    Masters of what is bestowed in the West,
Separate you me through your separation:[149]
    Allot[150] you what is evil to my adversaries,
    In accordance with my giving you my Truth.
Let your ordinances be according to your separations,
    Which I have undergone in accordance with the gods."[151]

Say they to Re:

"True of Voice are you, Re, resisting your adversaries;
    Now your conditions are as our conditions.
For you are that from which we have come forth:
    Our creation is for the salvation of its Presence.[152]
Your portions are yours in the Exulting Earth;
    The West is for your hallowed remains.

And your portions are yours in Nut;
   Now your Presence may rule the heavens."

Their extension is bread,
   Their scale-pans are hallowed vessels,
   Their cold refreshment is water.

Now, putting forth what is theirs on Earth
   Means taking as friends[153] the masters of what is bestowed.

Commentary

The Masters of what is bestowed in the West, ones who are of the gods and progressing through the Duat, are called to by Re and asked to judge Re. Just as everything that passes through the Duat is winnowed and weighed, so is Re. This process is repeated in various ways in the Duat, as the grinding and polishing is constantly revisited for perfection to emerge. Everything is constantly weighed and balanced so that order, Ma'at, can govern over everything—including Re.

Scene 52

Four upright mummies:

   Striving of Zeal

---

[149] Or: "Judge you me through your judgements."

[150] *wD.Tn*, usually **ordain**.

[151] *jr.n.j* "which I have undergone," a sense of *jrj* **make**. Re is asking the Assembly in the Duat to judge him at this point in his journey, perhaps because it is necessary for him to be separated from any imbalances that have accrued to him from his adversaries. The act of "judging/separating Re" happens as a result of attending to ones own "judgement/separation."

[152] Lamed vavniks.

[153] A sense of *Smsw*, usually translated **worshipping**.

Eighth Hour

The accompanying text reads:

> Says to them Re:
>
> "Uncovering for your veils, Striving of Zeal;
>   Unravelling for your wrappings.
> My brightness is yours, gods."
>
> Their extension is bread,
>   Their scale-pans are hallowed vessels,
>   Their cold refreshment is water.
>
> Now, putting forth what is theirs on the Earth
>   Means looking upon the brightness in the Duat.

Scene 53

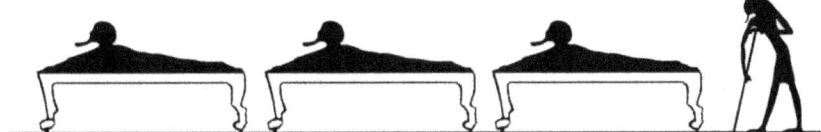

A figure leans on a staff...

> Hidden Mysteries

...before twelve sphinxes on biers:

> The Radiant who are dutiful and potent;[154]
>   The Radiant who are skillful.

The accompanying text reads:

> Says to them Hidden Mysteries:
>
> "Oho! the Radiant,

---

[154]This line of verse is damaged: what is legible is *Axw jr......mnxw* "Akhs, ... and potent." I have hypothesized that the partially missing word is something like *jrwt* "dutiful ones."

Oho! Underworlders!
An opening for you zealous ones;
   An uncovering for your pregnant darkness.
Radiance is of your Presences;
   Potency is for your shadows.
Wisdom for your mouths,
   Valour for your hearts,
Raising-up for your supports,
   Breath for your noses;
Delightful odour for your oils,
   Unravelling for your wrappings!
You depart, *and you come back*:
   You have come into power in your cold refreshment.
Be acclaimed, Presences;
   Be quick, and you can walk off with utterances,
   Though you be at peace in peacefulness.
Pour/receive[155] for yourselves your cold refreshment
   Into/From the winding/sunny[156] lakes in the Duat.
Stand you erect, who are in the possession of the opening of
      daybreak,[157]
   Which ascends a Radiant One belonging to He of the Akhet.

May you be dazzling inside what shall be your covering:
   Your brightness is the sunshine of Re.
Open for you is the Silent Land, being its equal;
   You shall enter the Hallows of Seat-of-the-Eye.
Oho! to you, the Radiant!"

They exist upon their supports;
   They are spending the night on their beds.

Their extension is bread,
   Their scale-pans are hallowed vessels,
   Their cold refreshment is water.

Now, putting forth what is theirs on Earth
   Means being Radiant, skillful, powerful[158]...and a shadow.

Eighth Hour

Commentary

This verse speaks to those described at the Geb posts as the "Empty Ones" or the sleeping ones: ones withdrawn from life, who are "spending the night on their beds." The lie on the cusp of life, birth, and dawn: "Stand you erect, who are in the possession of the opening of daybreak." They do not sleep in the depths of the Duat; rather they stay close to the dawn, but are not able, as yet, to participate in it. They are not bound in this place; it is more a state of waiting, where there is freedom to pass back and forth: "You depart, and you come back: You have come into power in your cold refreshment."

Remember the overcoming of the internal fire, which gives the candidate access to their coolness. The power within is tamed and worked with. So here we have those who have travelled deeply through the Duat, but are not quite ready for rebirth, joining the stars, or becoming Finished Ones in service. Instead they wait close to the dawn, where they learn to come into their power. Also, their sleeping presence is in itself is a form of service: they bring radiance to this place due to their presence.

Scene 54

Twelve figures:

> Assembly of Separations

The accompanying text reads:

> They are those who separate at this gate,
>   Hearing the conditions of those who are in it.
>
> Says to them Re:

---

[155] Usually **suck in**; a word which can have both senses of "pour" and "receive."
[156] See **winding** and **sunny** for the pun.
[157] The Crack of Dawn...
[158] *sxm*, see **come into power**.

"So Oho! Gods,
  Assembly of Separations,
Separating the Mortal, saving Presences,
  What is divine being placed on its base:
  Your Truth is yours, gods."

Say they to Re:

"So Oho! He of the Akhet,
  Great God, Master of Nine;
Now we work at separating what is mortal;
  Now we save the Radiant, they who are developing:
We give peace to a god who is upon his base."

Their extension is bread,
  Their scale-pans are hallowed vessels,
  Their cold refreshment is water.

Now, putting forth what is theirs on Earth
  Means being separated in the Assembly.

Commentary

These are the powers of Judgement/Ma'at that stand close to the threshold of the dawn/life. You will have noticed that there are different octaves of assessors or judges/judgement. Everything balances out everything else, everything counterweights everything else, and different thresholds, gates, and guardians filter and form the candidate as they pass through them.

These assessors are not judging the candidate's past deeds; they are assessing their readiness to make an important step back to life or up to being *as gods*, Finished ones, etc:

Now we work at separating what is dead;
  Now we save the Radiant, they who are developing:
We give peace to a god who is upon his base."

At each stage of the Duat, the candidates are tested, assessed, threshed, then held in a certain place or condition until they are ready to move a step further on the journey. So here we have souls waiting, resting, and preparing what is to come next.

Eighth Gate

The arrival by this Great God at this gate,
   The entry into this gate.

The worship of this Great God by the gods in her.

Gate caption:

Being Heated

Uraeus serpents caption:

She kindles for Re

Guardian captions:

Pellet: he bends his arms for Re.

Cycle: he bends his arms for Re.

Mummies caption:

The Eighth Nine:

"Come then to us, Foremost of the Akhet,
   Great God, who is parting the Mysteries;
Open to you are the hallowed gates,
   Revealed to you are the doors of the Mysteries."

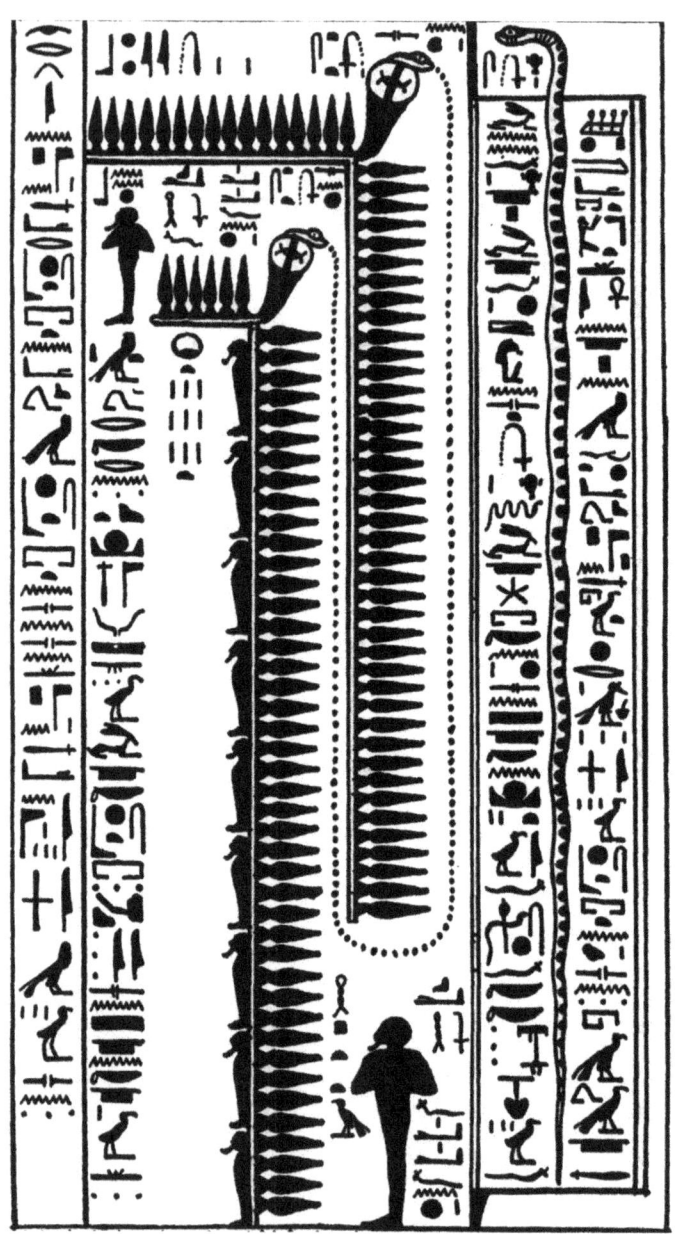

The Eighth Gate on Seti I's sarcophagus.

Doorway serpent caption:

Glister-Face:

He exists over this door,
    He opens for Re.

Perception to Glister-Face:

"Open your portal for Re,
    Reveal your door for He of the Akhet."

Now he makes bright the Original Darkness;
    He gives a lightening in/from the Hidden Region.

Sealed is this door
    After the entry of this Great God.
Alas, then, for the Radiant in this gate,
    Should they hear the shutting of this door.

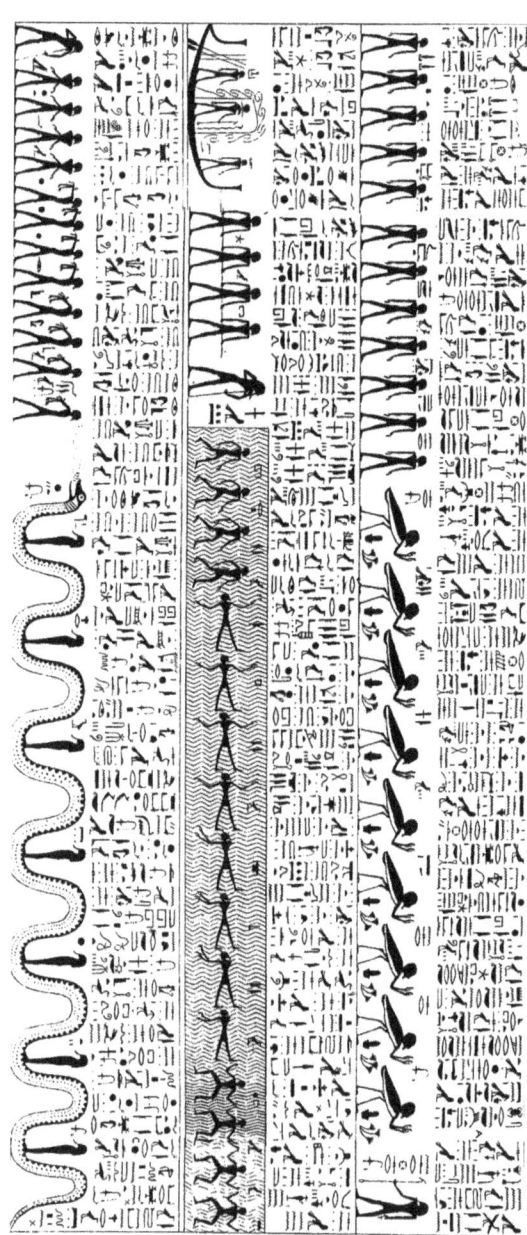

The Ninth Hour (Bonomi and Sharpe 1864).

Ninth Hour

Scene 55

Twelve standing figures:

> Assembly rendering bread, steering completions[159]
> For Presences in the Flaming Isle

The accompanying text reads:

> They are those who steer Presences to/upon pastures in the Flaming Isle.

Says to them Re:

"O Assembly belonging to the gods, encircling the Flaming Isle,

> Putting Presences upon their pastures,
> That they shall come into power for themselves through their bread:
> Steer your bread, govern your pastures for those Presenting
> Whom I have ordained for breathing in the Flaming Isle."

---

[159] See **complete** in the Glossary for the explanation of a pun here.

Say they to Re:

"Now to steer bread, rendering pastures to those Presenting,
 Whom you have ordained for breathing in the Flaming Isle:
Oho! Behold the Path of Goodness![160]
Acclamation is for you from the Foremost of Westerners;
 Joyfulness is for you from whom is in the Exulting Earth."

Their extension is bread,
 Their scale-pans are hallowed vessels,
 Their cold refreshment is water.

Now, putting forth what is theirs on Earth
 Means being a wandering member of the flock of the Assembly.[161]

Commentary

The Assembly, or Convocation of Workers, are ones who are of the gods, or Finished Ones, who work in this part of the Duat and are focused on triggering knowledge and evolution in Presences, which are the souls of the living or dead passing through this part of the Duat.

Some adepts will recognize this assembly as the Convocation of Inner Adepts, also known as *The Gathering*, and as we will see, the process for both living candidates and the Justified dead is becoming more and more apparent.

We have come across the bread theme many times in this text, representing the sum total of wisdom and life actions which have matured into bread or nourishment. Here we are presented with a new motif: plants.

Plant metaphors are well known in magic and Kabbalah, and have to do with the mystical evolution of a life. We see this in a much later text in the Jewish story *The Four Rabbis Who Entered Pardes*. In this story, which you

---

[160] See **good** in the Glossary for the connotations of necessity and lawfulness. The final three lines of their speech may be directed at a Presence they are steering rather than Re.

[161] *m wDwy m DADAt*. See **wandering member of the flock**, and Scene 30.

can look up for yourself, Elisha ben Abuyah is said to have angered God by "cutting down the plantings." This is to say that he damaged the mystical evolution of his students with his heretical teachings.

Later in the Ninth Hour we will encounter another theme that also shows up in the stories of Elisha ben Abuyah, where he is cast out of the universal connection with God to become "Acher" or "The Other," one no longer recognized by God. I find it interesting that dynamics within a mystical and magical Egyptian text of the New Kingdom should eventually surface in Jewish teachings.

The plants represent aspects of a person evolving through mystical union with the Divine: they are their mystical evolutionary potential. They are both previous evolution given back to them and new, renewed potential.

In this scene in the Ninth Hour, the Assembled Ones hand to the Presences, i.e. those traversing the Duat, their mystical evolution, their plants, and their knowledge/wisdom, their earned potential.

As we have seen through the passage of the hours and gates, the candidate is processed, transformed, advised, and to an extent disassembled. Then they pass through the Fulcrum, or scales, and begin the process of reassembly in preparation for rising and becoming Finished. This is the point in that process where their evolutionary harvest is offered back to them, or is perhaps woken within them. They have been given breath by Re, which is to say, life.

Scene 56

Nine human-headed Presences raising their hands...

Those Presenting in the Flaming Isle

...towards a large figure brandishing a dominion-staff:

Who is flaming

The accompanying text reads:

> They exist in the Flaming Isle,
>   They receive their bread;
> They come into power in this Isle,
>   They acclaim this Great God.

Says to them Re:

> "Eat for yourselves of your pastures;
>   Peace is for you because of your scones.
> Soundness[162] for your bellies;
>   Valour for your hearts.
> Your pastures are for the Flaming Isle,
>   Without there being a penetration of the Isle.
> Acclaim you me, and be valiant for me,
>   I, the great one who founded the Duat."

Say they to Re:

> "Oho! to you, who is great, who comes into power;
>   Acclamation is for you, who is great of towings,
> Now, yours is the Duat, which is of your loving,
>   Which you have hidden for those who are in their caverns;
> Now, yours are the heavens, which are of your loving,
>   Which you have made Mysterious for those under[163] them.
> The Earth is for your remains, the skies for your Presence,
>   And you are at peace, Re, through/amidst what you have caused to develop."

> Their extension is in bread,
>   Their pastures are rejuvenating,
>   Their cold refreshment is water.

> Now, putting forth what is theirs on Earth
>   Means Presenting for this Flaming Isle.

---

[162] *mH*, usually full.
[163] *xr* see in the presence of

Commentary

Here they take back into themselves their wisdom, knowledge, and mystical evolution so that they can come into their own power in this place, this Flaming Isle, a place of mystical alchemy, a place that holds the magical Mysteries, and holds the plants until they are ready to be absorbed. It is not an island that can be stepped onto; rather it is a holding pattern that is approached.

Re tells them to take into themselves their plants, and gifts them with strong guts and a brave heart. Again, this is an obscure reference to a magical process that many adepts will recognize. When you take into to yourself, in vision, parts of the Mysteries and the power of the Mysteries, the physical body always has a strong reaction to the inner input. The gut literally processes the power/knowledge: the adept has a physical intestinal reaction to the input of the power. Therefore the gift of a strong gut is a great gift indeed.

The heart spirit is the overseer of an adept's magical actions, and is their true voice and conscience. A valiant heart is a major gift. They are then told to be "valiant for Re," which refers to the service and trials of the Finished Ones, the adepts Justified in life and death, who then serve.

The non-standard offering list in this scene reflects their absorption and renewal of the life harvest and their mystical evolution. Progress towards rebirth, renewal, and Justification is confirmed in their bread, and their mystical evolution is rejuvenated. See **rejuvenated** and **plants** for the pun between "plants" and "verdant, vigorous, rejuvenated." This play on words shows the inner meaning behind the use of the word "plant," and points to the plant being renewed.

Scene 57

The Sun Barque, in the centre of which is the Meat of Re, with Spiral over him. In the front of the barque is Perception; by the oars, Magic. The barque is towed by four Underworlders:

The towing of this Great God by gods, by Underworlders

The accompanying text reads:

Say they, at their towing of Re:

"Praise in the heavens for the Presence of Re;
   Reverence in the Earth for his remains.
To repeat,[164] the limits of the skies are subject to his Presence;
   To repeat, the limits of the Earth are subject to his remains.
Oho! We part for you the Place of the Mysteries;
   We set aright for you the paths of the Silent Land.
May you be at peace, Re, because of your Mysteries,
   For those who are of the Mysteries adore you in your forms:
Oho! We tow you, Re,
   We conduct you, who are great, who are Foremost of the
      Skies."

Commentary

An interesting point in this declaration to Re is the connection between Osiris and Re. Osiris is the remains of Re in the earth, which are left behind as Re rises to traverse the skies.

Scene 58

A figure leans on a staff…

   In the Nu

   …facing a rectangle filled with water, in which are sixteen figures, in fours, adopting various positions:

---

[164]Or "repeatingly."

Ninth Hour

    The Diving

    The Slack

    The Swimming/The Golden/The Molten

    The Expanded

The accompanying text reads:

    Arriving at those being filled, who are in the water, and voyaging over them,
        Says to them who are inside the Nu:

    "O those being filled, who are in the water,
        The Swimming/Golden/Molten, who are in the Nu,
    Look upon Re who is passing through
        In his barque, which is great of Mysteries.
    Now he ordains the designs of gods;
        Now he formulates the business of the Radiant.
    Oho! Stand up, ones who are of the Nu:
        Behold Re as he ordains your designs."

    Says to them Re:

    "A coming-forth for your heads/best, those who are diving,
        Plying for your arms, those who are slack;
    Swiftness for your hurrying, those who are swimming/golden/molten,

        Breath for your noses, those who are expanded.
    A coming-into-power for you through your water:
        Be you at peace in your cold refreshment.
    Your setting out is of the Nu;
        Your strides are of a stream.
    Your Presences, which are on Earth, they are at peace,
        Meaning they breathe, and there is no destruction for them."

    Their extension is the peace of the Earth.

> Now, putting forth what is theirs on Earth
> > Means coming into the power of one's peace on Earth.

Commentary

The Nu is the primeval waters preceding creation, an infinite expanse of still, dark water, described in the cenotaph of Seti I as uniform darkness or inertness. This is known to adept magicians as the Void: the nothingness from which everything in creation flows, an emptiness full of potential for creation. Magicians work in the Void as a threshold place, and as a place from which potential is called into being.

In this scene we have candidates in the Void in various stages of potential in the mystical alchemical process. Some are inert within the Void, and some are traversing or working within the Void: those being filled, those who are swimming, and so forth.

Re utters and triggers these different Presences in the Void, in the Nu, and tells the Diving to wake up, the Slack to become active, the swimming to traverse the Void, and the expanded to connect to life.

Then there is a very curious line, which speaks to those living candidates traversing this place in vision: "Your Presences, which are on Earth, they are at peace, Meaning they breathe, and there is no destruction for them." This is speaking about living adepts traversing the *Gates* in vision, either as part of the Justification in life process or in service as a Golden One. Re tells them that there is no destruction for them: they can cross safely and emerge from this place with his protection.

The traversing of the Void in vision is a magical action first introduced to the apprentice magician in training. First it is learned about, practised, and understood; then finally as an adept it is worked with as part of the magician's completion of the Mysteries. Working with the Void as an adept magician teaches the magician ultimate stillness and silence, ultimate potential, and connects a very deep part of themselves with the universe.

Through this, the magician learns to operate without emotion, in the peace and silence of the fulcrum at the centre of everything. This brings the adept to a place of peace and non-action in the face of Divine power: they come into the power of their peace on Earth.

Scene 59

A figure leans on a staff...

> Distant One

...before twelve figures divided into three groups of four, each group's arms being bound differently:

> Adversaries[165] of Seat-of-the-Eye, who are (for) roasting.

The accompanying text reads:

> What is done for (some)one who is distant from his father, Seat-of-the-Eye,
>   For these adversaries are in this plan:
> *The* Distant One, he ordains that their evil be against them.

> Says to them the Distant One:

> "Binding[166] for your arms,
>   Adversaries of my father![167]
> Your arms to your heads, idiots!
>   You are bound[168] behind you, evil ones!
> You are cut out,
>   So that you do not exist!
> Destroyed is your Presence,
>   So that it shall not live,
> Because of your working against my father, Seat-of-the-Eye.

---

[165] The odd plural determinative used, N33, "grain of sand, pellet," is a standard replacement in religious texts for signs depicting dangerous enemies such as A14 (Gardiner 1957, p.490).

You place the Mysteries behind you?
   You withdraw (from) the governance of the Place of the Mysteries?
True of Voice is my father Seat-of-the-Eye against you!
   True of Voice am *I* against you!
You, who decide to expose what is hidden
   Being in the peace of he who ejaculated me, who is in the Duat!
Rejoice, you who were Finishing...
   At being finished!"[169]

Commentary

This is a harsh warning to those who immersed themselves in the Mysteries, became Justified, and then debased the Mysteries by revealing them (as opposed to teaching them) in unbalanced ways or by misusing them. For them it is the greatest sin of all, *because they knew better.*

Working in ignorance is one thing, and the consequences of missteps through ignorance are all part of the learning and development process. However, when one who knows better intentionally and knowingly debases the Mysteries, then their fate is the most terrible of all: they cease to be on the path, and they are destroyed.

This brings us back to the tale of the rabbis in Pardes, when Elisha ben Abuyah cut down the plantings when he knew it was the wrong thing to do. This caused him to be cast outside the Divine realm, to become other; *Acher.*

---

[166] *snHw*, see **bind**.

[167] "Father" has god determinative: less literally, "divine father."

[168] *nTT.Tn*, see **bonds**.

[169] *jhb(y) tmm.Tn tmyw* i.e. "you who were working your way to becoming a Finished One, we are going to finish you off—destroy you." In the Egyptian it is a pun on *tm*, which can mean both "complete" and "annihilate," which we can mirror with the English word "finish." (Faulkner 1962, p.298)

It is a theme within all the Mysteries all over the world, that those Justified who know better but still act against the Mysteries are shown no mercy.

Scene 60

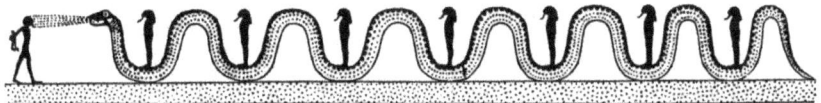

A great serpent, spitting red dots at the bound figures in Scene 59:

Fiery

Seven mummies stand between the serpent's coils:

Gods who are the upper part of Fiery

The accompanying text reads:

Says a Distant One to Fiery:

"O Fiery, who is greatly incandescent,
   This one, with my eye upon his mouth,
   With my offspring, who are guarding his coils:
Open your mouth, reveal your jaws;
   Flame you into the adversaries of my father.
Roast you their remains, sizzle their Presences,
   In that fiery blast belonging to what is upon your mouth
   And in the incandescence which is in your belly.
My offspring are against them:
   So they are destroyed.
The Radiant/Radiances, coming forth from in me,
   Are against them: so they do not exist.
The flame[170] comes forth which is in this serpent;
   Then roasted are these adversaries
   After Distant One calls upon him."[171]

---

[170] *xt*, see **Fiery**.
[171] "him" being the serpent.

>Now, being wise of the magic of this serpent
>>Means not touching[172] its fire.
>Now, putting forth what belongs to the upper parts of this serpent,
>>Means being one whose Presence is not on fire.

Commentary

This verse continues from the previous one. Horus casts Fiery against those who have debased the deepest Mysteries. The fire within consumes them (remember that fire?) so that they no longer exist.

Ninth Gate

>The arrival by this Great God at this gate,
>>The entry into this gate by this Great God.
>
>The worship of this Great God by the gods in her.

Gate caption:

>Great of Awe

Uraeus serpents caption:

>She kindles for Re

Guardian captions:

>Surrounding the Earth: he bends his arms for Re.
>
>Shouldering the Earth: he bends his arms for Re.

---

[172] *ar.f,* usually **penetrate**.

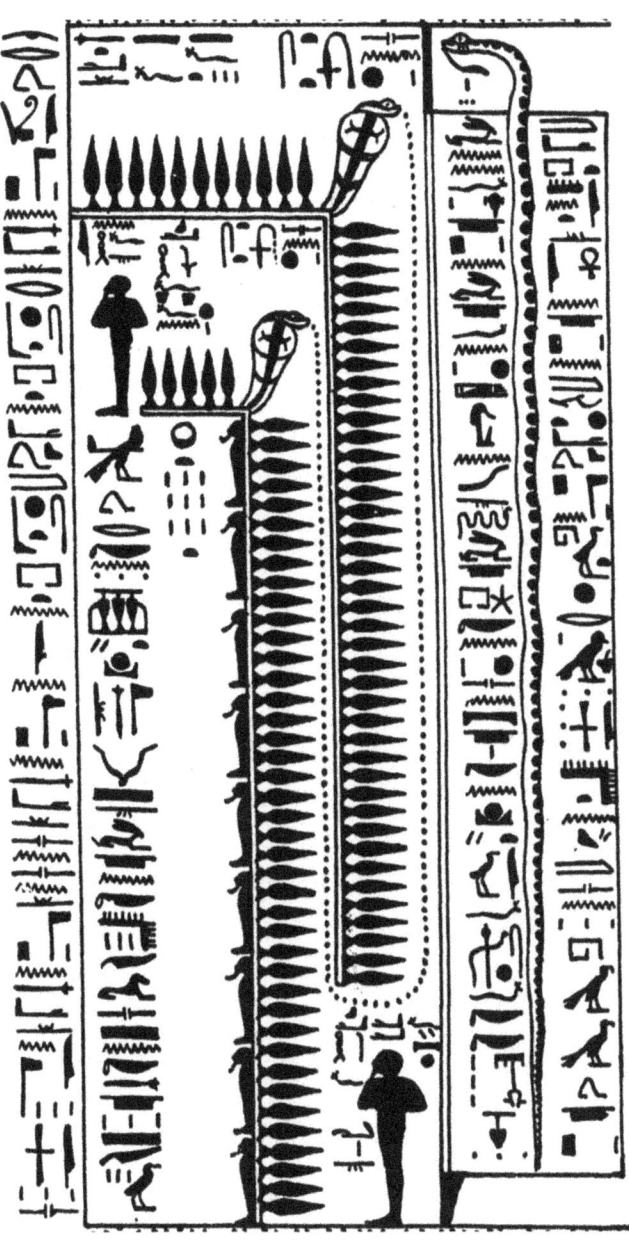

The Ninth Gate on Seti I's sarcophagus.

Mummies caption:

The Ninth Nine:

"Come then to us, Foremost of the Akhet,
    Great God, who is parting the Mysteries;
Open to you are the Prohibited Doorways,[173]
    Revealed for you are the doors of the Mysteries."

Doorway serpent caption:

Specification/Horn of the Earth:

He exists over this door,
    He opens for Re.

Perception to Specification/Horn of the Earth:

"Open your portal for Re,
    Reveal your door for He of the Akhet."

Now he makes bright the Original Darkness,
    He gives a lightening in/from the Hidden Region.

Sealed is this door
    After the entry of this god.
Alas, then, for the Radiant in this gate,
    Should they hear the shutting of this door.

Commentary

If you look at the name of the gate and the attendant guardians, then you can see what power lies beyond this threshold that they guard. It is the passage towards life.

---

[173] *sbxwt Dsrt*, "hallowed gates," but both words are spelled quite differently, and *Dsrt* has a knife determinative which seems to emphasize its cut-offness. I have selected different English words to mark the visual difference in the original text.

Tenth Hour

Scene 61

A hawk-headed sphinx, facing left, with a human head mounted on its rear. Both heads wear the White Crown.
   The hawk-headed sphinx, or the man holding the front rope:

   Distant One, who is in the Barque

The human head, or the man holding the back rope:

   Pleasing of Arm

Standing between the heads, on the sphinx's back, is a double-headed figure, the left head a hawk's, the right head a Seth-animal's:

   His Two Heads

Facing the sphinx on the left, four serpent-headed figures (or human-headed figures with Uraei) wearing White Crowns:

   Gods of the South Wind/Land, Gods who are Southern, Gods who are Vigilant/Awake.[174]

Facing the sphinx on the right, four serpent-headed figures (or human-headed figures with Uraei) wearing Red Crowns:

---

[174] *nTrw rsw* Several different meanings here, separated by commas and slashes.

The Tenth Hour (Bonomi and Sharpe 1864).

Tenth Hour

Gods of the North Wind/Land, Gods who are Northerners,
Gods of the Delta marshes, Gods of the flood-waters.[175]

The man holding the Southern rope, or the mooring-post or staff to which the rope is tied:

Overseeing the/a prow mooring rope

The man holding the Northern rope, or the mooring-post or staff to which the rope is tied:

Overseeing the/a stern mooring rope

The accompanying text reads:

They are in this plan:
    Their standing erect for Re.

Says to them Re:

"Receive for yourselves your best/heads, gods;
    Hold fast for yourselves onto your prow mooring rope.
Oho! The developings, (of) the gods,
    Oho! The Radiant, (of) the gods:
You have developed(,) gods,
    You have become Radiant(,) gods,
Being of my developing in/from the Place of the Mysteries,
    Being of my Radiance in/from the Place of Hidden Affairs."

Stands erect this god for Re:[176]
    His two faces must enter into this god
    After the passing of Re upon him.

Says to them Re:

"Your heads/best are yours, Gods:

---

[175] *nTrw mHt(yw)*. Without reading in the (missing) *jw*, only Gods of the Delta marshes or Flood-waters. With the *jw*, the other definitions.

> O receive for yourselves your Red Crown/Flood.
> Hold fast for yourselves onto the/a stern mooring rope,
>   Belonging to the barque which develops from within me.
> Thou art Distant One, refining your face."

Commentary

The scene opens with a series of cryptic images. The double-headed sphinx, with both heads wearing the white crown of the south, is the creative pattern of the monarch or Justified potential in life. The sphinx's body (watching, waiting) has the two heads, one of humanity and one of the Divine. Ra-Horakhty: Ra, Horus of the Two Horizons. This is pointed out by the names: "Distant One who is in the Barque" is Re, and the human name "Pleasing of Arm," which is the Justified human, the Finished One who will become as Re. Remember back to the Geb posts in the Seventh Hour, where the last step in the progression of the poles is to be *as Re*.

Conjoining Horus and Set brings together the two powers in an act of completion, *to make whole that which was parted.*

What we are seeing here is the pattern being created that allows the soul to manifest in life, or in the stars, as one who is of the gods on the cusp of the horizon. All the scattered powers and fragments of mortal and divine life that were separated out, weighed, and tested in the Duat are now brought back together in a process of completion in layers.

The deity powers of north and south, Upper and Lower Egypt, are brought together to join the powers of the Two Lands. Just as the life pattern of the soul is brought back together, so the life pattern of the land is also joined together, in this scene of preparation for life expression.

There is also a play of words on the magical dynamics of time: south is the future, hence "Awake," while north is the past.

Joining together the powers of the Two Lands is an important magical point that many miss. Ones of the gods (including the monarch), Finished Ones, Re, and the Land are all intricately linked in the weave of time and fate. They are not separate units, and humans are not separate from the power of the land. Each depend on each other, and you cannot make the human spirit whole if the spirit and energy of the land is not also made whole. The land is constantly being reborn and regenerated through the actions of Re.

---

[176] The two-faced figure standing on the sphinx.

Two powers oversee the rope of time, keeping it tight on its mooring ropes, keeping past and future equal so that the creation of time can be stable and allow the pattern of life in the centre, the sphinx, to be the fulcrum that expresses through time. The pattern of life is placed between past and future, north and south. So it is not yet in time, but it is ready to emerge into that stream of time.

Note the reference to the gods holding the rope as being developed and Radiant, and that they have become so as a result of Re's development in the Place of the Mysteries. In the last few hours, the helpers have been Finished Ones. But now we have come to those who have become godly, Radiant, like Re.

You will be starting to realize how the scene in the Seventh Hour with the Geb poles is like a key that unlocks the understanding of who is doing what in the Duat. As the candidates go through the Duat, they stay at certain hours for a while and act in service as Underworlders. In the Tenth Hour, the helpers are *as gods* like Re, which is the final stage of service before they, too, are ready to ascend at dawn.

Also notice again the reference to the development process: Re's passing through the Duat and undergoing transformation is what lets mortal candidates do the same.

We also see how Re triggers the Sphinx's pattern as he passes over it. Its two heads merge into the power of Re and partake of the regeneration.

The red and white are conjoined, the human and god are merged, and the soul becomes a Horus whose countenance is refined.

Remember, Pharaoh was interconnected with Horus as the monarch, which is why the king had a Horus name and a Golden Horus name. In the same line of thinking, the monarch was the ultimate Justified One of True Voice: the candidate who had joined with the Mysteries and undergone the trails of Justification in life. This was also connected with the Osirian Mysteries and the Heb Sed festival of the monarch's regeneration: being reborn, Justified, and regenerated after the Underworld trials.

The development of Horus in the Underworld as the two-headed sphinx is the pattern of Hor-em-akhet, or Horus in the Horizon. This pattern draws the soul into the pattern of one who is of the gods (Horus/Re) and a Justified human. This is the roots of the Pharaoh as divine and human monarch, and the candidate as "one who is of the gods."

Scene 62

A serpent with six or eight heads, on six or eight pairs of legs…

> Who Walks Abroad

…grasped by both hands by a walking figure:

> One who parts

The accompanying text reads:

> He exists in this plan:
>> Now he spreads across the Place of the Mysteries.
>
> He always returns[177] to the Place of the Towering Blade,
>> A hall of the West:
>
> Now, those who are in her,[178] their best/heads will be absorbed,
>
>> Should they smell the odour of Who Walks Abroad.
>
> One who parts guards him.[179]

Commentary

This interesting chap is a bit like a patrol officer: a serpent power that extends throughout the different regions and gates of the Duat. This is why his feet are shown going in two directions. He is governed, or tempered, by a worker

---

[177] *Hmm.f*, geminated from *Hm* return.
[178] In the West, which is feminine: *jmnt*.
[179] Break the connection?

Tenth Hour

who triggers and guides. He reaches back and forth through the areas of the Duat.

The last few gates that take us step by step to the horizon and dawn are heavily guarded, to make sure that everyone is where they should be, and that no one tries to reach the dawn before they are ready.

A cautionary note

Take note of the following after I had a dangerous encounter with Who Walks Abroad. This being is not to be trifled with. If he even gets close to you, he will utterly drain you of your sustenance. He does not have the limited remit of the guardian in Scene 63: he is not restricted to arresting trespassers and ne'er-do-wells. He is not even restricted to the Duat: he is capable of reaching through to the manifest world...as Josephine discovered firsthand.

The key to dealing with this being is in the name of the walking figure: *one who parts*. If you smell him coming in vision—he smells awful—then leave wherever you are at high speed, get back to your body, and *break any connection* you have with the Duat until it is safe for you to return.

The Duat has a way of sticking to one's feet and chilling one's bones. Merely not being in vision there is not necessarily enough to break the connection. Be safe.

Scene 63

A serpent with bearded heads at either end, wearing the White Crown. On it walks a serpent with four human torsos and heads at either end, the outermost torsos having arms raised as if in prayer, each torso having a pair of legs under it. A walking figure grasps this serpent.

The double-headed serpent:

Iron[180] of Earth

The eight-headed serpent:

Both being persecuted[181] /Being a group[182]

Figure holding the eight-headed serpent:

Bird-Trapper

The accompanying text reads:

> He exists in this plan:
>   He stands erect for Seat-of-the-Eye.
> The scrutinizing is his of those Presences
>   Who should be persecuted in the Duat.
> Now, he spreads across the Place of the Mysteries,
>   He is always returning to evict Presences
>   From a dwelling in the West.
> Then the group (the serpent) must enter Iron of Earth.
> Now, those who are in her, their heads/best is absorbed,
>   At their smelling of the odour of Iron of Earth.
> Now, Bird-Trapper is who guards him.

Commentary

This serpent is a reflection and higher octave of the previous scene's serpent, and makes sure that everyone stays in their assigned place. He wears the white crown of the north, which is also a play on the Underworld: he is a

---

[180] Please see iron, as there are many possibilities for this word, *bjA*.

[181] Reading *njkywy* "both being persecuted." A dual passive participle. (Allen 2014, p.403) The caption in Queen Tawseret's tomb is clearly N33 "pellet" with dual signs underneath, followed by *y*. N33 is used to take the place of dangerous signs in religious documents, such as *xftyw* "adversaries," and in fact the sign is used as the determinative for *njkw* "those to be persecuted" in this same scene. The reason for the participle being dual has to do with the serpent being divided in two halves, both of which end in heads.

[182] Reading *DADA* "body of men," (Faulkner 1962, p.319). For details on the sign D1, see Gardiner 1957, pp.449–450 The title on Seti I's coffin.

Tenth Hour

major power of the Duat, the king of the Duat, literally the power of the depths of the Duat. He is overseen by Bird-Trapper, a godly one whose power is to oversee the netting of souls.

We see here that this serpent is in service to the Osiris process, the coming-together and regeneration of the soul. He, too, roams throughout the Duat, absorbing the heads/best of trespassers.

We saw the reverse of this dynamic earlier in the *Gates*, in Scene 35, where the heads/best emerged from a serpent that had absorbed them:

> O heads/best, absorbing for yourselves that which absorbed you,
>
> Consume you him from whom you have come forth."

Scene 64

Two figures each hold a net above them.

The accompanying text reads:

> These gods are ensorcelling
>> For Distant One, Re, He of the Akhet,[183] in the West.
>
> They ensorcel the upper parts of the Net,
>> Which are in the Net, and in their arms.

---

[183] Or "Re-Horakhty."

Commentary

These workers use magic to catch the developing candidates and those who are soon to be *as gods* in their "nets." The nets are patterns of magic woven by the magic of the hands. The nets are images that outline the magical weave of the future, and the soul of the candidate is scooped up into the pattern so that they may express in life or in ascent. The arms are very important in Egyptian magic, as they hold specific powers within them. The left arm holds future potential, and the right arm holds harvest/completion.

Scene 65

The Sun Barque, in the centre of which is the Meat of Re, with Spiral over him. In the front of the barque is Perception; by the oars, Magic. The barque is towed by four Underworlders.

The accompanying text reads:

> The towing of this Great God by gods, by Underworlders.
>   Say they, towing Re:
>
> "The coming of a god to his remains:
>   The towing of a god to his shadow.
> You shall be in the peace of your bodily form, you who are
>   being towed,
>   Who are safe, being in his Mysteries.
> Comes Re, and you shall be at peace in your bodily form:
>   You are saved by those who oversee their Nets."

Commentary

This verse outlines the process of joining together the parts of the candidate or deity. The remains/shadow refers to the vessel for life, i.e. the form the body will take. The **shadow** is the outer form or vessel that the soul will flow into. This word is also used for the statue of a deity. It is the bodily vessel that receives the soul of a deity or human.

"You shall be at peace in your bodily form" refers to Re—and therefore also the candidate—aligning with his vessel, ready for rebirth or ascent. This is to say that the future life expression is lined up and ready for the completed soul when it emerges at the dawn. The form is chosen, harmonized, and connected to the soul that will flow into it.

Scene 66

Six male figures hold nets above them, four monkeys hold nets above them, and four female figures hold nets above them.

First three male figures, which in some versions have a human head, a double serpent head, and a bird's head:

>Overseeing the Words

Second three male figures:

>Ensorcelling

Four monkeys:

>Guarding Re

Four women:

>Guarding Re

The accompanying text reads:

They exist in this plan:

By their voyaging in front of Re,
    They ensorcel for him Apep.
They always return to the hall of Akhty:[184]
    They pass in his presence to the heavens,
They develop for him in both conclaves:
    It is they who cause him to appear in glory in Nut.

Say they, as they ensorcel:

"Oho! Trespasser! Being corded[185] is Apep,
    To whom is being rendered his evil.
Destroyed is your countenance, Apep;
    A path is made for the Place of Execution.
Knives are for you: you shall be cut out;
    The Old One is against you: you shall be destroyed.
Those who are spearing place them[186] into you:
    We ensorcel you through what is in our arm.
Oho! Being resisted, being destroyed,
    And being blotted out is the one being restricted.

Commentary

Here we have a gathering of powers and ones who are *as gods* whose job is to magically suppress Apep, while opening and bridging into the stars for Re to be reborn. They keep the threshold safe while opening the way ahead. The arm—it does not say which one—holds the magical power used to suppress Apep. Magically, these days we would assume it to be the left arm, as it holds the power of the Limiter and the serpent staff.

---

[184] Here a place rather than "He of the Akhet."
[185] *wAyw*, see *wAwAt* cord.
[186] The spears.

Scene 67

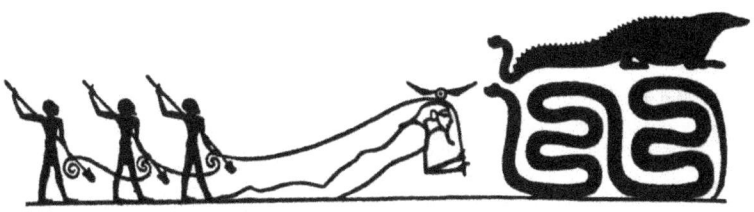

Three figures brandishing spears...

> Those who are spearing

...holding coils of a rope held by a half-lying god...

> The Old One

...facing Apep, above whom is a crocodile with a serpent's head for a tail:

> Sh-s-sh-s[187]

The accompanying text reads:

> They exist in this plan:
>> Being in the possession of their spears,
>> They guard the ropes of the Old One.
>> They do not permit[188] the arising of this serpent
>> To the barque of the Great God.
>> They pass as followers of this god into the heavens.
>> These are those who are of the gods
>> Who strive for this god in Nut.

---

[187] Possibly simply the hissing of the crocodile, onomatopoeic as with *sSSt* "sistrum"; possibly reduplication of *Ss* "rope, cord," picking up *sswnt ssy* "blotted out is the one being restricted." Possibly an "X is Y" type of non-verbal sentence, as many words are spelled *Ss* (Faulkner 1962, pp.271–272).

[188] *jwty dd.sn* lit. "they do not give."

Commentary

Here we are introduced to the Old One or Oldest One, the progenitor of humanity. He is the oldest human, or the god of the human line. His time is no longer of life, and he is holding the coiled rope of time/measurement which is not straightened: his time has passed in terms of life. Behind him are the nets which catch the souls ready for harvesting in life, and behind those is the Barque of Re.

He confronts Apep head-on. Though this old power is kept in the Duat, he is not chaotic: he is a deep, ancient power and he challenges Apep to protect the barque.

The workers watch over the Oldest One who acts as barrier to Apep. The very roots of human existence, the Oldest One, challenges the power of chaos in Apep to protect the barque.

Scene 68

Many figures all holding the same rope, which is pulled tight and passes under a double serpent...

>Developing One

...in the centre of which perches a falcon wearing the Double Crown:

>Distant One of the Duat

On the left, four groups of four:
Human figures:

>Presences of the West

Ibis-headed figures:

>Those in the following of Who Is Of The Ibis/Plummet/Lead[189]

Hawk-headed figures:

Those in the following of Distant One

Ram-headed figures:

Those in the following of Re

On the other side of the double serpent, eight human figures in two groups of four:

Those coming into power

The accompanying text reads:

They exist in this plan:
    The tiller-rope is in their arm,
    And it is at the foot of the Developing One.
He is returning to the hall which is of the Akhet:
    They must free this tiller-rope
    From this god (when he is) at the Akhet.
They are those who are towing him into Nut:
    They live in the South Wind/Land;
Their breathing is the North Wind,
    Meaning what is going forth from the mouth of Re.
Now, the voice of this Developing One, it travels round the
       Place of the Mysteries,
    After the arrival of Re in the heavens.

Say they to Re:

"Coming is the one who comes after his developing;
    Comes Re after his developing.
Comes forth who comes forth after his developing;
    Comes forth Re after his developing.
To the skies,

---

[189] There is, as usual, punning at work here. Among other things, we see here a progression from mere human Presences, to lead/the plummet, to "Distant One," to the gold of Re. See **Who Is Of The Ibis**.

> To the skies, Great One!
> Oho! We shall throw you upon your base
> > Through the tiller-rope which is in our fingers:
> > A great thing of the forms in the Place of the Mysteries."

He exists in this plan:[190]
The/A Distant One who is of the Duat, his coming forth from
    in him is first;
    (Then) Comes forth the developments from the coil.
Re, he calls upon this god,
    His two divine ones,[191] they unite with him,
And Distant One must enter into the Developing One
    After Re calls upon him.

Exists the tiller-rope in their arm,[192]
    Which exists at the foot of the Developing One.

Say they to Re:

> "Open for you are the paths of the Place of the Mysteries,
>   Revealed for you are the doors which are in the Earth,
> For your Presence, that it may be at peace in Nut,
>   We conduct you into the Lakes of the Vagina.
> Oho! You shall enter the East;
>   You shall voyage through the cultivator of your mother."[193]

Commentary

This scene is about the development of the soul into life. The scene centres around an image of a double serpent of Khepri, the Developing One, who brings things into creation. The name does not have a god determinative, so we may be talking about a power who develops like Khepri. Similarly, we have the crowned falcon but no god determinative—literally, Distant One of

---

[190] The Developing One
[191] *nTrtj.fj*, with two I12 "cobra/uraeus" determinatives (Gardiner 1957, p.476).
[192] Those coming into power.
[193] A **cultivator** is a triangular agricultural instrument; a hoe, in fact. Whether this appears as a cheeky joke or a mystical revelation depends greatly on the spiritual heights attained by the reader.

the Duat—so we have a power akin to Horus in the Duat: the new Justified life, the son of the Sun waiting to be rolled into life by the Developer.

Holding onto the rope are those in service to Djehuty, Horus, Re, and Justified, Finished humans.

The rope of time is anchored in the Developing One—time connected to life. It is then released, and the voice of the Developing One, the sound/call that triggers life, echoes through the Place of the Mysteries as Re is bridged into the sky, into Nut. Nut is the sister of Geb, the earth, and the sky and earth circle together as a container of the cosmos. Her hands and feet mark out the four directions, and she 'contains' all the powers of the skies.

So we are at the point where the bridge has formed between the Duat, the Underworld, and out into the sky.

The collected workers declare the development of Re: life and time for Re. They cast him into time by the tiller-rope in their fingers. The specific use of the word "fingers" denotes intricate weaving or time. The time of the rope has been fixed, and through that time developed in the Place of the Mysteries, Re can crossover the threshold into the sky and *into time*.

The emerging life (Horus power/Distant One) time (rope/coils) and Life (Developing One) enclose Re when he calls upon them. This is the joining of the potential/Justified with time and life, which all come together within the deity to form the new life. Note the use of sound/voice: calls and utterances are magically connected to creation/life, and Re's calling upon them draws those different powers and qualities to him.

Finally, the human workers use their voice to declare and trigger the new life into pregnancy.

Tenth Gate

> The arrival at this gate by this Great God,
> The entry into this gate by this Great God.
>
> The worship of this Great God by the gods in her.

Gate caption:

> Hallowed (place)

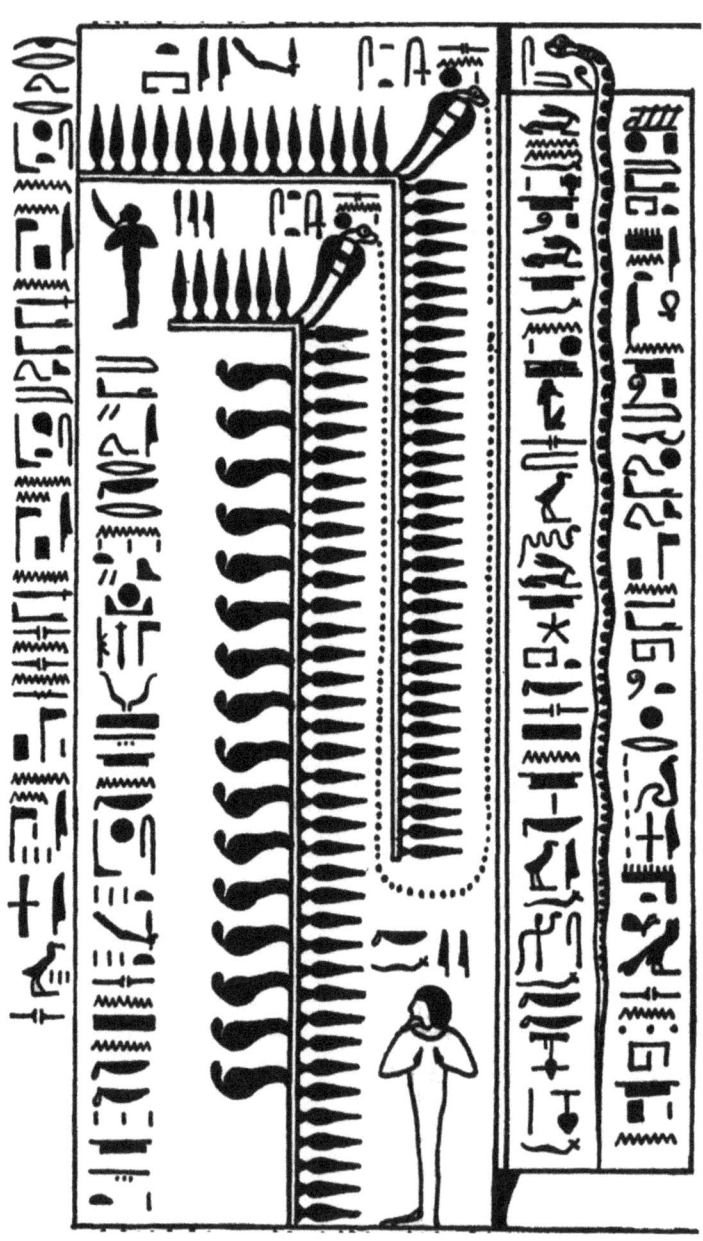

The Tenth Gate on Seti I's sarcophagus.

Uraeus serpents caption:

She kindles for Re

Guardian captions:

Moaner: He bends his arms for Re.

Uncoverer: He bends his arms for Re.

Mummies caption:

"Come then to us, Foremost of the Akhet,
    Great God, who is parting the Mysteries;
Open to you are the hallowed gates,
    Revealed for you are the doors of the Mysteries."

Doorway serpent caption:

Glister:

He exists over this door,
    He opens for Re.

Perception to Glister:

"Open your portal for Re,
    Reveal your door for He of the Akhet."

Now he makes bright the Original Darkness,
    He gives a lightening in/from the Hidden Region.

Sealed is this door
    After the entry of this Great God.
Alas, then, for the Risen Ones who are in this gate,
    Should they hear the shutting of this door.

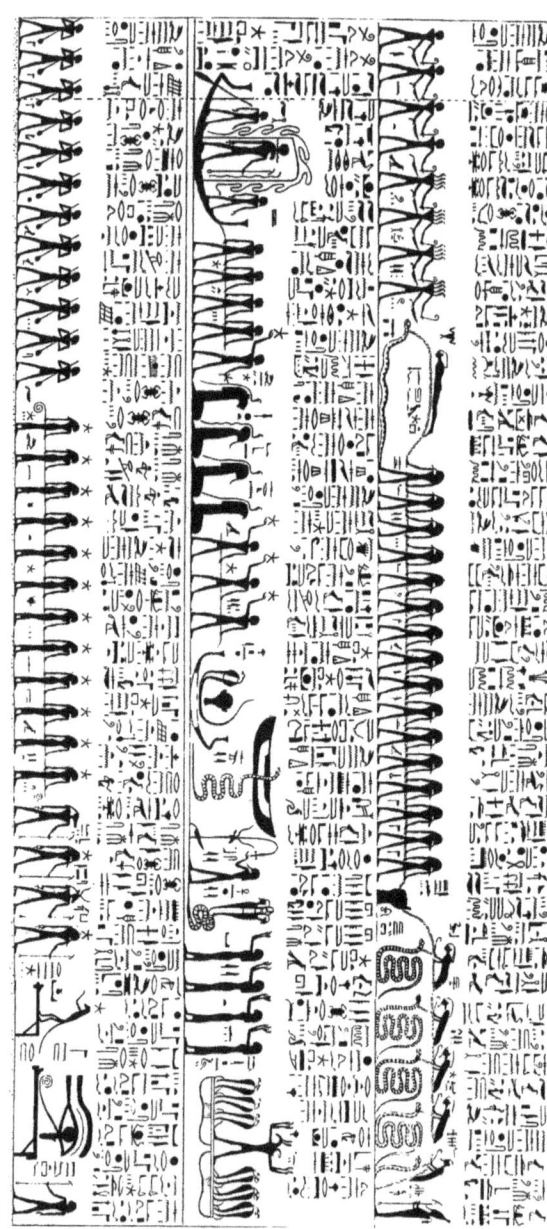

The Eleventh Hour (Bonomi and Sharpe 1864).

Eleventh Hour

Scene 69

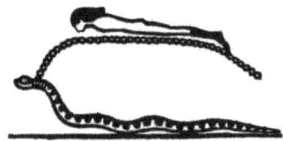

Serpent with a rope around his neck:

    Apep

Caption under the rope:

    His voice: it travels round the Duat

Lying over the rope is a figure:

    Who Permits Breath

Facing Apep are two sets of four figures:
Human figures, brandishing a knife in their right hand and a coil of rope in their left:

    Fetterers

Figures with four snake heads each, brandishing a knife in their right hand and a coil of rope in their left:

Slaughterers

At the front of the long queue holding the rope, facing Apep:

Endowing ones

In the middle of the rope, facing away from Apep:

Influential ones

At the back of the rope, facing away from Apep:

Stabilizers (divine ones)

An enormous fist rises out of the floor:

Whose Remains Are Hidden.

Four figures, wearing headdresses and carrying the crook, each hold a small chain attached to the main rope. The other end of each chain lassos a smaller serpent round the neck.
First figure and serpent:

> *Figure:* Geb/Overflowing
> *Serpent:* Who Conspires Against Rightness

The remaining serpents are not named.

Second figure:

>Staff

Third figure:

>Who Is Of The Course

Fourth figure:

>Who Adores His Mother

Fifth figure:

>Cold Refreshment Is His Companion

A mummified figure carrying the Was staff and wearing the White Crown faces all the assembled beings described above:

>Foremost of the West

The accompanying text reads:

>They are in this plan:
>>They stand erect for Re
>
>As he appears in glory who is Re;
>>As he approaches them.
>
>Say they to Re:
>
>"Appear in glory, Re;
>>Come into power, He of the Akhet.
>
>Behold us as we force into place Apep,
>>Who is rendered to his fettering.
>
>You need not arise, Re, against your adversary;
>>Your adversary shall not arise (against) you:
>
>Developed is your hallowedness, who are in Spiral;
>>Apep is being smashed into his blood."
>
>He is persecuted; Re stands erect for the peaceful hour;

The Great God must pass through, after his fetters have been
    tied.

The serpent exists in this plan:
    She Who Permits Breath puts out his bindings.
Now the barque of this Great God, it can go aground
    At this juncture, which is of Apep.
Smoothly goes this Great God,
    After the tying of his fetters.

They[194] are in this plan:
    They hold fast the abundance[195] of this one who is evil.

Say they to Re:

"Go smoothly, Re;
    Travel on, He of the Akhet.
Behold: daggers are placed into Degenerate of Zeal,
    Which is Apep, who is in his disorders."

They[196] are in this plan,
    Meaning being as guards for the Offspring of the Exhausted
        One.
They guard them through what weakens and persecutes,
    Which is in the hand of Whose Remains Are Hidden.
He is given a mortal grapple by means of his entourage,
    At the gate which is Foremost of the West.

Say these who are of the Gods:

"Pregnant darkness to your zeal, Who Conspires Against Right-
    ness;
    Destruction to you, who are Offspring of the Exhausted One.

The hand of Who Is Hidden (re)places your evils
    Through what weakens and persecutes, which is in him.
Geb, he is the guard for your bonds;
    The offspring of the bindings, they give you a weakening:

You are guarded through the scrutiny of the Foremost of the
West."

They exist in this plan:
   They add weight to the bindings of the Offspring of the Exhausted One.
Now the barque of the Great God may go aground
   At this juncture of Apep:
   He goes smoothly after their bonds have been put (on).

Commentary

In Scene 69, Apep, chaos, is held in check and disabled so that it can have no part in Re's dawning. In this scene, various powers come together to make sure of Re's safe passage towards rebirth. Just as labour is a dangerous time for mother and baby, so the labour of Re moving towards the gates of dawn is fraught with danger.

Towards the end of the *Gates*, instead of the usual troupe of human Underworlders working in service, we start to see some of the bigger players appearing: Deep Underworld ancestral presences and deities.

There is still a human presence, however, in the form of the Fetterers. Each of these carries a partially coiled rope in one hand and a blade in the other, as do the snake-headed beings called Slaughterers. Their tools show a clear division of magical power between the hands, something well known to adepts. The left hand is life, time, and limitation; the right hand is harvest, death, and release.

Carrying a serpent rope in the left hand indicates that they are able to hold time and life. This is reflected in the magician's serpent staff, which is always held in the left hand. The blade in the right hand is the harvesting, chopping blade that disassembles form. So they are limiting the time of Apep, and disassembling his form.

Apep is a root power of chaos that acts as a counterbalance to Ma'at, order. As such, Apep cannot be destroyed, but he can be limited and subdued.

---

[194] The figures holding the rope.

[195] *sDfAw* written here as *sdfw*. Usually **foundation** or **provision**.

[196] Geb/Overflowing, Staff, Who Is Of The Course, Who Adores His Mother, and Cold Refreshment Is His Companion.

The four human figures and the four serpent-headed figures confront the power of Apep to limit and disassemble chaos in the Re's difficult labour at the cusp of dawn.

"Who Permits Breath" is Serqet, the scorpion goddess who opens or closes the throat. She protects humans and deities from venom and snake bites, and is another adversary of Apep. She guards Apep in the manner of a prison guard, keeping him in check. In this scene she lies across the chained Apep to keep him in check and *close his throat*, to disable and silence him, protecting Re and the surrounding deities and workers from his venom.

Serqet oversees the suppression of Apep, and is the overarching power in this scene, as she is for a living candidate at this threshold. She will protect the candidate from any power of Apep that would try to destroy them or divert them from their path at this crucial, exposed point in the process.

The "endowing ones" hold a chain that fetters Apep and keeps him in check, while Serqet closes his throat and guards him. The "influential ones" and "stabilizers" are "divine ones," i.e. *as gods*, working to subdue Apep and give weight to the chain that binds the power of chaos.

The fist rising out of the depths of the Duat is very interesting indeed. When working with deep ancestors, the magician reaches down into the Underworld or into the sands of the Inner Desert in search of the oldest ancestor, a power we have already come across in the Duat. The fist or hand is the collective consciousness of the roots of ancestral lines: the original ancestor who is the combined hive of all ancestors who join together as one to assist humanity when truly needed.

It also connects to the visionary presentation when magicians work at the Abyss, to the vast hand that rises out of the Abyss to uplift the adept in the ascent process. This is Metatron, the human who walked with God and was not, which is to say *developed beyond humanity*. In the Abrahamic religions he appears as an angel, a servant of God; in more shamanic magical systems, he is approached as a root ancestor. This is the hand of the Old One, the sum total of a racial ancestral line.

"Foremost of the West," Osiris Khontamenti, is a guardian deity aspect connected to both Anubis and Osiris. He is the guardian of dead kings. In this scene, Osiris Khontamenti is connected to the Four Sons of Horus. The assembled parts of the dead are protected from Apep before everything is brought fully together for the dawn/ascent.

In the accompanying text, the workers and deities tell Re that they are subduing Apep so that Re does not have to. Re is in his "peaceful hour,"

Eleventh Hour

waiting for the dawn to break on the threshold. This is a vulnerable time, so the workers and deities come together to protect those who wait at this threshold.

The workers draw Re's/the candidate's attention to the knives they plunge into Apep to neutralize him. The names they use for Apep declare him as an abomination, the opposing the order of Ma'at, and as a perversion of an ordered quality.

Similarly, when a candidate waits in this holding pattern, the powers of adversity and chaos are held back, so that the candidate, when they are ready, can step through the gate towards the final threshold of the dawn.

"The Exhausted One" refers to Apep: he has been suppressed. The Offspring of the Exhausted One are Apep's children, or his aspects. Geb and the Four Sons of Horus[197] keep them in check by way of the chain. The hieroglyphs point to the chain being the weakness of the offspring's harvest: their weaknesses were used against them to bind them.

Finally, with Apep's offspring/aspects properly suppressed and bound, and with that suppression declared, Re is able to pass by safely.

Scene 70

The Sun Barque, in the centre of which is the Meat of Re, with Spiral over him. In the front of the barque is Perception; by the oars, Magic. The barque is towed by four Underworlders.

The accompanying text reads:

> The towing of this Great God by the gods of the Duat.
> Say they, towing Re:

---

[197] Staff, Who Is Of The Course, Who Adores His Mother, and Cold Refreshment Is His Companion.

"We tow for the skies,
> We tow for the skies!
> We escort Re to Nut.
You are coming into power, Re, in your countenance;
> You are great in your peace, Re, meaning your countenance of the Mystery.
Open/initiated/revealed is the countenance of Re;
> Clear[198] are the two eyes of He of the Akhet.
He dispels the pregnant darkness in the West;
> He gives dawnings through what brightens,[199] for his sake, what is obscure."

Commentary

Workers take Re closer to the threshold. We also get a little fragment of the magical path for the candidates in the declaration of service, "we escort Re to Nut." By working to get Re to the threshold so that he can dawn, they too are brought to that threshold. They can move closer to the dawn due to the service they give to Re.

Scene 71

A striding figure holds a star aloft in his right hand, behind him; his left hand, in front, carries a second star by his legs.

> Belonging To The Hour

---

[198] *baq*, also has the connotations "bright" and "innocent." See **clear**.
[199] *HDt*. One would expect this to be his Eye.

Eleventh Hour

The accompanying text reads:

> Giving his standing erect for Re,
> He is in the peace of the skies, which Belongs To The Hour.
>
> This god is who conducts him;
> The hour, she is doing her duty.

Commentary

The star held in the hand of a human Underworld worker is linked to the magical lantern held in the right hand of the adept. In magic, harvested and developed wisdom, and Ma'at, shines like a light that opens the way in the darkness. This is the imagery behind the Tarot's Hermit.

In this scene, the worker is holding two stars. The right star, which indicates his Justification, is held back to light the way for Re in the barque. The left star is held close to his leg, to light the path ahead. The left star is light gifted by deities in order for progress to occur. In a magician, it shines over their left shoulder. But in a Justified adept, a deity will flow that Justified light onto the path ahead in times of darkness and danger to ensure the magician's safe passage.

Here, Justified Finished Ones are working in service to facilitate the safe passage of Re. Human workers join with deities to move Re forward. Sekhmet is directly on the path before this human worker, helping with their service to move Re to the gate.

Scene 72

Four kneeling figures without arms, each with a Uraeus sitting on their head. Their captions:

> *Lion-headed figure:* Having come into power

Bald bearded human figure: Sousing

Human in headdress figure: Breathing

Falcon-headed figure: Distant One[200]

The accompanying text reads:

> They exist in this plan:
> Those in the Earth[201] are guarding them.
> Giving their standing erect for Re, they abide:
> The Great Guide/Counterpart is in their presence/holding.
> They must pass through, following Re,
> For what is held by Guide/Counterpart of the Mystery is in their possession.

Commentary

By their presentation and the presence of the Uraeus, we know that these four figures are either deity powers or humans who are *as gods* embodying these powers.

The first figure, **Power**, is Sekhmet. Her name is clearly marked in hieroglyphs, so it is more likely that this is an aspect of the deity Sekhmet as opposed to a human.

The second figure appears to have Ptah's head; however the hieroglyphs aside the image say **sousing** and are certainly not the hieroglyphs of Ptah.

---

[200] These four figures address stages of development we have already encountered, which were outlined in detail in Scene 30. First, **Power** in her form as the Eye brings you forth as a mere human, as a tear of her eye. Then you **souse** yourself with the waters of development, with you as the pot to contain the water. That is the Asiatic stage. Then, being at peace in Infinity, the Nubian stage, you must breathe: "Breath for your noses, you who are expanded." (Scene 58.) The way out of the Nubian stage, given in Scene 30, is "there should develop for them Distant One, as it is he who can save their Presences." This brings us to the Libyan stage: "it was the seeking of my Eye which ended in your development."

[201] Receives a serpent determinative, I14.

The third one, Breathing, is a Divine human form, and the final figure is Horus, the Distant One—up high—who is also identified with Pharaoh.

When you put all these together in a critical part of the eleventh hour, you get a very interesting pattern that is crucial to the process at hand. It is also one of those things that Ancient Egyptians loved so much: a powerful key hiding in plain sight. So it is worth taking a bit of time to look at this pattern in detail, as it has wide magical significance.

It is a pattern of emerging creation in action, a pattern that opens a road for rebirth, not only for Re, but also for a human travelling towards being reborn *as a god*, and being born as Pharaoh, both human and Divine.

In the four figures we have a family progression of power (Memphite theology) that starts by creating the Inner Desert and ends with one who is of the gods. The first figure is of Sekhmet, literally **Power**. She breathed the Inner Desert into form, the place where creation is played out. She is the bringer of both disease and cures, the warrior who protects Pharaoh/one who is of the gods, and protects and nurtures Ma'at. She is also the 'wife' of Ptah.

Next we have the Ptah figure, the husband of Sekhmet, a god who thought, then uttered, the world into form. Thus he oversees architecture, craft, and the rising of the Djed: the backbone of man, temple, and god. He also oversees the Heb Sed, the regeneration of the Pharaoh and the one who is of the gods. He is a god of the creation of form, and of renewal.

His and Sekhmet's son was human and became *as a god*, and was Imhotep, "In Peace," an Old Kingdom architect, Tjaty, and physician. By the eighteenth dynasty he was considered a demigod, and by the twenty-sixth he was a deity in his own right. The hieroglyphs do not say Imhotep, they say *srq*, **breathing**. But he is sitting where you would expect the son of Sekhmet and Ptah to sit. So I dug a bit deeper, and looked again at the literal translation of the word *sqr*.

The word is rooted in the name of Serqet (*srqt*). The priests of Serqet were doctors and magicians, and they had special focus on respiratory problems—venom and so forth. So we have an enigmatic figure, a semi-divine human, whose parents are both involved in creation and medicine, who is opening the path ahead for Re. That also made me think of Imsety, one of the four sons of Horus, a power that opens the south (the future, the way ahead), and Imsety helped bring life back to the corpse for renewal.

So I strongly suspect this figure is a composite meaning that plays on the three personalities of Imhotep, the priesthood of Serqet, and Imsety. The

Egyptians loved their puzzles like this, and would often point to something as 'being like' something else. It also leads me to wonder if this is the root of what would later become known as the "thrice great."

The last figure is human with a falcon's head: the king or godly one as Horus, the One Who Rises High.

So we see the magical power progression from the right conditions (creation, the presence of the Inner Desert), the thought (creation and mind forming), the magical medicine that raises the corpse and is himself raised, and finally the Rising One who expresses Divine power in humanity.

This magical pattern has many layers, and I am sure many adepts who work in both vision and ritual will draw much from it. It is a pattern of stages, filters, and bridges for regeneration and renewal. The four power personalities, guarded by their Uraei, uphold the Mystery in their possession. They keep the pattern of regeneration, recreation, and healing filled with power to benefit Re and those who pass through.

Scene 73

Three figures...

>Ones who are being stars

...hold a rope in front with their left hands, and stars behind them in their right hands. The rope connects to a barque containing a serpent on which sits an enormous head:

>This is the countenance of Re/the sun-disc

The accompanying text reads:

> They exist in this plan:
>
> They acclaim through their stars;
>> They hold fast the prow mooring rope of this barque,
>> They who are entering into Nut.
>
> This is the countenance of Re.
> Now, he is plying the cycle from/into the Earth;
>> There is acclamation for him by those who are in the Duat.

Commentary

These workers light the way and pull the barque which holds the face—the countenance—of Re.

Scene 74

A winged serpent:

> Guide/Counterpart

The accompanying text reads:

> She gives her standing erect for Re:
>> She is who conducts this Great God
>> To the portal of the Akhet of the East.

Commentary

This is the winged serpent who will lead Re and the godly ones forward to the threshold.

Scene 75

A staff topped by a bull's head, with a knife crossing it at the base. The smoke from a brazier drops onto this assembly of objects. A figure lifts the brazier:

    Inducer

The accompanying text reads:

> Giving his standing erect to Re,
>   He places fire through what is parted;
> Comes forth a knife in the arm of one who strives,
>   One who is an escort of this god.

Commentary

A godly one pours fire into the bulls horns: he is awakening and enlivening the warrior bull power of Pharaoh/the godly one. The bull, in the form of the Apis bull, was connected to kingship. The bull was the fighting spirit, strength, and renewal of the godly one's life, and was connected to Ptah and Osiris.

    It is a staff with bull's horns, not a bull: it is the enlivening of the power staff or tool that carries the warrior power for Pharaoh/the godly one, that will serve them in rebirth and beyond.

Scene 76

A serpent with three heads: a snake's in the middle, and two human heads facing left and right:

> Living

The accompanying text reads:

> Giving her standing erect to Re,
>   Established is the lifespan, which is written in years in this
>   Risen One.
>   Now she causes ascension, in his presence, to the heavens.

Commentary

Now we are back to the power of the Fates. Remember, the first Fate we met took fate/time away to dissolve the connection between the dead and their old lives. Then we met the Fate who oversees weaving a new fate pattern. Here we meet the middle fate: Decima or Lachesis (Roman and Greek names, respectively). This power of fate holds the lifespan tight, just as the rope of time is held tight, and records it: the lifespan is now set, and cannot be adjusted.

She rises into the skies (the constellations at birth) and holds the lifespan/fate pattern so that the new life can express through it.

Scene 77

Four female figures, their arms aloft:

> Evokers

The accompanying text reads:

> They say, at their calling upon Re at Re's passing through:

> "Oho! Come, infant!
>   Oho! Come, born of the Duat!
> Come, nursling of the heavens!
>   Oho! Developed is Re!"

Commentary

These are the birthing cheerleaders, a sort of ancient mystical version of the midwife screaming "push!" as the baby's head presents itself. Remember the barque with the face of Re?

Scene 78

Eleventh Hour

Two bows, face down, three Uraei rearing upon each, facing out, and a two-headed, four-armed being straddling the two. The face facing left belongs to the Seth animal; the face facing right is a falcon's.

> His Two Faces

The accompanying text reads:

> This Spiral belongs to Risen Ones;
>   He spreads across the Duat.
> The two bows, they are the equals/ladder-uprights/carriers[202]
>   Of His Two Faces, into/being his Mystery.
> They are who make known Re,
>   Who are in the Eastern Akhet of the skies.
> They travel on (into) the heavens after him.

Commentary

Here we have the conjoined brothers of Set and Horus who together balance opposing powers—completion. They stand on the two bows of Neith, the battle goddess connected to weaving creation and the rebirth of the Sun each day in her form of Mehet-Weret. The conjoined brothers are joined on the two bows by six Uraeus serpents who guard and announce Re to the Eastern Horizon.

Scene 79

Twelve figures holding oars:

> Gods, the Ignorant Of Wiping Away[203]

---

[202] *rmnj.sn* see **equal**.

The accompanying text reads:

> They exist in this plan:
> Giving their standing erect to Re,
> They receive their oars at this cavern of the hour;
> They develop into themselves in accord with the births of Re
> in Nut.
> Their developing accords with the births of Re;
> They come forth into/from the Nu in his presence.[204]
> They are who ply for this Great God
> After he is at peace in the Eastern Akhet of the skies.
>
> Says to them Re:
>
> "Receive for yourselves your oars,
> For yourselves, be in the peace of your stars.
> Your developings are but[205] my developings;
> Your births are but my births.
> My ones who ply, for you there is no wiping away;
> Being gods who are ignorant of wiping away, being stars."

Commentary

This is essentially a new barque crew of oarsmen. Their job is to row Re into the stars and sky, and this honour comes from their having Developed. Going once more back to the Geb posts of the Seventh Hour, you will remember that the final step to becoming a godly one was becoming as Re.

These oarsmen have developed beyond being Finished Ones, and now get to partake of rising into the heavens by way of their service to Re.

The godly ones who get to rise in the skies with Re have succeeded in stepping forth into becoming immortal: now one with the stars, they can never be destroyed. Through service to the Divine, they become *as a god*, and this is the stage where their service is no longer in the Duat, but out in the stars and the world of creation.

---

[203] In the Pyramid Texts, *jxmw sk* "those who are ignorant of wiping away" refers to the circumpolar stars (Faulkner 1962, p.29).

[204] The Asynchronous Swim Team from Scene 58.

[205] *swt* "but, and." (Allen 2014, p.221, §15.7.9) But also see *swt* "wheat," Faulkner 1962, p.218: "your developing is the wheat of my developing..."

Scene 80

Twelve female figures holding a rope, a star above each of their heads:

Hours, who tow/flow/injure[206]

The accompanying text reads:

> They exist in this plan:
>   They receive the tiller-rope of the barque
>   So that Re is towed through Nut.
> They are who tow/injure Re,
>   Who govern the courses in Nut.
> It is these same goddesses
>   Who govern this Great God in the Duat.

Says to them Re:

> "Receive you the tiller rope, and be you at peace.
> Tow, according to yourselves, my followers to the heavens,
>   And govern you me according to your paths.
> My births are but your births,
>   My developings are but your developings.
> Oho! Establish you a/the lifespan,
>   Render you the years according to what is inside you."

---

[206]There is a play on two senses of the verb *sTA*: "tow" and "flow." The flow of hour to hour seen as beings who pull other beings through time. However, note that they are grabbing the tiller-rope, not the tow-rope: they are holding a straight course by keeping the rope tight that is tied round the tiller: they are not directly pulling beings forward, but rather forcing the rudder to point in the right direction. There is also a pun here between *sTAwyt* "those who tow/flow" and *sTAw* "injury." (Faulkner 1962, p.255) The hours can be thought of as dealing injuries to any being subject to time.

Commentary

These twelve goddesses hold the rope of time and the stars that light the way to the future. They hold time and limit it by causing "injury." Creation must be balanced with destruction, else you get overgrowth. Their caption is therefore ambivalent, standing for both the flowing of time and the limitation of time: the finite creation of the cycle of life and death. These goddesses put the cycle of day and night in time with the sky.

Those who have moved beyond being Finished, who are now moving towards being *as a god*, as Re, also partake of the bridge of time. They move with Re into the stars, into ascent.

Also note how Re speaks about the power of the sun and the power of the hours: they depend on each other and are woven together.

Scene 81

Seven figures with their own verses:
A crocodile-headed figure carries an ankh in his right hand behind him, and a dominion-staff in his left, before him.

> Throaty:
>
> This god is in this plan:
>   He is who cries out at/for the opening of gates for Re.
>   He passes through in his presence.

A human-headed figure with a star above his head, carrying the same implements as Throaty:

> Whisperer:
>
> This god is in this plan:

He is who calls upon stars at/for the births of this Great God.

He passes through in accordance with him.

A bull-headed figure with the same implements as Throaty and Whisperer:

Sustenance/Bull of the West:

This god is in this plan:
    He is who calls upon the gods of the barque of Re.
    He passes through in his presence.

Another human-headed figure with another star on his head, with the same implements as Throaty, Whisperer, and Bull of the West:

Who Nurses Stars:

This god is in this plan:
    He is who places stars according to their red linen.
    He passes through in the presence of this Great God.

A monkey stands on a standard, facing these beings:

From the sky below:

He acclaims for Re;
    He makes praise[207] for He of the Akhet.

An enormous eye on a standard:

Goddess:[209]
    This is the Eye of Re.
This god, he is at peace with her
    When she is in the peace of her seat in the barque.

---

[207] There is a really weird pun here, as *jrj.f hnw* can also mean "prepares a jar," a jar being a measure roughly equivalent to a pint. See 8th sense of *jrj*, "prepare food and drink," and *hnw*, "jar, measure of about 1/2 litre." (Faulkner 1962, p.26 and p.158) The reason for this pun is, I think, to link the Eye of Re to the *wDAt* eye, the source of measures of capacity, (Faulkner 1962, p.75) the eye that was magically restored by Thoth and which particularly had to do with the *grain measure*.[208] Thus it is linking together Re's journey with that of the Radiant: here is the Eye of Re; here is the Eye of a Distant One...
[208] Gardiner 1957, p.197 §266

A figure stands facing this collection of beings, holding a dominion-staff and no ankh:

> Overseeing his base:
>
> He is initiated, and a companion of the door of this cavern.[210]
>   He is established in his seat;
>   He shall not pass through in the presence of Re.

Commentary

These seven figures, seven being a mystical number to do with developing, are involved in the release of Re and his retinue into the pattern of life. Four carry the Ankh held back in their right hand: life in death. This shows that their presence and actions are rooted in the Duat. The *wAs* staff of power in the left hand is the power that opens the path ahead in life.

One utters the gate open, one utters the star alignments to come together for the birth, one identifies those who go forward into the pattern, and one fixes the stars once they have gathered in the right alignment: the weave of the *red linen*.

The Divine eye of Re equates with the right eye, the eternal eye that sees into the netherworld, the eye that is the face of the sun, and the eye of perfect proportions. The Divine eye is female: it can create by casting a glance. For example, Sekhmet was created by the fiery glance of the eye of Re. So first we had the face of Re, which appeared apart from his body—the face of the sun. Now we have his Divine eye on a throne.

The figure standing before the gate is a worker fixed in this position. He does not travel through the gate; he does not leave the Duat. He is a human sentinel, a Finished One, at the threshold of the gate, working in service. We know he is a Finished One because "he is initiated, and a companion of the door of this cavern." His job is merely to be a human presence at the threshold, and to bear witness. Just his being present and actively observing brings a power and influence into the whole developing process as the entourage passes through.

---

[209] *nTrt*. The Eye functions almost as a giant determinative for this word: the goddess *is* the Eye.

[210] Mundane reading: "He opens, who is the door-keeper of this cavern." *wn.f jrj aA nj qrrt tn*. For "he is initiated," see **open**. For "companion," see **companion**.

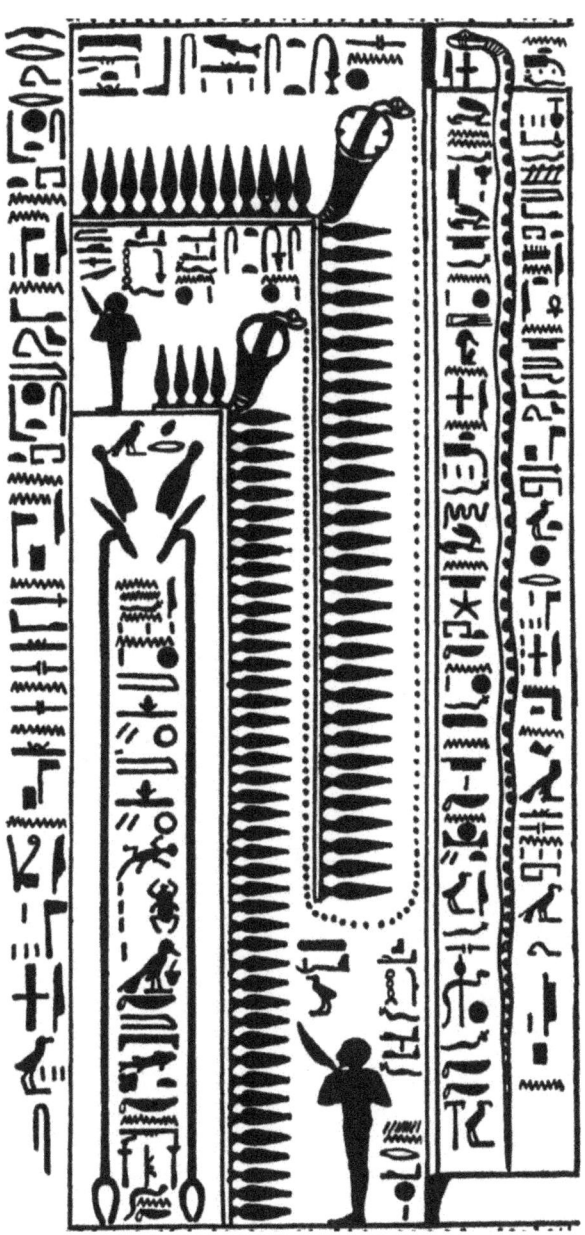

The Eleventh Gate on Seti I's sarcophagus.

Eleventh Gate

> The arrival at this gate by this Great God,
>   The entry into this gate by this Great God.
>
> The worship of this Great God by the gods in her.

Gate caption:

> The Mystery of Initiation

Uraeus serpents caption:

> She kindles for Re

Guardian captions:

> Ardent: he bends his arms for Re.
>
> Hewer: he bends his arms for Re.

Dominion-staff with falcon's head and White Crown:

> Distant One

Dominion-staff with human head and White Crown:

> Seat-of-the-Eye

Text between the staffs:

> Say they to Re:
>
> "In peace!
>   In peace, Re!
> In peace!
>   In peace, Myriad of Developments!
> Your presence to the skies,
>   Your remains to the Earth,
> You who have (been) ordained as great by yourself."

Doorway serpent caption:

Who Is In His Flood:

He exists over this door,
   He opens for Re.

Perception to Who Is In His Flood:

"Open your portal for Re,
   Reveal your door for He of the Akhet."

Now he makes bright the Original Darkness,
   He gives a lightening in/from the Hidden Region.

Sealed is this door
   After the entry of this Great God.
Alas, then, for the Gods who are in this gate,
   Should they hear the shutting of this door.

Commentary

The gate's name, "The Mystery of Initiation," and the two *wAs* staffs, indicate that this is a crucial threshold where everything is brought together for ascent. The power of Osiris is the power of one who will rise again, and the power of Horus is the one that rises far in the sky. The king or godly one is dismantled, reassembled, and given back his face and eye to complete the initiation of the Mysteries.

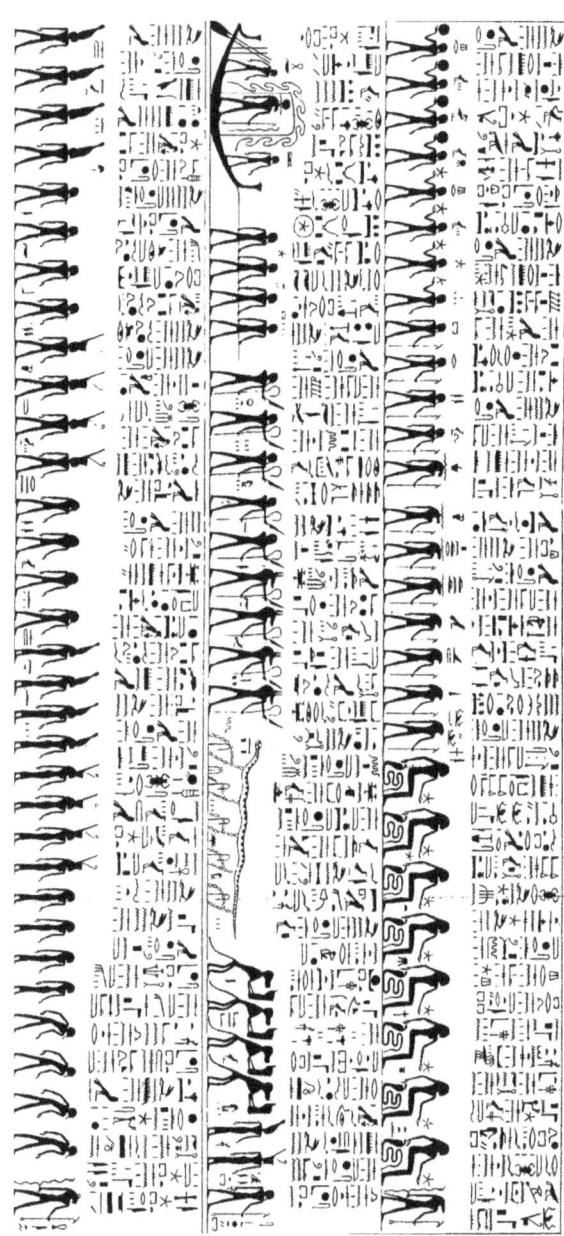

The Twelfth Hour (Bonomi and Sharpe 1864).

Twelfth Hour

Scene 82

Four figures, each carrying behind them a disc in their right hand:

> Those in the possession of Radiance

The accompanying text reads:

> They exist in this plan:
>   They shoulder/equal the sun-disc belonging to Re.
> They are those who join the Duat to the heavens,
>   Though this counterpart/guiding which is in their arm;
> Who guard words at the gate of the Silent Place
>   So that Re shall be at peace in/on the belly of Nut.

Commentary

The twelfth and final hour of traversing the Underworld is all about bridges and bridging. Powers and presences come together to facilitate the passing of Re and the godly ones from the threshold of the Duat to the sky and the stars.

You will also notice that the final gate is two doorways instead of one. The passage into the Duat is easy, as it is the natural flow from life to death.

However, overcoming the trials of the different hours becomes harder and harder as you get closer to the final gate, and passage out of the Duat as a godly one is the hardest task of all. The final hour is heavily guarded, and the double gates make sure that no one escapes the Duat who has not earned the right of safe passage.

Similarly, the road into magic is easy, but the emergence as 'one who is magical' is very hard indeed; and the final threshold that takes a person from one who *does* magic to one who *is* magic is also heavily guarded. The passage of Re through the Duat is also the passage of the human candidate towards Justification; and the passage of the aspirant magician towards becoming Justified is also the passage of Re. The two are inextricably linked.

The beings/workers in this scene act as mediators and a bridge for the vital force of the sun to ascend into the sky. They are also the same mediators that bridge the vital force of 'brightness' of the newly-formed godly ones who are releasing into the living world, or into the realm of the stars and sun.

Scene 83

Four figures carrying a star behind them in their right hand:

> Those in the possession of stars

The accompanying text reads:

> They exist in this plan:
>   They shoulder/equal stars.
> Receiving both arms: the Nu, and Re,[211]
>   They acclaim through their stars.
> They pass, in his presence, into the heavens;
>   They are at peace in/on the belly of Nut.

---

[211] *Ssp awj nww ra.* Hornung has "when the arms of Nun receive Re" (Hornung and Abt 2014, p.412).

Twelfth Hour

Commentary

These are godly ones who carry their star, their Justified brightness. They move with Re into Nut to take their place in the stars.

Scene 84

Four figures, each with a dominion-staff in their left hand:

> Coming forth

The accompanying text reads:

> They exist in this plan:
>   With their dominion-staffs in their arm,
> They are those who establish boundaries for this god in the
>   skies
>   In accordance with Re's ordaining of their bases.

Commentary

These are the powers that step into the boundaries previously marked out for the presence of Re and the godly ones. Their job is to hold the boundary in place. By limiting and holding the boundary, the emerging consciousness that flows out of the Duat into the heavens can be contained, and so be part of the order of the heavens.

Scene 85

Four figures with the heads of rams, individually named, each with a dominion-staff in their left hand:

Presence

Union

Upend Resistance

Butcher/Quest[212]

The accompanying text reads:

They exist in this plan:
With their dominion-staffs in their arm,
  They are those who supply the peace which belongs to gods
     in the skies,
Which is of the emission of the Stream;
  Which is of[213] Re's arrival to the Nu.

---

[212] *dnd* **butcher**. Translating as **quest** requires assuming an unwritten final *n*, *dndn*, which is indeed possible.

[213] Here *n* is D35, "arms in gesture of negation." Gardiner 1957, p.454. However, in this case I have translated as "belonging to" rather than a negative of some sort. The odd use of this sign is, in fact, consistent with 18th Dynasty practise, and so we might reasonably expect to see it in this text, considering its suspected date of composition. (See Josephine's Introduction for date of composition, and Gardiner 1957, p.126, §164 for the unusual use of D35 here.)

Twelfth Hour

Commentary

These four powers also hold the boundaries, and hold back or give access to the forming bridge. They connect to the deities in Nut, and to the deep, ancient collective deity powers of the Nu; and they hold a tension between the two to keep everything in place while Re proceeds.

Scene 86

Four figures with the heads of falcons, individually named, each with a dominion-staff in their left hand:

Distant One

Who Is Of The Breast

Quick

Who Is In Both His Barques[214]

The accompanying text reads:

They exist in this plan:
With their dominion-staffs in their arm,
    They are those who establish the shrine;
Who give arm to those in the belly of the god's two barques
    After their coming forth from the mouth of one who joins.
They place the hurrying in Nut
    At the developing of the hour which is before the Third Hour.[215]

---

[214] Reading *wjAwj.f*. Alternative reading, *dptj.f*, "who is in both his boats," and *dptj* also means "loaves".

[215] i.e. the Second Hour.

Commentary

Here are more boundary-keepers who are also navigators. They assist and instruct the crew of the two boats (one with Re and another with Re's face) about the course to take through the heavens.

"At the developing of the hour which is before the Third Hour" is a rather enigmatic reference to the twilight of dawn, before the sun's face appears risen in the sky.

Scene 87

Eight female figures sitting on Uraei, each supporting, before them, a star in their left hand:

> Those who adore; those who save.

At the front, a crocodile-headed being with a dominion-staff before him in his left hand and a serpent behind him in his right hand:

> Discovering A Mouth[216]

The accompanying text reads:

> They exist in this plan:
> Their Spiral is in the possession of them;
>   Their arm is in the possession of stars.
> They come forth, meaning the two conclaves of this Great God:
>
>   Four to the East/Left,
>   Four to the West/Right.
> They are those who call upon
>   Presences who are of the East.

---

[216] *sbq r*, words provided by Hornung, and which he translates as "He with a wise mouth" (Hornung and Abt 2014, p.418).

It is they who are acclaiming this god:
  Adore they him after his coming forth
  A Child at his coming forth through his developments.
It is they who are governing the plying of the crew
  In the barque belonging to this Great God.
They call to this god;
  They hold fast for themselves their Spiral.

Who passes through the heavens as his followers[217] is in this
    plan:
  Now his stride is as their stride.
They stand erect for this god,
  When this god twists himself at this gate.
Coming forth, he stands erect in respect of[218] the Hall of the
    West.

Commentary

These female figures are risen deities and godly ones in their stars. They sit upon their Spiral/Mehen, their earned divine serpent protection, in the company of the gods. They rejoice in the coming of Re to join them, and they draw close to Re from the two directions of life and death. They offer their help and guidance to the crew who navigate the boat, while maintaining their safety with their Mehen.

The crocodile-headed figure is a deity who functions at the twelfth gate and who has 'students,' Developing Ones, following in his footsteps. This is a scene in which we see subtle reference made to candidates who spend time at various hours and gates, working in service, learning and developing, until it is time to move forward. This deity power oversees such candidates, and they move with him to be of service and to learn.

---

[217] Discovering A Mouth
[218] "in respect of" is just the preposition *r*, nothing to do with *having* respect for anything.

Scene 88

The Sun Barque, in the centre of which is the Meat of Re, with Spiral over him. In the front of the barque is Perception; by the oars, Magic. The barque is towed by four Underworlders.

The accompanying text reads:

>Say the Gods of the Duat:
>
>"Come forth from the West,
>>One who is at peace on both banks of the Nu;
>>One who makes developments upon both arms of the Nu."
>
>This god is not entering the heavens;
>>He is but parting the Duat from the heavens
>>Through his developments which are in the Nu.
>
>Regarding "parting the Duat from Nut,"
>>This is both arms which belong to him whose identity is hidden.
>
>He exists in the Original Darkness;
>>And at their[219] coming forth, Re is in (his) first light.

Commentary

This deep threshold between the Underworld and the skies is where the bridge forms. It is a place between the Duat and the skies where the point of transformation occurs, a bit like a birth canal. Here the Divine collective presence of the Underworld is present. The consciousness of the Underworld is like a hive and vessel of the powers, oldest ones, ancient deities, ancestors, and Underworlders that make up the different regions of the Underworld: "him whose identity is hidden."

---

[219] The two arms.

Scene 89

Five human figures and four jackal-headed figures. They each carry a ruling-staff in their left hand, and a knife in their right, before them:

> Nine persecuting Apep.

Before them, a great serpent in chains:

> Apep

The chains connect to five peasant's crooks:

> Offspring of Distant One(s)[220]

The accompanying text reads:

> They exist in this plan:
> With their words/staffs in their arm,
>   They receive their butchering knives
>   That they may persecute Apep.
> They are those who ever[221] work his slaughtering,
>   Who ever carry out the restoration/mutilation at the shallows of the heavens.
> The thousands who are of this trespassing one
>   Are in the hands of the offspring of Distant One:
> They must evaporate this god,
>   Their ropes being in their fingers.

---

[220]"Distant One" is singular or plural depending on whether you read its plural determinative as referring to the whole phrase "Offspring of Distant One" or merely to "Distant One." I have gone for the latter, because *ms* "offspring" receives its own plural determinative here. I think these are metaphorical 'children' of Distant Ones, which have the power to restrict Apep. Also note that the peasant's crooks, S39, have the phonetic value *awt*, which also means "flocks," recalling the Flocks of Re. It also somewhat recalls *Awt*, the "extensions." (Gardiner 1957, p.509)

Then this god collects up his parts[222]
    After the opening up[223] of what was hidden in his arms,
That a path be made for Re.

This serpent exists in this plan:
    Offspring of Distant One, they hold him fast,
    They who are at peace in Nut.

They[224] exist in this plan:
    They put forth his bindings.
Now, though his shallows exist in the skies,
    His semen drops into the West.

Commentary

Here the power of Apep is defeated once more, to make absolutely sure that he cannot interfere with the passage of Re or emerge from this threshold place. There is often confusion when magicians read about the various attacks on Apep, as they assume that once he is fettered he is harmless or destroyed. This power cannot be destroyed. Instead, his emergence is suppressed at critical points in the final stages of the journey to make sure that chaos does not inadvertently rise along with Re.

Scene 90

Four baboons, each holding in front of them a large human hand, its index finger pointing upwards:

Baboons/Greeters

---

[221] *jrj* geminated here.
[222] *jp...Haw.f,* see **reckon up** and **members**.
[223] *wp,* usually translated **part**.
[224] Offspring of Distant One.

The accompanying text reads:

> They exist in this plan:
> They are those who make known Re
>   In the Eastern Akhet of the skies.
> They make known this god,
>   Who created them, in their habit,
> Two upon the East/Left,
>   Two upon the West/Right,
>   Meaning/In both conclaves of this god.
> They are ever coming forth after him;
>   Valiant is his Presence at his looking upon them.
> They are those who establish his sun-disc.

Commentary

The baboon is an aspect of Djehuty: knowledge and foresight. They utter the story of the rise of Re and point out which direction Re has to go. This also has deep connections to the various stages of creation where the power of Djehuty utters the deeper aspects of creation into words that form paths within the patterns. These beings give Re and the godly ones directions, and by uttering the way ahead they also create the pathways of the future.

This is of great importance to magicians. By casting the mind in a specific direction, not only can one *see ahead*, but the mere action of doing so changes what is ahead and creates the formation of shifts within the pattern.

Scene 91

Three figures.

A female figure wearing the White Crown:

The West

A female figure wearing the Red Crown:

The Place of the Loins

A male figure with life in his right hand behind him, and a dominion-staff in his left hand before him:

Who is of a gate

The accompanying text reads:

They exist in this plan:
They twist themselves at this gate belonging to One of the Duat,[225]
   One who is/Those who are ever parting the caverns and establishing the Gates of the Mysteries.
Their Presences, they pass through in his following.

Commentary

These two very interesting female figures are likely the *Two Ladies*, Nekhbet and Wadjet, goddesses who can appear as two women or two cobras. They are the powers of Lower and Upper Egypt, the spiritual, magical, and kingly powers of the land, and are depicted as wearing the two crowns of Egypt.

Nekhbet wears the **White Crown** of upper Egypt, and Wadjet wears the **Red Crown** of Lower Egypt. The red crown, *nt*, was connected to the goddess Neith, also *nt*, the Mistress of Sais who bore Re. Both Nekhbet and Wadjet are deeply connected with childbirth and the protection of Re.

Here they work closely to oversee the birth of Re over the threshold, and they are joined by a godly one who guards and oversees the portal.

---

[225] Receives a god determinative.

Scene 92

Four figures wearing the White Crown:

> Refining the best.[226]

The accompanying text reads:

> They exist in this plan:
>   They are those who establish the White Crown/Bright One
>   for gods who are followers of Re.
> They are established in the Duat;
>   Their Presences, passing through,
>   They stand erect at this gate.

Commentary

It may be helpful to explain something about the imagery behind the White and Red Crowns. The White Crown is Upper Egypt, which encompasses the sacred places, like Waset (Thebes), Abydos, and so forth. Upper Egypt is the country's spiritual/magical heart. The Red Crown is lower Egypt, which encompasses the Delta region, the kingship centre of Egypt, and takes in Memphis, and so forth. It is the heart of the power of kingship.

Deities that wear the White Crown are often connected to the development and upkeep of the spiritual soul of Egypt. Deities that wear the Red Crown are often connected to the development and upkeep of the country's temporal power base. The two parts woven together make a power pattern that is both sacred and temporal.

These godly ones with White Crowns are workers who oversee and protect the principles of spiritual evolution at this gate.

---

[226] *sTnw tp*, punning on "those who are crowned of head," which is visually how they are displayed here.

Scene 93

Four figures:

> Mourning

The accompanying text reads:

> They exist in this plan in this gate:
> > They are mourning Seat-of-the-Eye after Re's coming forth
> > > from the West.
>
> Their Presences pass through, following him;
> > Yet they exist in the following of Seat-of-the-Eye.

Commentary

These Finished Ones are still part of the Osirian process.

Scene 94

Four figures wearing the Red Crown:

> Uniting

The accompanying text reads:

> They exist in this plan:
> They are those who unite with Re,
> > Who cause to develop his offspring through the Earth.
>
> Their Presences pass through as his followers;
> > Their remains are established in their seat.

Twelfth Hour

Commentary

These are godly ones who work to trigger the birth of those about to rise. They stay in this place to act as midwives for the birth.

Scene 95

Four figures:

> Nursing

The accompanying text reads:

> They exist in this plan:
> They are those who nurse Re,
> > Who cause to be great the identities of all his developments.
> Their Presences pass through as his followers;
> > Their remains are established in their seat.

Commentary

These are godly ones working in service who nourish Re and give vital force to all aspects of Re. They rise with Re as they pass over the threshold.

Scene 96

Four female figures wearing the White Crown:

> Refining

The accompanying text reads:

> They exist in this plan:
>   They are those who cause Truth to arise,
> Establishing her in the shrine of Re,
>   In accordance with his being at peace in Nut.
> Their Presences, they pass through as his followers;
>   Their remains are established in their seat.

Commentary

These female godly ones awaken the Ma'at within Re and those who rise with Re. Remember, the White Crown is about the spiritual soul of Egypt, and at the heart of the spiritual soul is Ma'at: Truth, Order.

Scene 97

Four female figures wearing the Red Crown:

> Uniting

The accompanying text reads:

> They exist in this plan:
> They are those who establish a lifespan,
>   Who cause to develop the years
> For those who are reddening in the Duat
>   (Who are) For living in the skies.
> They exist as followers of this god.

Twelfth Hour

Commentary

These female godly ones make sure the lifespan has enough vital force to fulfil its destiny in the Duat and in the skies. Remember, the Red Crown is also connected to Neith, the weaver of life and creation. These powers make sure that the destiny, which has been measured and dispensed, has the vital force necessary to bring itself to completion.

Scene 98

Four female figures:

> Mourning

The accompanying text reads:

> They exist in this plan in this gate:
> They uplift/mourn through their hair,
>   Before this Great God in the West.
> They twist themselves at this gate;
>   They do not enter into the heavens.

Commentary

These ones are still in the stage of the Osiris development.

Scene 99

Four figures with bent backs:

Old Ones

The accompanying text reads:

> They exist in this plan:
> They adore Re, they acclaim for him;
> > They cause him to be valiant through their Duats/acclaiming.
>
> These gods, who are in the Duat,
> > Are door-keepers of the Place of the Mysteries.
> They are established in their seat.

Commentary

These are the ancient ancestors, the old ones who witness the birth of the new ones.

Scene 100

A figure with a cat's head, holding a serpent behind him in his right hand and a dominion-staff before him in his left:

> Pussy

The accompanying text reads:

> This is the door-keeper of a/the cavern;
> > He is established in his seat.

Twelfth Hour

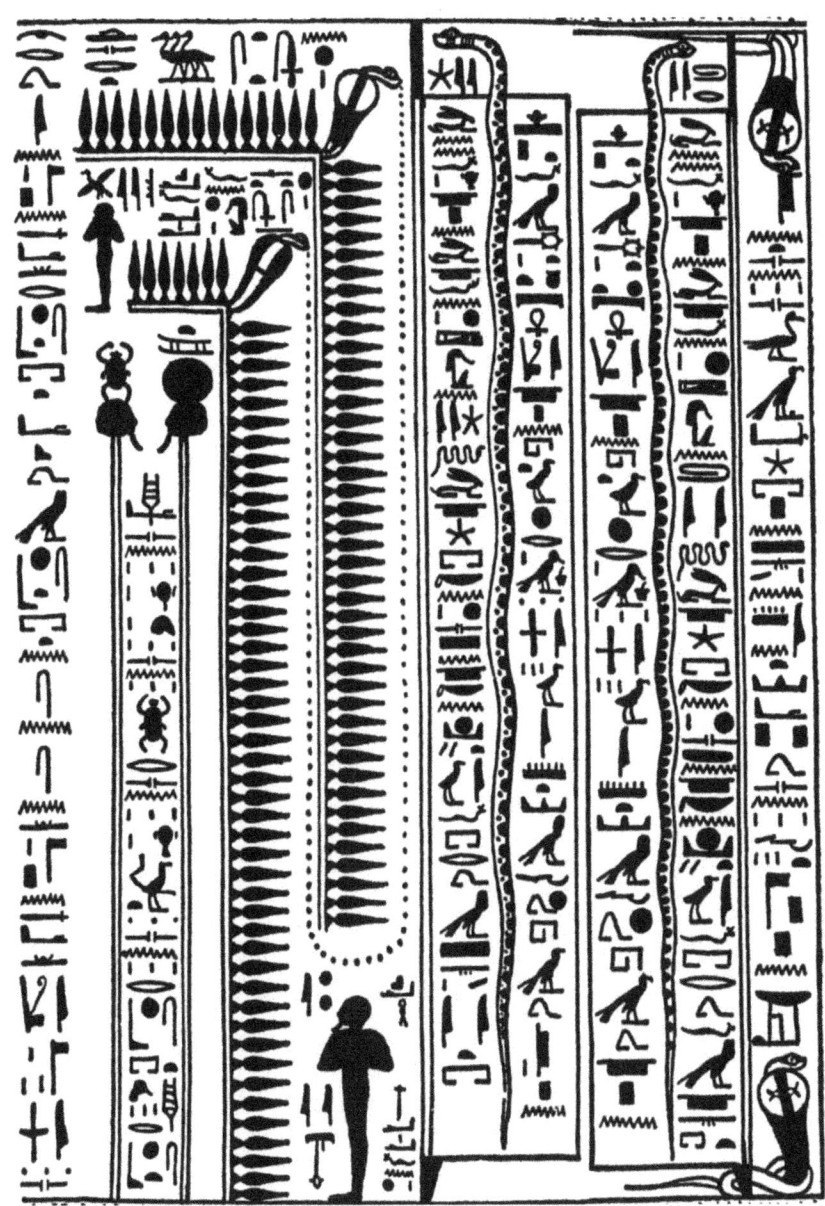

The Twelfth Gate on Seti I's sarcophagus.

Twelfth Gate

> The arrival by this Great God at this gate,
>> The entry into this gate.
>
> The worship of this Great God by the gods in her.

Gate caption:

> Hallowing Presences

Uraeus serpents caption:

> She kindles for Re

Guardian captions:

> Destroying/Providing: he bends his arms for Re.
>
> Who Is Of The First Light: he bends his arms for Re.

Staffs with human heads:
Facing right:

> Developing One

Facing left:

> Finished One

Text between the staffs:

> They stand erect upon their best.
> They develop upon their new start at this gate;
>> They stand erect upon their best at this gate.

First doorway's serpent caption:

Who Is Of The Portal/Star/School:

He exists over this door,
    He opens for Re.

Perception to Who Is Of The Portal/Star/School:

"Open your portal for Re,
    Reveal your door for He of the Akhet."

Now he comes forth from the Place of the Mysteries;
    He is at peace in/on the belly of Nut.

Sealed is this door.
Alas, then, for Presences who are in the West
    After the shutting of this door.

Second doorway's serpent caption:

Who Travels Round:

He exists over this door,
    He opens for Re.

Perception to Who Travels Round:

"Open your portal for Re,
    Reveal your door for He of the Akhet."

Now he comes forth from the Place of the Mysteries;
    He is at peace in/on the belly of Nut.

Sealed is this door.
Alas, then, for Presences who are in the West
    After the shutting of this door.

Two Uraei:

Seat

Mistress of the Enclosure

They are those who guard this portal, the Mystery of the West;

They pass through as followers of this god.

Commentary

It may be interesting to point out the two human-headed staffs. Most of this gate's text is obvious, but the human staffs talk about the power presence of humans in their development.

The one who faces west is still developing. All the developing happens through the death/rebirth process, which repeats until the development is done.

The Finished One faces east. He has done all his developing in the west, but he has yet to move forward from being Finished to being *as a god* and rising to the heavens. So he faces east, as becoming *as Re* is the next step.

These two staffs embody those dynamics and form part of the structure of the gate. It is the dynamics of human striving to becoming *as Re* that creates the threshold that allows it.

The first gate is for those who are "of the star": godly ones about to launch with Re into the heavens to become the stars.

The second gate is for those who are "travelling round." It is a serpent power very similar to the Greek idea of the Ouroboros, an idea that is also present in Egyptian texts. It is the power of completion where the end becomes the beginning.

The two goddesses who present as Uraei (serpent form = Underworld) are, between them, the Gate of Ascent, both in the Mysteries of death and rebirth, and in the magical Mysteries of completing the cycle and becoming Justified. These two goddess powers create the gate and give safe passage and protection for those who pass through them.

The Final Image

A figure bending back on himself:

> This is Seat-of-the-Eye.
> He encircles the Duat.

Twelfth Hour

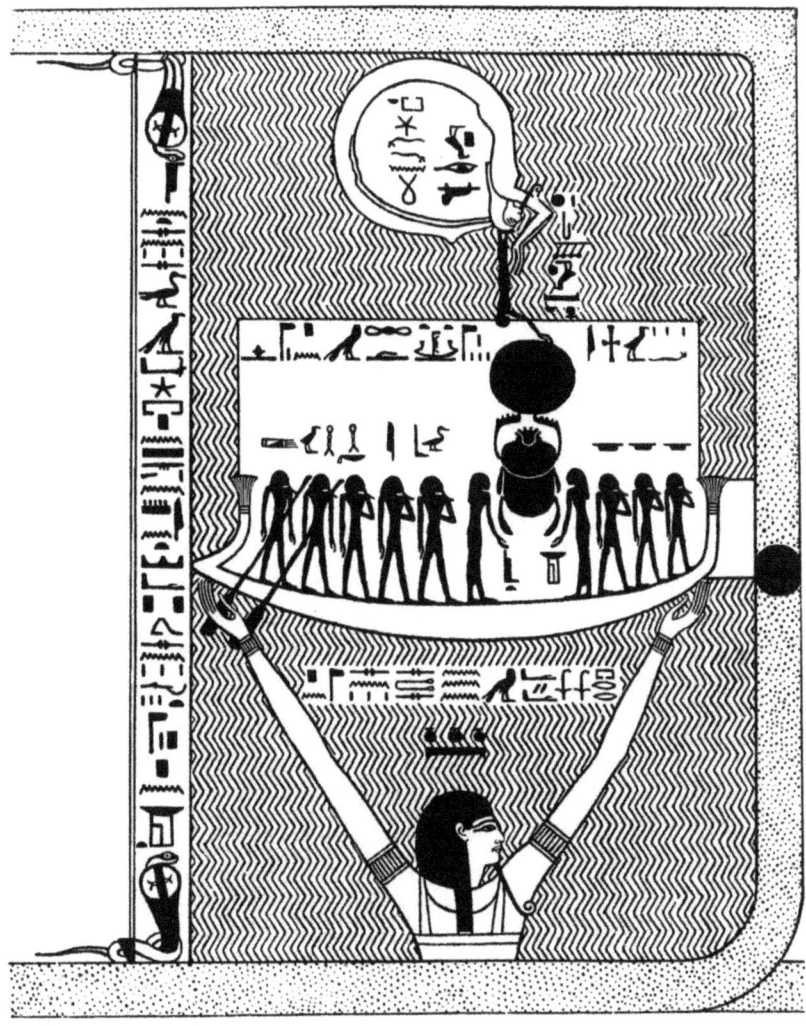

The Final Image on Seti I's sarcophagus.

A female figure standing on the previous figure's head, her hands touching the sun-disc:

> This is Nut.
>   She receives Re.

Caption above the Sun Barque:

> At peace is this god in the Dawning One.

> Gods who dwell in it:

> Doors/Door-keepers,
> Mistress of the Enclosure,
> Seat,
> Geb,
> Shu,
> Magic,
> Utterance,
> Perception.

Caption between the arms of a large figure supporting the Sun Barque:

> The coming-forth of both these arms from the water as they
>   cause this god to be raised up.

The large figure:

> The Nu.

Commentary

These are the elements that draw together to fulfil the destiny of those rising out of the Duat to traverse the stars: the seat (Isis), the boundary (Nephthys), the body (Geb), the breath (Shu), Magic (Heka), and Perception (Sia). These are the powers and qualities, all balanced within Ma'at, that the godly one lives through and by.

> And so they become clothed in gold:
>   Their faces in the stars,
>   Their feet in the waters,
> And their minds cast to the road ahead.

The Great Swimmer

Glossary

This glossary was prepared using Faulkner 1962 as its main reference.

abide *Hmsj* "sit, sit down, dwell, occupy (a place), sit at ease, remain inactive, stay."

absorb *am* "swallow, breathe in, absorb, realize, know, recognize, be discreet, dissemble, regret, forget, be unconscious."

Absorbing One, the *amw* from *am* **absorb**, with I14 serpent determinative. See Scenes 34 and 49.

acclaim *Hkn* "be joyful, acclaim, thanksgiving, acclamation."

add weight *wdn* "be heavy, weigh, become difficult, be copious, burdensome, oppressive."

adjudication *wpt* "judgement, adjudication," related to *wpj* **part**.

adoration *jAw* from the verb *jAj* "adore, praise, hail, exalt."

adore *dwA*, "praise, worship, adore"

adversary *xfty* "enemy, foe, opponent."

Akhet *Axt* (Johnson 1990, p.7)

Alas, then, *hwt xr*, see *hwjw* alas! This seems to be an onomatopoeic word; we read *hwt xr* as "Alas, then..." See Allen 2014, 18.11 and 19.11. This is much lighter than Hornung's reading of the word as "wail."

allotment *psSt* "part, division." See also *psSt* "carpet, matting (of reeds)."

Apep *aApp*

appear *wbn* "rise, shine (of sun), glitter (of precious metal), appear (of god or man), overflow, be excessive (of justice), dawn, brighten."

appear in glory *xAj* "rise (of sun), appear in glory (of god or king, esp. of king's accession), be shining (of king)"

approach *tkn* "approach, draw near, reach, counter, oust, chase away."

Ardent *mds* "sharp (of knife), acute (of vision), forceful (of character), firm-planted (of foot), cut down (quarry), ardent, excellent, powerful."

arise *ar* "mount up, penetrate."

arm *a* "arm, hand, item, sign, portion, habit." The phrase "in the arm of" can mean something like "under the control of," not just literally "in the arm/hand of."

Armless *nn-a*, The name of the being second in the queue in Scene 7.

aroura *sTA* "measure of capacity." We are reading this, where it occurs in Scene 24, as *stAt*, "aroura." "Aroura" is the Greek term for this measure of a hundred square cubits, 2,735 square metres, or roughly two thirds of an acre. (Gardiner 1957, p.200, §266)

arrive *spr* "arrive, reach, come."

ascend *sTsj* "raise, lift up, display (beauty), carry aloft."

ashlar *wdnt* "heavy block of stone," from *wdn* "be heavy."

Asiatics *aAmw* "Asiatics," and with a throw-stick determinative, "throw-sticks."

Assembly, the *DADAt* "magistrates, assessors, councils, judges, conclave."

attend to *aHaw + Hr* "attend to." Also a potential pun for **lifespan**, for instance in Scene 20.

Atum *jtm(w)* from *tm* "finish, complete, fulfil, exact, perfect." We translate this as "Finished One" rather than "Atum" when there is no god determinative.

authority, has authority over *Hry-tp* "who is upon, having authority over, chief, headsman, master."

Glossary

awake *rs* "wake, watchful, vigilant, keep watch, guard, be awake." See **vigilant**

awe *SfSft* "respect, awe." Also potential pun with *SfSft* "ram's head."

baboons/greeters *janw* plural of either *jan* "baboon," which is also a constellation, or *janw* "greeting, grief, cry out, groans, attention."

back of, at the *m sA* "m-sA: at the back of," from *sA* "back."

Balm *nsrt*, from *nsr* "anoint (injury)," or *nsr* **flame**. Pun on *nsrt* "royal serpent," .

bank *jdb* "river-bank, riparian land, shore (of flood), (of sky)."

barley *jt* "barley."

barque *wjA* "sacred barque, boat, ship, barge."

base *nst* "seat, throne, base." This word is rendered in Scene 24 in such a way as it could also be read as *gt*, "shrine."

bear *fAj* "raise, lift up, carry, support, present, transport, deliver, gather in, weigh."

bearers *fAyw* from *fAj* bear.

beat down *jr*, var. of *Ar* "drive away." *Ar*: "drive away, oppress (the poor)" See also **thresh** and **winnow**.

beauty, beautiful *nfr* "beautiful, fair, kindly, good, fine, goodly, happiness, good fortune, benefactions, good thing." . Also see **good**.

become Radiant *sAx* "spiritualize, glorify, illuminate, transfigure." Causative of *Ax*, "be, become a spirit." See also **Radiant**.

bed *aTwt* "bed."

beer *Hnqt*

before (him) *m-bAH* "in the presence of."

beget *jrj* "create, beget, make, construct, fashion, lay out (a garden), cultivate (crops), perform (a miracle), garner (corn), read aloud (a book), recite (a spell), + *m* = change/transform into." See also **make**. Generally we translate this as **make**, except when the sense absolutely requires "beget."

behind you *HAw.Tn*, from *HA* "occiput, back (of ear), behind, around." Only used in Scene 58.

behold *m.k*, *m.T*, *m.Tn*. Because "look you" was too Welsh. (Allen 2014, pp.141-142, §10.4.1)

belly *Xt* "belly, womb, body, sole (of foot), stomach, abdomen, offspring, generations, people, group."

Benben Enclosure *Hwt-bnbn* with O1 "house" determinative. See **Benben Stone** and **enclosure**.

Benben Stone *bnbn* "the sacred stone of n, point aloft, become erect, stretch out, loaf." Note the recurrence of the bread metaphor! The Benben stone is the small pyramid where the sun's first rays fell, found in the Temple of Re at Heliopolis. Related to the capstone of the pyramid.

bend *qaH* "bend (arm)"

best *tpw* "the best of..." Also means "heads," "on top of." See the best/heads punning theme in this book, which includes on occasion visual puns.

bestowals, what was bestowed *xrt* "state, condition, requirements, products, quantity needed, needs, possessions, dealings." For the sense of bestowal, see *xr* "with, near, under (a king)," and *xr-nsw* "(favours, etc.) from the king."

bind *snH* "bind, bind fast, entwine, fasten."

bindings *qAsw* "bonds, rigging of ship."

Bird-Trapper the human figure in Scene 63, from *jbT* "bird-trap." In what form are drawn Presences and the Radiant?

birth *msj* "bear, give birth, calve (of gazelle), lay (of bird), be born, create (of god), bring forth (of field), make, fashion, brood."

Glossary

Black Land, the *kmt* "the Black Land, Egypt." See also the pun on *kmt* "completion, final account" under **final reckonings**.

blackened *ss* "burn, ashes." In Scene 10, the heads are drawn as black, so the sense of this word, as used in this text, appears to be "like soot" rather than "burning."

blade *dmt* "knife, blade, sword, be sharp."

blood *snfw* Note interesting similarity to *snf* "cause to breathe."

blot out *sswn* "destroy, destruction, punish, blot out, be parched."

bodily form *Dt* "body (of person), figure (of a land), (a word describing an obelisk), image/bodily form (of a god)." An almost identical word means **eternal sameness**.

bonds *nTTw* "bonds, cordage, tie, 'sparrow (?) bread'"

born *ms* from *msj* "bear, give birth, calve (of gazelle), lay (of bird), be born, create (of god), bring forth (of field), make, fashion, brood."

boundaries *Hnbwt* "confines of district, delimited land, farm?."

boundary-beings *Hnbyw* with god determinative. From *Hnbwt* **boundaries**. Beings who set the boundaries of an allotment in the Marsh of Rushes. See Scene 25.

bow *Smrt* "bow."

bread *tA*

bread-measure *nDA* "measure (for loaves and dates)"

breakfast *jSt* "possessions, morning meal."

breath *TAw*, "wind, breath"

breathe *srq* "inhale, permit to breathe, breathe."

brewer *afty* "brewer"

bright *HD*

brightness *HDDwt*

brood *wA* "brood (*n* on), conspire (*m* against)."

bull *kA* with bull and/or penis determinative.

bun *a* "loaf." Punned with **arm** in Scene 42. Translated "bun" because I quickly ran out of synonyms for "bread" in this translation. I briefly toyed with translating it as "bagel," but it seemed to detract from the seriousness of the scene.

burn *Am* "burn up, burn (of brazier)."

butcher *dnd* "slaughter (animals)."

butchering knife Sign T34, "butcher's knife," phonetic meaning *nm*, "knife." (Gardiner 1957, p.515)

cake *Sayt* "cake, biscuit, shortbread, barley meal, date cake." Punned in Scene 33 with *Sat* "document."

calamity *mr* "sick, ill, diseased, painful, sorely, pain, ailment, illness, sorrow, woe."

call forth *njs* "make summons, make invocation, summon, call forth."

call, call upon *Dwj* "call upon (god)"

Care *nhp*, "care." The name of the serpent in Scene 40.

carnage *aDt* "slaughter, massacre," from *aD* "hack up, destroy."

carry out *wdj* "place, put, implant, plant, appoint as, be bent on, follow after, put forth, throw, shoot, utter, send forth, extend, compete with."

cast down *xrw* "fall, cast down, destroy."

cater for *drp* "offer to (god), present (dues), grant," related to *drpw* "offerings, provisions, meals, sustenance."

cause (the) destruction *sHtm*, causative of *Htm*, **destroy**.

cavern *qrrt* "cavern, hole, burial chamber"

chamber *at* "room, chamber, dwelling, department."

Glossary 275

Child *sDty* "child, foster-child (of king)," The seventh figure in the queue in Scene 7. Potential pun with **fire**.

circumference *dbnw* "circumference (of sky), circle." Also see *dbn* "mortar."

clear *baq* "oily, white, clear (of character, innocent), fortunate, bright, clear."

cloth *aAt* "linen cloth, thread, webbing."

coils *qAbw* "coils." Compare with *qAb*, **fold**.

cold refreshment *qbHw*, see "libation" and "cold water," . For the sense of this word as meaning "refreshment," see (Hornung and Abt 2014, p.25). These are cold waters that purify.

Cold Refreshment Is His Companion *qbH-snw.f* "one of the four Sons of Horus."

come *my* "come!, please!, pray!."

come forth *prj*

come in *jj* "come (of persons, of things, of future events), return, 'Welcome!', send, pass, wonder, occur, be disbursed."

come into power *sxm* "powerful, have power over, take possession of, possessed of." Undifferentiated power.

come, come back *jw* "come, return, arrive, delivered." Translated "come back" when preceded by **go**, as they are opposites.

companion *jry*, see *jr*, jry: "fellow, companion, mate, accomplice"

compass *dbn* "go round, travel round (a region), encircle."

complete *skm* "make complete, finish out, spend, bring to an end, blacken." In Scene 55, punned with *smw* **pastures** by giving it determinative M2, "herb," which is in fact associated with the word *jswt* "old times." (Gardiner 1957, p.478)

concerning one of the large number of words used to render the preposition *r*, whose basic meaning is "with respect to." (Allen 2014, p.107, 8.2.7)

conclaves, in both *jtrtj*, dual of *jtrt* "row (of men or shrubs), of shrines at jubilee, in the two conclaves, chapels, niche (for statue), box (for us-abtis), side."

conditions *xrt* "state, condition, requirements, products, quantity needed, needs, possessions, dealings." For the sense of bestowal, see *xr* "with, near, under (a king)," and *xr-nsw* "(favours, etc.) from the king." See **bestowals**

conduct *sSm* "lead, guide, rule, govern, show (the way), instruct (people), reveal, marshal, direct, manifestation." Also note the pun in Scene 20 on *sSm(tj)*, "butcher."

conducted *sbj* + *n* "conduct to." Note: "conducted" is always *sbj* in this translation; "conduct" is always *sSm*.

conformists *snjw* from *snj* "be like, resemble, copy, imitate, conform."

consecrate *snTr* "incense, consecrate."

consider *hnn* "attend to, consider."

conspire against *wA m*, "conspire against." See also **brood**.

consume *wnm* "eat, eat of, feed on, consume, devour."

cord *wAwAt* "cord." Distinct from **Magic Cord**

corner-place *Knbt* "corner, angle" with house determinative. Literal translation of *Knbt* "court (of magistrates)."

corruption *jwtyw* "corruption"

countenance *Hr* "face, mask, head, mind, zeal." See **face** and **zeal**.

counterpart *sSmw* "statue, portrait, image, counterpart."

course *mTn* "road, way, course, path."

cover *Hbs* "clothe, be clothed, don, furnish, hide, cover up, give shelter."

create *qmA* "create, produce, hammer out." Also see the related word (though seemingly in opposition) *qmAw* **winnower**

crew *jst* "crew (of ship)." Potential pun with *js* "be light (of weight)."

criminal *xnr* "criminal, prisoner."

crookedness *XAbt* i.e. who made a crooked path, who made themselves crooked, who did imbalanced deeds.

cry out *sbH* "sob, mourn, low."

cultivates the differences *jrj.f Tnwt*, from *jrj* (see **garner**) and *Tnt* "difference."

cultivator *jHwtj*, a variant of *aHwty*, "cultivator," which is a triangular agricultural instrument.

cut out *Hsq* "cut off, cut out, behead." In this text, the notion is of being cut out of existence.

cuttings *Saw* from *Sa* hew

cycle *Hptt* "course (of sun and moon)."

dagger *sft* "knife." Translated "dagger," which isn't really quite the right term, to distinguish it from **knife** and **blade**, which were already used. Also note possible puns: *sf* "yesterday, mix, be mild/merciful, mercy, gentleness," *sfw* "the gentle man," *sft* "clemency."

daily bread *mjnt* "daily fare," and with a different determinative, "a kind of land." Notice the equivalence made between bread and the land provided to the Righteous in the Duat.

darkness/greed *snkw* We translate this weird word in Scene 9 as "darkness/greed." From *snkw* "greed" and *snkkw* "darkness, obscurity." Like several words in this text, it possesses some odd features which seem to wave at the reader to pay careful attention. The question to be answered is: is this word "greed" or "darkness"? It is possible that the second *k* for *snkkw*, "darkness," has been omitted; but then why the *sun* determinative? The expected determinative for the word is N2, the sky with a broken *wAs* sceptre, not N5, the sun-disc. (Gardiner 1957, p.485) In our opinion, the word's spelling evokes both concepts: darkness and greed, and the sun determinative is to direct our attention to the *things that shine* in the scene: Glister the serpent, the "flesh of the gods" in the shrines, and Re.

dawn *anDw* "dawn."

Dawning One, the *anDtt* with barque determinative, the name of the Sun Barque in the final image. See **dawn**

daybreak *wnyt* "light, daybreak."

dazzle *sSp* "be white, be bright, make bright, lighten (darkness), sheen, brightness, splendour."

dazzling *Sp*, by removal of the causative *s* in **dazzle**. Possible connotation of blinding light from *Sp*, "be blind, make blind"?

decide to expose *sHAj*, causative of *HAj* **expose**. "strip (someone), reveal (secret)."

dedicated to *twr* "show respect to." See also **devotion**, and note potential pun with *twr* "be clean, purify, be cured."

deep darkness *wSAw* "deep darkness."

degenerate *nHA* "contrary, perverse, alarming, terrible, abnormal (?), infested, wild, dense, impracticable, troubled, dangerous, untended, rough, wild, hard."

Degenerate of Zeal Title of serpent in Scene 69. See **degenerate** and **zeal**.

delightful *nDm* "sweet (of flavour or odour), pleasant, pleasing, well, hale, please, delightful, rejoice, pleased, be glad, happy, of good cheer, comfortable."

Delta marshes, the *mHt* "the Delta marshes,"

depart *Sm* "go, opposite of *jw* "come", walk, set out (on journey). depart, return, emerge." see **come back**.

Desert *smyt*

designs *sxrw* "plan, council, determination, preparations, dispositions, advice, designs, decisions"

destroy *Htm* "perish, be destroyed, overwhelm, annihilate, liquidate, pay (debt)." Note the very similar word *Htm* "provide."

Glossary

develop *xpr* (Allen 2014, p.526)

Developing One *xprj*, generally transliterated as (the god) Khepri.

devotion verb *tr*, noun *tryt* "greet respectfully, show respect, worship, esteem, adore."

Discovering A Mouth *sbq r*, from *r* mouth and *sbq* "find, discover." But also possibly from *sbq(j)* "legitimate, precious, excellent, clever, splendid, fortunate, felicitous, wise, skilled, short, cool places, uplift."

dismember *stp*. We translate as "dismember" when the word occurs with a wounded man determinative. The word also means **selection**.

disobey *thj* "go astray, transgress, attack, lead astray, mislead, overstep (path), falsify, impugn, disobey, neglect, reject, violate, do wrong, damage, interfere with."

disorders *abw* "disorders, impurity."

dispel *xsr* "dispel, drive away, clear (a road), remove (dirt)."

displace *tkn m*. From *tkn* **approach** "be near, approach, draw near, reach, counter, oust, chase away."

dispute *DAjs* "dispute, argue, oppose (actions), argument, dispute, civil war."

distant *Hr* "distant, be far from, apart from."

Distant One From *Hr*. Generally the name for Horus We suggest that the title sometimes applies to a student of the Mysteries who has reached a particular stage.

divide, division *pSn* "split (heads), fracture (bones), separate (combatants), slice (bread), be rid of, be separated, stretch, divide"

divine *nTry* "divine, sacred." Also see **Magic Cord**.

Diving, the *hrpyw* from *hrp* "sink, be immersed, suppress, dive."

dominate, dominion, have dominion *wAs* "dominion, have dominion." A power that has to do with static dominating, and often, in this text, having to do with stopping or limiting the movement of Apep/chaos. Represented by a staff with a Set animal/shoulder head and a forked bottom.

dominion-staff a *wAs* staff.

door *aA*

door-keepers *jryw-aA* from **keeper** and **door**.

dream *qdd* "sleep, slumber, dream."

drop *hAj* "come down, go down, descend." Also see **shut**.

Duat *dwAt*

duty *jrt* "duty, use, purpose."

dwelling *arrwt* "gate, leaf (of double door), hall of judgement, dwelling, home." Also translated **hall** and **home**

ear *msDr* "ear."

Earth *tA*

Earth Barque, The *wjA tA*. See **barque** and **Earth**.

East *jabt* "the East, left."

eat *wnm* "eat, eat of, feed on, consume, devour."

egg, the *swHt* "egg."

ejaculation *aAa* "ejaculation."

embrace *jnq* "unite, collect, gather together, embrace, come together, encompass, enclose."

eminence *bwA* "become high."

emission *wddt*, geminated infinitive of *wdj* **put out**, giving a sense of continuous output.

emmer *bdt* "emmer."

empty *Sw* "be empty, be lacking, be devoid, be missing, free (of)"

encircle *Snj* "encircle, encompass, embrace, cut mortise, enclose, surround, cover."

enclosure *Hwt* "enclosure." (Allen 2014, p.524)

endow *sDfAw* "endow, provide, foundation, endowment, supply (with offerings), give abundance, furnish." See also **provision**

enduring *rwD* "hard, enduring, permanent, firm."

ennobled one *saH* "noble, dignitary, be noble, (trans.) ennoble, eternal image, mummy." This word is used to refer to mummies, but in this text it does not mean a physical dead body. Also note the pun betwen *saH* and *saHa* "cause to stand erect, raise up."

enquire about *nD* "take counsel, ask advice, enquire about."

ensorcel *HkA* "magic, magic spells, enchantment, bewitchment, charms." We translate as "ensorcel" when it is a verb, to avoid it sounding like a simple act, as "charm" or "magic'd" might make it seem.

enter *aq* "enter, come in, enter into a state."

Entering-Into *aqn* with god determinative. From *aq n* "enter into (a state)" . Usually just transliterated as "Aqen," this intriguing character also appears in Spell 99 of *The Book of the Dead*. Possibly "one to whom entry belongs."

entourage *Snwt* "entourage, courtiers."

entrust *wD* "command, make a command, ordain, commit, assign, decree, allot, decree (+ *n* "to"), entrust (+ *n* "to"), command, decree, despatch, precept, send away." Usually translated **ordain**.

equal *rmnj* "shoulder, carry, support, match, equal, bearer, support." Compare with *rmn*, "shoulder, arm," which in dual is "arms of a balance, uprights of a ladder."

Equalled *rmnj* "shoulder, carry, support, match, equal, bearer, support." Compare with *rmn*, "shoulder, arm," which in dual is "arms of a balance, uprights of a ladder."

equip *apr* "provide, equip (+ *m* "with"), acquire, incur (injury)."

escape *Sp* "flow out, depart, break out." In the Sixth Gate, the being called "Escaped" could also be called "Blind": *Sp* "blind, make blind."

escort *Sms* "follow, accompany, bring, present, escort, guard, retinue."

establish *smn* "Make firm, establish, make to endure, pepetuate, make fast, set in place, set up." Causative of *mn* **establish**.

established *mn* "be firm, established, enduring"

estrange *jwd* "separate (x r 'from' y), lie between, distinguish."

eternal recurrence *nHH* "eternity." For a discussion of *nHH*, which is specifically "eternal recurrence," and how it fits into the dynamics of creation, see (Allen 1988, pp.25–27).

eternal sameness *Dt* "eternity." For a discussion of *Dt*, which is specifically "eternal sameness," and how it fits into the dynamics of creation, see

evaporate *axx* "evaporate, consume."

evict *Dsr*, more normally "holy, sacred, hallowed," etc., but can be used to mean "segregate."

evil *Dwt* "evil, dirt, fault, difficulty, badness, ill"

evoke njs "make summons, make invocation, proclaim, formulate, call forth."

Evokers *Dwywt* from *Dwj* "call upon." Beings in Scene 77.

exaction *xbt* "deduction, exaction, lessening of moon, lessening of tax."

excess *aAy* "excess, (+ *r* "over" = math. 'difference')"

exhausted *bdS* "become faint, weak, exhausted."

exist *wnn* "be, exist, live."

Expanded, the *pgAw*, from *pgA* "open, be open, enrol, extend." Dive in, relax, concentrate, expand.

expert *Hmt* with A2 "man with hand to mouth" determinative. (Gardiner 1957, p.442) From *Hmt* "skill, craft (of sculptor)."

exposed *HAy* "be naked, exposed, shine over, illuminate."

expression *tpy-r* "utterance, financial principle (?), base (of triangle), radius (of circle), speech, expression." Note how this can mean both expression as "what you loaned out to start with," and expression as in "utterance."

extension *Awt* "length (of time), stretch (of foot)." Generally translated "gifts" when paired with the bread roll determinative, and viewed in funerary contexts as offerings presented to the deceased. We adopt a translation that is arguably more literal, though it seems more abstract. The word is related to *aw* "long, length (of space)," and from the verb *Awy* "extend (the arm), present (an offering), stretch." See also the phrase *r Aw*, "to the extension," to mean "entirely," (Allen 2014, p.233) which suggests a sense of *Awt* as reaching ones fullest extent.

extinguish *aSm* "extinguish," translation given by Hornung for this word. (Hornung and Abt 2014, p.105)

exult *Tnj* "lift up, promote, distinguish, exalt."

Exulting Earth *tA-Tnn* "Memphite earth-god." Generally transliterated as Tatenen, "Exulting Earth" is the literal meaning of the name. It is generally translated as "risen earth,"(Wilkinson 2003, p.130) but we render it here as "Exulting Earth" both for consistency with *tA* **Earth** and *Tnj* **exult**, and also because here *Tnj* is geminated, *Tnn*, giving a sense of continual exulting/raising/refinement.(Allen 2014, p.166) "Exulting Earth" means both the original rising of the mound from the waters of creation but which is in some sense eternally recurring/continuing, and also the fertile silt left behind after the Nile's inundation.

Eye *jrt*

face *Hr* "face, mask, head, mind, zeal." Also think "countenance," as in the KJV.

faint *gAH* "be weary, become easily tired, be faint, be soft."

fall upon *hAj* "come down, go down, descend, fall, drip, drop, grasp the meaning of." We translate this as "shut," because in English to speak of "the coming down of a door" brings to mind a portcullis rather than a pair of double doors. Also see **shut**.

father *jt*

feed *xfA*, see *xfAt* "food," .

fen *Sa* "field, meadow, country, marsh, swamp, fruit, trees, date groves, flowers, bushes." . As we are running out of different common English words for marshes, we translate this as "fen": "low marshy land often, or partially, covered with water; a morass or bog." (Schwarz 1991, p.380)

ferry *DAj* "ferry, cross over, traverse." Note that the same word, with a different determinative, can also mean **extend**, just as *Awt*, "gifts," can also mean "extension." Including this word in Scene 10 just before the 'offering list' is, I think, intentional, to help prime the reader for making the gifts/extension link.

fetter *jnT* "fetter."

Fiery *xty* from *xt* "fire." The name of the serpent in scene 60.

fiery blast *hh*, "blast (of fire), (of heat of sun), (as symptom of disease), fiery hot breath, wind."

fill *mH* "fill, pay in full, finish." See also **full**

final reckonings *kmwt* "completion, final account," from *km* "total up to, amount to." It is written with a plant determinative to link it to the barley that is to be threshed, and contains an extra *t* "bread loaf."

find *gmj* "find."

fine gold *Damw* "fine gold, electrum." See also **sceptre**.

finger *Dba* "finger" (Gardiner 1957, p.456).

finish *tm* "finish, complete, fulfil, exact, perfect."

Finished One *jtm(w)* from *tm* "finish, complete, fulfil, exact, perfect." We translate this as "Finished One" rather than "Atum" when there is no god determinative.

fire *sDt* Potential pun with **child**.

first light *jxxw* "twilight, dusk."

Glossary

flame *ns* "flame," potential pun here with *nsr* "royal serpent."

flaming *nsrsr*, formed by doubling *nsr* "flame" for emphasis. (Morrow 2015, p.27)

Flaming Isle *jw nsrsr*, see **flaming** and **isle**.

flesh of a god *Haw-nTr* See **members** and **god**.

flock *awt* "small cattle (i.e. sheep and goats), goats, sheep, herds in general, flocks, wild cattle." Compare with the Biblical flock/shepherd metaphor.

flood *nt* "water, inundation, flood." See also **Red Crown**

flood-waters *mHt* "flood-waters,"

flourish *rd* "grow, flourish, prosper, restore, become firmer."

fluid *nX* "fluid (of body)."

fly away *aXj* "fly, fly away."

fold *qAb* "fold over, double over, double quantity, doubled, intestine, rectum." Compare with **coils**.

follower *xt* "student, follower." Notice the similarity with the derivation of "disciple."

foot *rd* "foot, heels, paces;" note the related word *rdw* "stairway."

force into place *sxr* "overthrow, throw down, cast down, force into place (a dislocated bone), worry, banish, lay low." Also "exorcise": (Ritner 1993, p.48)

forecourt *wsxt* "hall, court, forecourt."

foremost *xnty* "who, which is in front of, southern, who is at the head of, foremost, before, presider over, outer chamber, front part."

Foremost of Westerners *xnty-jmntyw*, "epithet of Osiris," . See **foremost** and **Westerners**, and **Seat-of-the-Eye**.

form *jrw* "shape, form, nature."

formulate (your) business *jrt mxrw*. For *mxrw* "dealings, business, ordinances, arrangement," see

found *snT* "measure out (land), found (house), create, foundation, custom."

frame *qS* "bone, frame."

free *wHa* "loose (fetters, etc), release (someone, something), interpret, explain, solve, unfurl."

Freed of Heart *wHa-jb*, the fifth figure in the queue in Scene 7.

front *xnt* "face, brow."

full *mH* "fill, pay in full, finish, make whole, complete, be pregnant, hold fast."

garner *jrj* "create, beget, make, construct, fashion, lay out (a garden), cultivate (crops), perform (a miracle), garner (corn), read aloud (a book), recite (a spell), + *m* = change/transform into." Usually **make**, but we translate as "garner" occasionally to help bring out the barley/bread metaphor.

gate *sbxt* "portal, doorframe, gate, porch?, doorway, screen, pylon-shaped receptacle."

Geb *gb* "the earth-god Geb." Also see **overflow**.

give *rdj* "give, put, place." Also see **place** and **render**.

give up *jmj* "(imperative) give! place! cause! let, have to, bring, give up, sell."

Glister *sty* literally "glittery one." From *stj* "glitter, shine, strew." We translate this being's name as "Glister" purposefully to bring to mind the phrase "All that glisters is not gold." (The Merchant of Venice, Act II, Scene 7.)

glow *nbj* glow.

go aground *SAy* "go aground, founder."

god *nTr*

goddess *ntrt* "goddess," and with eye determinative, "divine eye." Similar words when spelled *nTryt*, as in the Fifth Gate, *ntry* "magic cord," *ntryt* "natron," *ntrty* "adze."

godhood *nTr* "godhood, divinity."

gold *nbw* "gold" Compare with *nbj* **molten**

good, goodness *nfr* "beautiful, fair, kindly, good, fine, goodly, necessary, pleasing, kind, happy, well, good, well-supplied, lawful, wise, favourable, pleasant, kind, excellent, sage."

govern *sSm* "lead, guide, rule, govern, show (the way), instruct (people), reveal, marshal, direct, manifestation." Also note the pun in Scene 20 on *sSm(tj)*, "butcher."

grace *jmAw* from *jmA* "kind, gentle, well-disposed, pleasing, be gracious, be delighted, charmed, amiable, sympathetic, befriend, be dear to, pleasant, graceful, good, kind, grace." Also see *jma* "tree, wood."

grain *npr* The name of one of the figure at the front of the queue in Scene 7.

grain-rations *dj* "provisions, grain rations, gift, wages."

great *aA*

Great God *nTr aA*, only used to refer to Re in this book.

guard *sAw* "guard, ward off, restrain."

guardian *sAw*

habit *a* "arm, hand, item, sign, portion, habit."

hail *hy* "hail!, shout, jubilate."

hair *Snw* "hair, wool, woolen?, lack of hair, coiffeur, grass."

hall *arrwt* "gate, leaf (of double door), hall of judgement, dwelling, home." Also translated **dwelling** and **home**

hallowed *Dsrw* "seclusion, holy place, holy ground, sacred area." Compare with the similar word *Dsrt*, **strong ale**.

hand *Drt* "hand, trunk (of elephant), handle (of jar), *m Drt* in the service of, in the hand of."

He of the Akhet *Axty*

head *tp* See also **best** and the best/heads punning theme in this book, which includes on occasion visual puns.

hear *sDm* "hear, listen, understand."

heart *jb* "heart (physical, and seat of thoughts and emotions), understanding, intelligence, will, desire, attention, sense, passion, opinion, take thought."

heat *bxxw* "heat."

heavens, one of the *Hrty* from *Hrt* **heavens**.

heavens, the *Hrt* "sky, heavens." We translate this as plural, though the Egyptian word is singular, to avoid confusion with the concept of "heaven" as "Paradise." See also: **Nut, skies.**

heir *rpat* "hereditary noble, heir, crown prince."

helpful person *aHaw* "stand-by, helper."

hew *Sa* "cut up, cut down (trees), diminish, hew (ship)."

hidden *jmn*

Hidden Region *at jmnt* "region, chamber": "room, cell, hall, dwelling, department, pantry, orchard.

His Hind Leg Is Forward *xnty-mnt.f* Literally "Foremost is his thigh."

hold fast *nDrw* "grasp, hold fast, take possession of, follow, observe, draw tight, pursue."

hold secret *HAp* "secret, mysterious, hide, conceal, hold secret."

hollows *bAwt*, noun from *bA* "hack up (the earth), hoe (crops); see also *bAj* "water-hole." . Hornung has "cavities." (Hornung and Abt 2014, p.117)

Glossary 289

home *arrwt* "gate, leaf (of double door), hall of judgement, dwelling, home." Also translated **dwelling** and **hall**

honour *Sf* "respect, honour (?)"

hot *tA* "hot, hot-tempered, temper."

hour *wnwt* "hour, division of time." Other words written *wnwt* are "duty, service, office, (lay) priesthood."

humans *rmTw* See pun on **tears**.

hurry *Hpt* "travel," *Hp* "to hurry, run, ritual race?"

identity *rn* "identity, name." (Allen 2014, p.523)

idiot *xm* "ignorant man," from *xm* "know not, be ignorant of, (with reflexive:) not know oneself, be unconscious of (one's limbs), forget, have no regard for, not to acknowledge, be unacquainted, ignore, be witless, unmindful, heedless."

Idle, the Literally "idle ones." From *nnyw*, "be weary, inert, drag (of foot), reluctant, neglect, fail, be idle"

ignorant *jxmw*

Ignorant Of Wiping Away, the *jxmw sk* "indestructable stars, i.e. circumpolar stars." See *jxmw* **ignorant** and *sk* **wipe away**.

illumination *tkAw*, see *tkA*, "torch, taper, flame, illumine, burn, rite of torch-lighting,"

in accordance with *xft* "in front of, in accordance with, as well as, corresponding to, when, according as, at the time of, when, during, since, at."

in the possession of *Xr* "under, carrying, holding, possessing, in possesion of, in tenure of, held by." Note the ambivalence: it is not clear whether A is possessing B or B A.

in the presence of *xr* "with, near, under (a king), to, in presence of, before, from."

incandescent *wAwAt* "fiery one," perhaps related to *wAwAw* "sheen."

incite *ddb* "sting, incite." See also **subject to**.

increase *HAw* "wealth, increase, excess, surplus, interest, addition, payment, food."

Inducer *bsy*, from *bsj* "flow forth, influx (of foreign migrants), come forth, bring forth, introduce." Perhaps related to the god Bes.

Indwelling Gods *nTrw jmyw* literally "gods who are in(side)."

infant *xy* "child, young, plant."

infiltrate *Dfy* "penetrate." In Scene 45, spelled *dfy*. Translated "infiltrate" rather than "penetrate" mainly to distinguish from **penetrate**.

Infinity *HH* "million, a great number, + *n* many." The god Heh, the personification of infinity,[227] whose name we thus can translate, almost literally, as Infinity.

influence, influential *wsr*, "strong, powerful, influential" Power that influences, steers, directs, manipulates. Represented by a staff with a jackal's head.

Initiation *bsw* "secret image of god, introduction, initiation." See also *bs* "introduce, initiate, bring in (a state of affairs), reveal (a secret), enter, come forth, bring forth, flow, extend, induct, emerge flowingly, admit into."

inlay *sam* "wash down (medicine), swallow, inlay, cause to eat, overlay."

inundate *mHj* "drown, be drowned, overflow (of Nile), inundate, swim, launch (a vessel)."

investigate *wHa*

iron *bjA, bja(t)* "heaven, firmament." In Scene 62, could also be "heaven, firmament, a mineral, bronze, meteoric iron quarry, gritstone, mining-region, mine, produce of a mine, wonder, marvel." Also note that *bja-sH-nTr* "the bronze/iron which reveals the god," is the implement for Opening the Mouth.

---

[227] Wilkinson 2003, p.109

Glossary 291

isle *jw* "island, be boatless, strand, leave boatless."

issue instructions *wD n* "make a command for the benefit of"

jackal *sAb* "jackal"

jaw *art* "jaw."

join *smA* "unite, join (a company)." Would have been translated as "unite" but for that word already being more needed elsewhere.

joyful *Haj* "joyful, rejoice, acclaim, exult, shout for joy."

juncture *hAw* "time, neighbourhood, environment, circumstances, affairs, whereabouts, vicinity."

keep safe *swDA* "make healthy, keep safe."

keeper *jry* from *jry* "relating to." e.g. *jry-at* "hall-keeper," *jry-aA* "door-keeper."

kindle *stj* "shoot (arrow), throw, thrust, spear, kindle (light), pour (water), glitter (of sky), hurl, shine, strew." We translated this word as "Glister" when used negatively; we translate as "kindle" when used positively. Note that the same verb, with a different determinative, means "beget."

knife *ds* "knife, flint, slaughter."

Labour *tj(A)wyt* Literally "place of acute pains/shrieks." For *tjA* "pain, shriek," see

lacking *gAw* "be narrow, constricted, languish, lack, be lacking, deprive, lie."

lake *S*, "lake, pool, pond, garden, basin for liquids."

Lakes of the Vagina *Sw knst* with N25 "foreign land" determinative. (Gardiner 1957, p.488) See **lake** and **vagina**.

lamplight *tkA*, "torch, taper, flame, illumine, burn, rite of torch-lighting," This definition is given more to distinguish between the different words for "flame" than for its literal meaning.

lapping *wAw* "wave of sea," but here applied only to the lake in Scene 10.

lashes *rwD* "cord, bow-string, sinews, lashes."

Libyans *TmHw* "Libyans, Libyan dancers."

lick *nsbw* "lap up, lick, swallow."

life, live *anx* See also *spj* **live on**.

lifespan *aHaw* "lifetime, period, space of time, span, duration, pause, noon."

lift up *wTs* "raise, lift up, wear, weigh (goods), extol (god), display (beauty), announce (someone), extol, exalt, proclaim, support."

lightening *Ssp* "white, bright, dawn."

limb *at* "limb, member (of body); note also *at* "room, chamber, cell."

limit, limits *Dr* "limit." (Allen 2014, p.535)

linen *sSrw* "linen." Also note the word with different determinatives can mean "things, actions, cause, utterances, expressions."

live on *spj* "remain over, be left out, excluded, be left over, abandoned, spare, occur, live on, continue."

loaf *xnfw* "cake, bread." This is translated loaf primarily for differentiation between the different types of bread referenced in this text.

look upon *mAA* "see, look upon, regard, behold, inspect."

love *mrj* "love, want, wish, desire, cherish, prefer, covert, beloved, demand."

lowing *jm* "moan," which in Scene 11 is interpreted as the lowing (mooing) of bulls. We say "lowing" because "mooing" does not quite provide the necessary gravitas.

magic *HkAw* "magic, magic spells, enchantment, bewitchment, charms."

Magic *Hkaw*, "Magic," the name of a god who travels with Re at the back of his Barque.

Magic Cord *nTry* "magic cord." Also a pun on *nTry* "divine."

Glossary

make *jrj* "create, beget, make, construct, fashion, lay out (a garden), cultivate (crops), perform (a miracle), garner (corn), read aloud (a book), recite (a spell), + *m* = change/transform into."

make bright *sHD* "illumine, gladden, reveal, make bright, enrich." Causative of *HD*, **bright**, which see.

make known *sr* "foretell, make known, spread abroad, reveal."

make Mysterious *sStA* "make secret, mysterious, secret, confidential matter, religious mystery." Causative of **Mystery**.

make Radiant *sAx* "spiritualize, glorify, illuminate, transfigure." Causative of *Ax*, "be, become a spirit." See also **Radiant, become Radiant**.

make the designs *jrt sxrw*

make towering *sqAj* "make high, set upright (a person), exult (a god), extol (beauty), victories, prolong (lifetime), exult, raise, praise." We translate as "make towering" for consistency with **towering**. Note the connotation of *setting upright*.

marsh *sxt* "marshland, field, country, district, countryside, plains, burial ground." Note that a phonetically identical word means "offering loaves," recalling the bread in Ma'at's scale-pan in an earlier scene.

Marsh of Rushes *sxt jArw* See **marsh** and **rushes**.

Master *nb* "lord, master, owner, possessor."

meadow *AHt* "field, arable land, earth, mould, soil, holding, meadow, tilled land." We translate as "meadow" rather than "field" to emphasize its membership in the Marsh of Rushes.

means preposition *m* in sense of "is," "namely." *m* of predication. (Gardiner 1957, p.125, §162)

meat *jwf* "flesh (of man), meat, diaphragm."

Meat of Re, the *jwf ra*. See **meat** and **Re**.

meddle with *snj* "pass, pass by, surpass, transgress, outstrip, swerve, meddle with."

members *Haw*, "members," plural of *Ha*, "flesh, body." In plural "limbs, members," even "self."

Mistress *nbt* feminine of *nb*, **master**.

Mistress of the Enclosure *nbt-Hwt*, "Nephthys."

moan *mnj* "shout (of people), low (of cattle)."

molten *nbj* "melt (metal), cast (objects in metal), model, fashion, blaze, flame up, put on, assume."

monkey *ky* "monkey." Note pun on *ky* "other."

mortal *mt* "dead man, mortal man." The temptation is to translate this as "dead man." However, in this text mortals are usually contrasted with Radiant ones, so we prefer to translate as "mortal," which does seem to make much more sense of the text.

Mortal, the *mtw*, plural of *mt* **mortal**. Humans who are not the Radiant.

mortal-grapple *mt* rendered with Z6, "hieratic substitute for A13 or A14," , *mt* "perish (of ship), death, kill self, be dead, sink, death's grapple."

mould *qd* "form, nature, character, disposition, condition, duty, contour, mould."

mountain *Dw* "mountain, hill."

mourning *jAkb* "mourning."

mouth *r* "mouth, opening (of cave), door, utterance, speech, language, intent, spell, dictate, deposition, voice, word, saying."

multitude *aSA*

myriad developments *aSAw xprw* (Allen 2014, p.526)

Mysteries, the *StAw* "secrets, religious mysteries."

Mystery *StA* "mysterious, secret, hidden, difficult, hiding, difficult, secret place, quiet, composed." Note the similarity of the word to **tow**.

neck *wsrt* "neck."

Net *amamtyw* with F18 "elephant tusk." From *am* "absorb," reduplicated to make *amam* (Allen 2014, p.168, §12.5.6), "continually absorb (?)," with F18 denoting a hunting implement or perhaps even wonder (Gardiner 1957, p.463).

new start *mAwt* "a new thing, newly, anew, new land, fresh."

Nine, the *psDt* "group of nine, Ennead of gods, the Nine Bows (= the nations of the world)." Note similarity with *psD*, "shine." We translate this as "the Nine" rather than "the Ennead," since the latter tends to refer to a specific group of gods; here the term generally refers to the groups of nine mummies found on the gates, whose natures are not specified.

noise *xrw*, "voice, noise, plea."

nonexistence *tm wnn*, literally "not do existing." See *tm* (Allen 2014, p.533)

North Wind, the *mHyt* "north-wind, storm from the north, 'norther'."

northerners *mHtyw* "northerners,"

nose *fndw* "nose."

now *jw* a particle meaning something like "it happens that," (Gardiner 1957, p.384, §461) or demonstrating that a statement is only temporarily true (Allen 2014, p.213, §15.6) Translated here as "now" because it fits both senses: "Look here..." and "At the moment..."

Nu *nww* "primeval waters." The Nu are the primeval waters preceding Creation, an infinite expanse of still, dark water which the Cenotaph of Seti I describes as existing in "uniform darkness" and "intertness."[228] For Quareia students, think of the Void.

Nu, ones who are of the *nnyw* "inert ones," either from *nnw* "weariness, inertness, slackening, settle (of flood-water), hence the translation elsewhere as the **Idle**, or from *nww* "primeval waters," hence the translation in Scene 58 "ones who are of the Nu."

Nubians *nHsyw* "Nubians, drugs or medicines."

---

[228] Allen 1988, p.1

nurse *rnn* "extol, caress, nurse, young ones, lad."

nursling *Atw* "who is nursed," from *Atyt* var. *ATyt* "nurse."

Nut *nwt* "Nut the sky-goddess, sky." See also **heavens, skies**.

O *j* Interjection used before a vocative. (Allen 2014, p.221, 15.8.1)

oars *mw-Hw* "water-threshers," i.e. paddles. There may also be a pun here: "water of the Divine utterance." See **water** and **Utterance**.

obscurity *snk(t)* from *snkt* "darkness, obscurity." . See also **dark greed**.

odour *sty* "odour, smell."

offering, make *Hnk + m* "make offering of."

offerings *Hnkt*

offspring *ms* "child, young, offspring, descendents."

Offspring of the Exhausted One The serpents behind Who Conspires Against Rightness in Scene 69.

Oho! *jhy*

oil *mrHt* "oil, grease, caster oil, wood tar, pitch, liquid asphalt (?), unguent, ointment."

oipe *jpt* A grain-measure equal to four hekats, or about twenty litres. (Gardiner 1957, pp.197–198, §266)

Old One, the *jAy* plus god determinative, from *jAwj* "be aged, attain old age, old age."

One In The Egg *nty m swHt*, "one who is in the egg." See *swHt*,

open *wn* "open, rip open, uncover, reveal, initiate." See also **wide open**

open up *wbA* "drill (stone), open, open up, explore, reveal, bore, pierce, gain access to, delower."

oppose *xsf* "drive away, ward off, oppose, repress, drive, prevent, frustrate."

Glossary

ordain *wD* "command, make a command, ordain, commit, assign, decree, allot, decree (+ *n* "to"), entrust (+ *n* "to"), command, decree, despatch, precept, send away."

ordaining words *wD-mdw* "govern," literally "command speech." (Allen 2014, p.518)

ordains the designs *wD.f sxrw*

Original Darkness *kkw smsw* twilight, primeval darkness, from *kkw* "darkness, twilight" and *smsw* "elder, eldest, senior." . This is usually translated as "Primeval Darkness." We translate it as "Original Darkness" to make it clear that it is the Darkness preceding creation, not just really, really old darkness.

outer chamber *xnty* "who, which is in front of, southern, who is at the head of, foremost, before, presider over, outer chamber, front part." Generally translated as **foremost**.

outside *r-rwty* "outside." Possible pun in Scene 39 with *rwty*, "double lion-god."

overflow *gp, gb* "overflow." Also note *gb* "the earth-god Geb."

oversees, one who *Hry* "who, which is upon, who is higher, having authority over, superior, overseer, captain, chief, master." In my first draft, this was rendered as "captain X," for instance "Captain Perishing" was the "one who oversees destruction." But this anthropomorphised these beings far more than the original text.

part *wpj* "open, open up, inaugurate, part, separate, divide." In this text it generally means "open." However, we translate this word as "part" to distinguish it from *wn*.

pass, pass through *apj* "traverse, fly."

pastures *smw* "pastures, plants, herbage, vegetables."

path *wAt* "road, way, path, causeway, resource, direction."

peace *Htpw* "peace, contentment, good pleasure, favour." We also translate the verb *Htp* as "being at peace."

pellet *bnn* "bead, pellet." Also note, with penis determinative, *bnn* "beget, become erect."

penetrate *ar* "mount up, extend, penetrate."

Perception *sjA*, "Perception," the name of a god who travels with Re at the front of his Barque.

persecute *njk*, as verb, action done to criminals, see *njk* "evil-doer, criminal," Hornung translates this as "punish." (Hornung and Abt 2014, p.41) We translate as "persecute." Both 'goodies' and 'baddies' do this verb in this text, and we wanted to avoid it seeming something that can be meted out *only* to criminals.

Perverter, the *nwDwy*, from *nwdw* "swing away, act perversely, make a travesty of." See also *nwd* "turn aside, vacillate, lie crookedly, falter."

place (noun) *bw* "place, with N25 (hills determinative) in reference to desert."

place (verb) *rdj* "give, put, place." Also see **give** and **render**.

Place of Destruction *Htmyt*, see **destroy**.

Place of Establishing Designs *mnt-sxrw* with O1 "house" determinative (Gardiner 1957, p.492). From *mn* **established** and *sxrw* **designs**.

Place of Execution *nmtj* with O1 "house" determinative, from *nmt* "slaughter-house, execution block."

Place of Hidden Affairs *jmnt xrt* with O1 "house" determinative. From *jmn* **hidden** and *xrt* "affairs," normally translated **bestowals**.

Place of Preparation *sAyt* with O1 "house" determinative, reading literally an apparent 'misspelling' in Scene 31. From *sA*, prepare." This brings to the fore the "liquidation" and "pay a debt" aspect out of **destroy**, in "Place of Destruction."

Place of the Loins *sAwt* with O1 "house" determinative. From *sAwt* "loins."

Place of the Mysteries *StAyt*, literally "place of *StAw*," where *StAw* means "secrets, religious mysteries."

plants *rnpwt* "herbs, vegetables, plants."

pleasing *an* "beautiful, bright (of face), pleasing, be kind, comely, lovely."

Pleasing of Arm *an a*, see **pleasing**. Other options: *ana* "var. of *jan* 'baboon,'" *any* "writing-board."

plummet *tx* "plummet (of balance)"

ply *Xnj* "row, convey by boat, ply, transport, sail, ferry, fetch, carry."

portal *sbA* "door." See also **star**, **teach**.

portion *Xrt* "possessions, belongings, share, portion, requirements, necessities, supply, rations."

possessing *Xrjw* "which is under, having, possessing, carrying, bearing, and containing, bearer." See also **possessing** and **portion**.

post *sxnt* "post, supports, the four posts of the sky."

potent *mnx* "potent, efficacious, pious, capable, efficient, well-disposed, devoted, splendid, excellent, well-famed, well-established."

pour forth *kAj* "think about, plan, plot, reflect, pour forth (from mind)." Note the mental nature of this pouring forth.

Power *sxmt*, "power, might, fury," and with goddess determinative, the goddess Sekhmet. See also **come into power**.

praise *hnw, hnj* "praise (of god or king), jubilation." Also see *hnw* "jar, measure of about 1/2 litre."

pregnant darkness *kkw* We translate this as "pregnant darkness" to emphasize that it is the darkness that precedes birth.

Presence *bA*

presence of, in the see **in the presence of**

protect *xwj* "protect, exempt (from dues)."

provide *DbA*, "(1) repay, replace, restore, (2) clothe, adorn, provide."

provision *sDfAw* "endow, provide, foundation, endowment, supply (with offerings), give abundance, furnish." See also **foundation**

prow *HAt* "forehead, forepart (of animal), vanguard (of army), foremost, chief, the best of, beginning (of region, book)." In Scene 20, we use the words "prow" and "stern" for the beginnings and ends of the hours to pick up the nautical term for the **Rope**.

prow mooring rope *HAtt* "bow-warp, prowrope."

pure, purify, purifications, keep pure *wab* "pure, purify oneself, bathe, cleanse, purify, purification, purity, be neat, unoccupied, be calm, pacify, innocent, exhaust." Also see *wabw* "sacred robe" and *wab* "serve as priest."

Pussy *mjwtj* literally "who is like a cat." From *mjw* "cat."

put forth *wdn* "offer, make or bring offerings," and also "install (as god or king), record (royal titulary), affix, be heavy, weigh, be copious, burdensome, oppressive." Compare *wdnt* "heavy block of stone."

put together *sAq* "pull together, join together, assemble, fit, put together, carry, be armoured, be cautious, compress, shape."

put, put out *wdj* "place, put, implant, plant, appoint as, be bent on, follow after, put forth, throw, shoot, utter, send forth, extend, compete with."

putrefying *Hw(A)t*, from *HwA* "foul, offensive, rot, putrefy, smell offensive, spoil enjoyment."

Quarry Place, the *XA-st* from *XAt, XAw* "mine, quarry."

quest *dndn* "traverse (a place or way)."

quick *spd* "sharp, effective, skilled, restore to order, set in order, acute, clever, apt, unwavering, keen, ready, well-prepared, dextrous." We translate "quick" to get the connotations of a sharp knife and a sharp person.

radiance *Ax* "be, become a spirit, glorious, splendid, winnow with a broom."

Radiant One *Ax* "spirit, glorious one, the spirit-state, glorious, splendid, beneficial, useful, profitable, efficient, serviceably minded towards." The word is closely related to *Axt* "the Akhet, Uraeus-serpent, Eye of

Glossary 301

God, flame," and *Axw*, "sunlight, power of god, have magic, mastery over work, worth, benefactions, good, excellent things, glorification, advantage, magical charms, ability, efficiency."

Radiant, the *Axw* plural of *Ax*, which we render as "Radiant One." See also **become radiant**

railing, rail against *tryt*.

raise up *Tsj* "raise, lift up, extol, go up, mount, rise up, exalt, climb." See also the causative *sTsj* **ascend**.

ram *bA* with ram determinative.

Re *ra* Literally means "sun." However, whereas other god names are translated for meaning, we have kept Re transliterated, so as not to confuse the reader with the physical sun. Quareia students may like to compare how Re is spoken of in this text with 'Divinity.'

reap *Asx* "reap."

receive *Ssp* "take, accept, assume, purchase." See also **lightening**

reckon up *jp* "count, reckon up, make reckoning, assess (dues), pay, allot, exact, detail (someone for work), examine, recognize, revise (schedules), take heed of, set in order, muster, assemble, accounting, estimation." Possible pun with *jpt* "grain measure, box, granary, fittings, cakes."

red *Tms* "red, ruddym violet, be besmeared, filthy, coloured red, "evil injuries," violet, red (hue), fury, rage."

Red Crown *nt* "Red crown of Lower Egypt." In Scene 61, punned with *nt* "water, inundation, flood."

Red Land, the *dSrt* "the Red Land, the desert." And with other determinatives: "red pot, red vessel, wrath."

red linen *dmjw*, alternative spelling of *jdmj* The red linen is described as over a person's head in the Pyramid Texts; it is the fate pattern, and it is red when the dawn light of creation shines through it to manifest its results in the created world. You can see how the god who makes sure that the new star is placed according to their fate pattern could be thought of as their extoller, caresser, and nurser. See **Who Nurses Stars**.

refine *sTn*, "distinguish, honour, refine." The causative of *Tnj*, which we render as "exalt."

rejoice *jhhy* "rejoice."

rejuvenated, be *rnpy* "be young, fresh (of water), vigorous, healthy, rejuvenated, flourish, youthful."

remains *XAt* "corpse." (Allen 2014, p.527) We translate this as "remains," because of the sense in which it is used in this book. It does not appear to refer to the literal corpse of a dead person, but to what *remains* of the dead person that must be got rid of. See the reference for how this word can be written as a fake plural, suggesting a possible parallel with **members**.

remobilize *dmD* "reassemble (dismembered body), assemble, bring together (people), associate, join (someone), accumulate (grain), compile (spell), extend (hand) mobilize, collect."

render *rdj* "give, put, place." Also see **give** and **place**.

repeat *wHm* "repeat, bruit abroad, do again, take anew." For grammar of use, see Gardiner 1957, p.562.

repel *rwty* "repel."

resist *dr* "subdue, expel, repress, wrongdoing, remove, clear, overwhelm, dispel, resist, deter, cast down, repel.

resistance *dryt*, from *dr* "subdue, expel, repress, wrongdoing, remove, clear, overwhelm, dispel, resist, deter, cast down, repel.

respect *snD* "fear, be careful regarding, respect, be fearful, afraid, timid, deferential."

restoration/mutilation *sDb* "restore to life, slur, abomination, evil, worry, impediment, obstacle, opposition, penetrate (of injury)."

restrict *ssy*, verb related to *ssw* "stockade, enclosure."

Glossary 303

retire *xtj* "retire, retreat, travel, desist, turn back."

return *Hm* with legs determinative, "retire, retreat, return."

reveal *snw* "reveal" See also *snj* "pass, pass by, surpass, transgress."

reverence *sA-tA* "reverence (?)"

Ribbon *sSd*

Righteous, the *mAatyw* "just men, the righteous, the blessed dead, blessed spirits"

rightness *mty* "straightforward, precise, proper, trustworthy, just, traditional, exact, regular, customary, usual, exactitude, exactness."

Risen One *jart*, usually translated as "Uraeus." However, this word does not always refer to a literal uraeus-serpent in this book, so we have preferred to translate its literal meaning. See (Johnson 1990, p.5).

roar *hmhmt* "war-shout, quacking of wild-fowl, roaring, battle cry."

roast *wbd* "burn, heat, be scalded, roast."

Rod, Master of a *nb mAwt*. *mAwt* "spear-shaft, staff, stalk (of corn), measuring-rod, rays of light, new, be renewed, new land island, mound."

Rope (capitalized) *Hrrt*, from *Hr* "a rope (aboard ship)".

rope (uncapitalized) *nwH* "rope, band (of metal), bind (enemies), lead (cattle), bandage."

Royal Child *jnpw* "royal child, Anubis." . The meaning of Anubis's name as "Royal Child" is uncertain,[229] but fits well with the way the name is used in this text.

ruler *HqA* "rule, ruler, provincial, district governor, headman, chieftain."

ruling-staff A staff in the shape of the *Hqa* sceptre (S38, "crook." Gardiner 1957, p.508).

---

[229] Wilkinson 2003, p.187

rushes *jArw* "rushes"

safe *wDA* "hale, uninjured, safe, intact, be sound, whole, keep well."

sail south *xntj* "sail upstream, travel southward."

save, salvation *nD* "save, protect, guard against (magic), make good, protection, protector."

say *xrw* as a verb. (Allen 2014, p.303)

scale-pan *Hnkw* "scale-pan of balance." For substituting it for *Hnqt*, **beer**, see Scene 21.

Scales, the *mxAt* "balance, scale," from *mxA* "match, equal, adjust, counterpoise, make level, be like."

sceptre *Dam* "sceptre." When plural, puns with *Damw* "fine gold, electrum."

scone *Sns* "a cake or loaf." Translated "scone" purely because I am really running low on English words for bread. I guess the Egyptians really did have to make their own entertainment. Note the similar word *Snsw* "slab (for offerings)."

screech *khA* "raise the voice, utter a bellow."

scrutinize *sjp* "inspect, examine, revise, allot, assign, destine, organize, inspection, control, test, examiner, supervision."

seal *xtm*

sealed, what is *sDAyt* "seal." Also see *sDAwt* "precious things, treasures."

search out *gmH*, *gmHw* "catch sight of, espy, look, behold, spy on, stare, search out."

Seat *Ast* "Isis," from **seat**.

seat *st* "seat, throne, place, position, abode."

Seat-of-the-Eye *wsjr* "Osiris" from *js-jrt* "seat of the eye" (Allen 2005, p.438)

seek *HHy* "seek, search for."

Glossary

seek out *sxn* "embrace, seek out, meet, occupy, envelop."

selection *stp*. We translate as "selection" when the word is not written with a wounded man determinative. See "dismemberment."

self *Haw*, "members," plural of *Ha*, "flesh, body." In plural "limbs, members," even "self." Most of the time we translate this as "members," but occasionally we render it as "self."

semen *mtwt* "semen, seed, progeny, poison, ill-will, venom."

send out *sbj* "go, travel, attain, watch over, send, conduct, spend, pass time, attain, send on one's way, pass away, despatch, vanish."

separate the words *wDa mdw* "judge, litigate, have judgement, judgement." We translate more literally, to help bring out the theme of utterance that runs through this text.

separate, separation, separate out *wDa* "cut (cords), cut off (head), be parted, cut out (sandals), split, judge, have judgement, judge between, discern, assign, remove." Compare **divide**

serpent *HfAw* "snake, serpent."

set aright *smAa* "put in order, correct, present, pray, handle, offer, thrust, direct."

set out *Sm* "go, opposite of *jw* "come", walk, set out (on journey). depart, return, emerge." see **come back**.

sever *snj* "cut off (heads), sever (necks)."

shadow *Swyt* "shadow, shade (as part of man's personality), spirit (of god), sacred figure, image (of god), sunshade, kind of small temple." What gawpers at the wall of Plato's cave often confuse for reality...

shallows *Ts* "sandbank, shallows."

She Who Keeps *jryt* fem. of *jry* "keeper, relating to...", e.g. *jry-at* "hall-keeper."

shine *psD, psd* "shine." Compare with **Nine**.

Ship's Mast *dpw* "mast wood." To judge from the strange appearance of the "earth barque," it indeed looks like a mast.

shoulder *rmnj* "shoulder, carry, support, match, equal, bearer, support." Compare with *rmn*, "shoulder, arm," which in dual is "arms of a balance, uprights of a ladder."

shrine *kAr* "shrine, chapel, naos, portable shrine, cabin (of sun barque), vineyard."

shut *hAj* "come down, go down, descend." We translate this as "shut," because in English to speak of "the coming down of a door" brings to mind a portcullis rather than a pair of double doors. Also see **fall upon**.

sickle *HAb* "sickle."

side *gs* "side, border (of land)."

Silent Land, Silent Place *jgrt*. We translate "Silent Land" with a land determinative, and "Silent Place" with a house determinative.

sin *jsft* "wrong, wrong-doing, falsehood, deceit, evil, evildoers" Sin has a connotation of straying from the path.

sinner *jsfty*

sizzle *snwr* "make to tremble" with Q7 "brazier" determinative. (Gardiner 1957, p.500)

skies, the *pt* "sky, heaven." We translate as "the skies" for consistency with "the heavens," which we translate in the plural to avoid confusion with the concept of "heaven" as "Paradise." See also: **heavens, Nut**.

skillful *jqr* "trusty, trustworthy, skillful, excellent, pleasing, well-to-do, superior, diligent, worthy, precious, virtue, wealth, excellence."

sky below, the *nnt* "lower heaven."

Slack, the *jgyw*, from **lacking**. Characters in Scene 58. Hornung translates "those who have capsized," a definition I have not managed to confirm. (Hornung and Abt 2014, p.318) I translate "slack" to give the sense of being relaxed and underwater after having dived.

Glossary

Slaughterers ::/Hntyw/, from *Hnty*, "slaughterer." Snake-headed beings in Scene 69.

slaughtering *Sat* "slaughtering, terror, knife, massacre, dread, murderousness."

small *nds* "little, small, young, children, commoner, citizen, of low estate."

smash *Hsb* "break, smash, fracture." Also note potential puns: *Hsb* "count, reckon, reckon with (offenders), kind of bread" and *Hsbw* "reckoning, account, doom."

smell *ssn* "breathe, smell, take a breath."

smooth, go smoothly, smooth the way *naa* "smooth, undecorated, clear, smoothness (of complexion), mix smoothly."

son *sA* "son, pupil, son-in-law."

Sound Eye, the *wDAt* "the uninjured (sound) Eye of Horus, the source of notation of measures of capacity."

Souser *abS*, "wine-jar, a crocodile deity." "Who drowns." (Hornung and Abt 2014, p.383)

South Wind, South Land *rsw*. With P5 "sail" determinative, "south-wind." With O49 "village with cross-roads" determinative, "the South Land." For determinatives, see Gardiner 1957, pp.498–499.

spear *abb* "use the pitchfork."

specification *wp* "specification, details, namely, specify, disclosure, carver, double-edged knife." But also see quite likely more literal meaning *db* "horn." (Gardiner 1957, p.463)

speech *r* "mouth, opening, utterence, speech, door, language, intent, spell, dictate, deposition, voice, word, saying."

spend the night *sDr* "spend the night, sleep, lie, lie down, go to rest, be inert, inactive."

Spiral *mHn*, "coil, the Coiled one, a board game Schlangenspiel." Usually transliterated as "Mehen." Mehen's name literally means "Spiral," the combination of a cycle plus forward/outward/inward movement. There was quite a debate between Josephine and Michael as to whether to transliterate this word as "Mehen," or to translate the god's functional meaning, "Spiral." This was because there are various spiral forces, so translating "Spiral" risked losing specificity. However, the Spiral over Re being the granddaddy of other, smaller spirals is implied pretty heavily on one occasion in this text: *mHn pw nj arwt* "this is the Mehen/Spiral of Risen Ones." (Scene 78.) As a result, Michael decided ultimately to go with translating Mehen's name literally, just as he has translated the majority of the other god-names in this text, particularly since it would help to bring out other underlying spiral themes. But beware of equating all spirals, Egyptian or otherwise, with Mehen! Any time you read "Spiral" in this translation, it refers to Mehen; words such as **coil**, etc. mean something quite different.

spiteful *knj* "be sullen, sullenness, annoyance."

spread across *xns* "traverse, travel, spread, move in two directions." Note that the determinative for "move in two directions" looks a lot like the Earth Barque.

spring up *nhp* "pulsate, jump, copulate, mate, rise early in the morning."

Stabilizers *Ddyw*, from *Dd* "stable, enduring." The back group of gods in the "tug of war" in Scene 69. Reading the first two signs, *DA* and *tjw* or *A*, as their value when used as group-writing, which is *D*. For group-writing, see (Gardiner 1957, p.52, §60), and for *DA* (U28) and *jtw* as *D*, see [p.519]{gardiner1957}. We in fact use a very similar word to describe the person at the end of a rope in a tug of war: "anchor."

Staff *mst* "staff." Here understood as Imsety, one of the Four Children of Horus.

stairway *rdw* "stairway, steps (of throne), tomb-shaft."

stand erect *aHa* "stand, withstand, stand by, stand erect, raise oneself, rise up."

Glossary 309

star *sbA* "star." See also **portal, teach.**

stare at *sty* "stare, stare at."

steer *mAa* "lead, guide, direct, send, despatch, throw out (rope from ship), steer (ship), extend (limbs), paddle (water, of swimmers), set out (on journey), transport."

stern *pHwy* "hinder-parts, hind-quarters, back (of jaw), rear, rearguard (of army), stern (of ship), end (in both concrete and abstract senses), limit, base, extreme."

stern mooring rope *pHwyt* "stern-warp (of ship)."

stone vessel *aAt* "stone vessel, precious stone."

straight *aqA* "precise, accurate, exact, straightforward, use aright, correct, straightness, straight-dealing, straight-forwardness, exact sense (of speech), on a level with."

stranger *xpp* "stranger, unusual condition." Where this occurs in Scene 10, it is indeed written in an unusual condition, with the *jw* legs sign providing the plural to mask its meaning.

stream *nwy* "water, pool, stream."

stride *nmtt* "stride, gait, expedition, steps, movements."

strip, strip away *kf* "uncover, unclothe, doff (clothes), strip, deprive, despoil, strip away."

strive *aHA* "fight, oppose, reprimand, wrangle, war, battle, combat."

strong ale *Dsrt* .

subject to *xr* "with, near, under (a king), to, in presence of, before, from." See also **in the presence of.**

subjects *Xrw* "relatives, underlings, inhabitants," from *Xr* "under, carrying, holding, possessing, in possession of, in tenure of, held by." See also **possessing** and **portion.**

sucks in *xnp* "snatch, catch, steal, pour (water), present (offering), receive seed (of a woman), breathe, loaf." Note how the word can mean both "suck in" and "put forth/offer."

summon, he who is *njsw* "he who is summoned, reckoner."

sun-breeze *Sw* "the air-god Shu, the sun, sunlight, ascend." We translate "sun-breeze" where it is not specified as the god Shu to get at both connotations of light and air.

sun-disc *jtn* "sun, more specifically disc of sun, globe, sphere"

sunny *qaHw* "sunshine"

sunshine *jAxw* "sunshine, radiance."

supply *snm* "feed (someone), consume (food), supply (necessities), provision, pray, supplicate (someone), prayer."

support *mkAt* "support, pedestal."

surpass *swA* "pass, escape, surpass, pass away, remove"

surplus *DAt* "balance, remainder." Literally what is left over after a subtraction has been performed. (Please note that the connotation of "balance" her is "the change from a transaction," not "balance" as in "scales.")

surround *jnH* "surround, enclose, rim (a vessel with gold), envelop, encompass, hem in."

sustenance *kA*. For the Ka's its identification with life force and what sustains life force, see (Allen 2014, pp.100–101). We translate this concept uniformly as "sustenance" throughout this book.

swallow *sXb* "swallow."

swift, be swift *pHr* "run, be swift, runner."

Swimming/Golden/Molten, the *nbyw*, from *nbj* "swim." See also **gold** and **molten**.

taken *hqs* "steal."

Glossary

tape *mt* "strip of cloth."

teach *sbA* "teach, teaching, school." See also **portal, star**.

tears *rmwt* "tears, weeping." Punned with **humans** in Scene 30.

tell *mdw* "speak, address, speech, word, plea." Also note pun with *mdw* "staff, rod."

temple bread *Sbw, Sbt* "food offerings, in a temple, bread."

tenants of the Duat *xntyw dwAt*, from *xntyw-S* "tenants, smallholders." These are tenants of *dwAt*, "the Duat," rather than *S*, "a garden."

The Aged One Who Is Another One *jk-ky* + god determinative. From *jk* "be aged," , "miner, hewer of stone." (Gardiner 1957, p.444)

Third Hour *sHtpn.s* "third hour." Lit. "who causes her (own) peace," I think.

Thou *Twt*. An archaism at the time this text was written, which we therefore render archaically in English. (Allen 2014, p.63) (Gardiner 1957, p.53, §64)

thought *wAwA* "take counsel, consider, think about, deliberate, take thought, plan, plot, conspire."

thousand *xA* "1000, herds."

thresh *Hwj* "beat, strike, smite, thresh (corn)."

thresh by foot *aAgw* with foot determinative, "thrash," related to *aAgt* "hoof."

threshing floor *xtyw* "threshing floor, threshing platform, platform, dais, terraced hillside."

throat *Hty, Htyt* "throat."

Throaty *bantj*, lit. "belonging to the neck," from *bant* "neck." Note the other word used for **neck** and its meaning throughout the text.

throw *wDj* "place, put, put forth, throw, shoot (an arrow), utter, send forth (the voice)."

tie *Ts* "tie knot, cord, conceive, tie up, bind."

tiller-rope *nfryt* "tiller-rope."

torpor *bAgj* "be weary, languid, indolent, tired, scuttled, shipwrecked, lazy, be slack, remiss, weariness, langour, slackness, remissness."

tow *sTA* "drag, pll, pull out, draw off, admit, usher in, flow." See also Mystery.

towering *qAj* "tall, high, exalted, be raised on high, uplifted, presumptuous, overweening."

trap *HAd* "fish-trap, trap fish (as verb)."

travel on *SAs* "travel, tread on (enemy)"

travel round *pXr* "turn, turn about, revolve (of sun), move about (of limbs), surround, enclose, travel around, traverse, perambulate (a hall), circumnambulate (walls), pervade (hearts), unroll (a papyrus), twist/distort (what is said)."

treading out *hbj* "tread out (grain), tread (a place), explore, traverse."

tremble *sdA* "tremble."

tremor *nwr* "tremble."

trespass, trespasser *sbj* "rebel (verb and noun)." For its similarity to the verb *sbj* "go," we translate as "trespass" as a nice English equivalent.

Trespasser, the *sbj*, **trespasser** with a serpent determinative. See *sbj* "rebel-serpent" in .

True of Voice *mAa-xrw* "justified, vindicated, triumphant." We translate this phrase literally, to help bring out the utterance theme in the text.

Truth *mAat* "truth, fact, right-doing, righteousness, justice, rightness, orderly management,"

turned about *sxd* "upside down, disordered (of dress), reversed, inside out."

twist *ann* "turn back, come back, return, bring back, twist, controvert, hereafter, avert, retreat, relapse, subside."

Glossary 313

unbalance *rqw* "tilting (of balance), enmity."

uncover *kf* "uncover, unclothe, doff (clothes), strip, deprive, despoil, strip away." Most of the time, we translate this as **strip**.

Underworlders *dwAtyw*

Union *Xnm*, the name of the sixth figure in the queue in Scene 7, and the second one in Scene 85. The name is often transliterated when applied to the god Khnum.

Unite *Xnm* "join, unite with, enclose, enfold."

unravel *snfxfx* "(causative) loosen, release"

upend *pna* "turn upside down, turn back, go back on, overturn, upset, reverse, incline, bend, pervert, shift, return."

uplift *HAj* "mourn, wail, screech (of falcon or kite), dance (at funeral), uplift."

upper part *Hrw* "upper part, top."

Upright spelled *mAay* where it appears in Scene 40, which for the pun to work should be read as *mAaw(w)* "who are aright," from *mAaw* "aright? . However, also note other similar words: *mayt* "scabbard, shaft, sheath."

utter *wSA* "utter, recite."

Utterance, the *Hw* "(the god) Authoritative Utterance."

vagina *knst* "vagina, vulva, perineum (?)." See also *kns* "pubic region (?)."

valiant *wAS* "be honoured, be strong, honour (due to a god or king) push, force, batter." From its usage in this text, we translate "valiant" or "valour."

valour *wAS* "be honoured, be strong, honour (due to a god or king) push, force, batter." From its usage in this text, we translate "valiant" or "valour."

veil *afnt* "royal head-cloth," used metaphorically in Scene 40 as part of the trappings of the dead. See also *afnw* "covered, blindfold, blindness."

vigilant *rs* "wake, watchful, vigilant, keep watch, guard, be awake."

voice *xrw*, "voice, noise, plea."

voyage *sqdy*, "sail, travel, row, convey."

wages *jsw* "reward, exchange."

walk off (with) *jtj* "take (for use), take possession of (an inheritance), take, conduct, take away, carry off, remove (oneself), spend/pass (time), excel, move, use (one's arm)." Related to *jtw* "thief."

wandering member of the flock *wDww, wDy(w)* "wandering cattle." With god determinative. See **flock** and Scene 54.

water *mw*

weakness *jHw* "weakness."

wealthy *wsr* "wealthy man."

weigh *wDa* "weigh." Another sense of *wDa* **separate**.

weight *mwt* "weight, block."

West *jmnt* Often the feather-on-standard determinative (R14) helps distinguish this from "hidden."

Westerner *jmnty* from *jmnt* **West**.

Whisperer *sSS*, which Hornung translates as "rattling," I prefer to think of a sistrum "whispering," which fits better with the description of this being's activities.

White Crown *HDt* "the white crown," literally "the **bright** one." Note also the phonetically similar words *HDt* "white linen, white of the eye, loaves." Yet another potential bread pun...

Who Adores His Mother *dwA-mwt.f* "one of the four sons of Horus."

Who Conspires Against Rightness *wA-m-mty, wAmmty* "name of Apophis." Often simply transliterated as "Wamemty."

Who Is Of The Breast *Snbtj*, from *Snbt* "breast, flesh."

Who Is Of The Course *Hpy* "one of the four sons of Horus." Related to *Hpw* "course (of river, of life)."

Who Is Of The Ibis *DHwty* "Thoth." The derivation of this god's name appears to have been a matter of some discussion among the Ancient Egyptians, as well as Egyptologists.[230] Budge, whose claims one must always verify, notes that some Egyptians favoured a derivation from *tx*, a word he translates as "weight," and which Faulkner, writing half a century later, gives as "plummet (of balance)."[231] This links the literal meaning of this god's name to the plumb-line used to keep the scales true. However, note also the very similar words to *DHwty*, *DHty*, "lead," and *DHty HD* "tin?" (literally "bright lead".) If this god's name sounded like the word for the metal "lead," then the line of figures in Scene 68 demonstrates an alchemical progression.

Who Nurses Stars *rnn-sbAw* A variety of possibilities: this seemed to make the most sense. "Extol, caress, nurse, young ones, lad," are all possible translations of *rnn*.

Who Permits Breath *srqt*, fem. noun from *srq* **breathe**, more accurately "causes to breathe." The goddess generally transliterated as Serqet/Selket.

Who Walks Abroad *Smty*, from *Sm* "go, opposite of *jw* "come", walk, set out (on journey). depart, return, emerge, come and go." See Scene 62.

wicked *bjn* "bad, evil, dreadful, naughty, dangerous, wicked."

winding *qaH* "bend (arm), corner, cornerpiece, bend (of stream)." In Scene 53, punned with *qaHw* **sunny**.

wine *jrp* "wine."

winnow *jd* "assault (?)" Here translated "winnow" mainly to distinguish it from "thresh," but also due to the context of Scene 18, where it appears, and the A24 determinative, "man striking with stick." (Gardiner 1957, p.444)

winnowed kernels *DAHw* "winnowed kernels."

---

[230] Budge 1969 [1904], p.402
[231] Faulkner 1962, p.301

winnower *qmAw*,

wipe away *sk*

wise, to be wise of *rx* "know, know how to..., be able to..., be aware of..., learn, know of, acquire wisdom, can take notice of, find out, enquire about, attest, succeed in, be skilled, discern, list." The term "wise man" does not necessarily have magical overtones, though the term *rx-xt* "wise of things" does mean "professional magician." [232]

withdraw *Sdj* "take away, remove, cut out, dig (lake, etc), salvage (boat), stave off (event), exact (dues), save, preserve, restore, recover, keep safe, excavate, extract, pull, maintain, reserve, let resound, collect, greet, recover, exact, deliver, secure, withdraw, drag."

Witness *mtry*, from *mtr* "testify concerning, exhibit (virtues), instruct, be famous/renowned, recognize, educate, teach, advise, inform, assist, attest, examine, tell, bear witness."

wobble *dA* "become loose, wobble (of decaying limbs)."

word *mdw* "speak, address, speech, word, plea." Also note pun with *mdw* "staff, rod."

work *jrj* "create, beget, make, construct, fashion, lay out (a garden), cultivate (crops), perform (a miracle), garner (corn), read aloud (a book), recite (a spell), + *m* = change/transform into." Usually translated as **make**, except when context will not permit it.

worship *snsw* "worship, be brotherly, fraternize, mingle with, take as a friend, laudation, prayers, make friends with."

wrap up *wt* "bandage, bind, mummy-wrapping, smear, wrap up."

wrappings noun related to *wt*, **wrap up**.

writing (down) *sS* "write, inscribe, paint, draw, enrol (troops), document."

wrong *bgst*, from *bgsw* "wrongdoing."

yardarms *tpt* "yardarms, cord, thread, first, (top of) stake, prow."

---

[232] Ritner 1993, pp.229–230

years, making years *rnpwt* "make years (of life), spend, pass years."

Young, the *rnpw*, from *rnp* "young man."

zeal *Hr* "face, mask, head, mind, zeal."

Bibliography

Allen, J.P. (1988), *Genesis In Egypt: The Philosophy of Ancient Egyptian Creation Accounts*, New Haven, Conneticut: Yale University.

— (2005), *The Ancient Egyptian Pyramid Texts*, Atlanta: Society of Biblical Literature.

— (2014), *Middle Egyptian: An Introduction to the Language and Culture of Hieroglyphs.* 3rd ed., Cambridge: Cambridge University Press.

Bonomi, J. and Sharpe, S. (1864), *The Alabaster Sarcophagus of Oimenepthah I., King of Egypt*, London: Longman, Green, Longman, Roberts, and Green.

Budge, E.A.W. (1969 [1904]), *The Gods of the Egyptians Volume 1*, Originally published by Methuen & Company, London., New York: Dover Publications, Inc.

Clagett, M. (1995), *Ancient Egyptian Science, A Source Book, Volume Two: Calendars, Clocks, and Astronomy*, Philadelphia: American Philosophical Society.

Faulkner, R.O. (1962), *A Concise Dictionary of Middle Egyptian*, Oxford: Griffith Institute.

— (1985 [1972]), *The Ancient Egyptian Book of the Dead*, ed. by C. Andrews, Revised edition, London: British Museum Press.

Gardiner, A.H. (1957), *Egyptian Grammar*, 3rd ed., Oxford: Griffith Institute.

Hesiod and Anon (1914), *Hesiod, The Homeric Hymns and Homerica*, Loeb Classical Library, New and revised edition, 1936. Translated by Hugh G. Evelyn-White, London, England: Harvard University Press.

Hornung, E. (1991), *The Tomb of Pharaoh Seti I/Das Grab Sethos' I*, 1st ed., Zurich, Switzerland: Artemis & Winkler.

Hornung, E. and Abt, T. (2014), *The Egyptian Book of Gates*, Zurich, Switzerland: Living Human Heritage Publications.

Johnson, S.B. (1990), *The Cobra Goddess of Ancient Egypt: Predynastic, Early Dynastic and Old Kingdom Periods*, London: Kegan Paul International.

Kuckens, K. (2013), *The Children of Amarna: Disease and Famine in the Time of Akhenaten*, University of Arkansas.

Manassa, C. (2006), 'The Judgment Hall of Osiris in the Book of Gates', in *Revue d'Égyptologie 57*, Leuven, Belgium: Peeters, pp. 109-142.

Morrow, S.B. (2015), *The Dawning Moon of the Mind: Unlocking the Pyramid Texts*, New York: Farrar, Straus and Giroux.

Murray, M.A. (1913), *Ancient Egyptian Legends*, London: John Murray.

Pinch, G. (2002), *Egyptian Mythology: A Guide to the Gods, Goddesses, and Traditions of Ancient Egypt*, Oxford: Oxford University Press.

Ritner, R.K. (1993), *The Mechanics of Ancient Egyptian Magical Practice*, Studies in Ancient Oriental Civilization, 54, Fourth Printing 2008, Chicago, Illinois: The Oriental Institute of the University of Chicago.

Schwarz, C. (ed.) (1991), *Chambers Concise Dictionary*, Edinburgh: Chambers Harrap.

Wilkinson, R.H. (2003), *The Complete Gods and Goddesses of Ancient Egypt*, London: Thames and Hudson.

Biographies

Josephine McCarthy is an adept magician, author, and the director of the Quareia Magical Training School. She has authored twenty-eight books on various magical subjects and written countless articles for occult and magical publications around the world. She lives in Southwest England with her husband Stuart Littlejohn.

Stuart Littlejohn is a magical artist and classical ritualist whose artwork has featured in many books by leading writers on the subjects of magic, myth, and the occult. His original artwork can be found in collections around the world, and his detailed studies of Egyptian, Classical Roman, and Ancient Greek imagery are renowned in the international magical communities.

Michael Sheppard edited the Quareia course and was its ancient languages consultant.

www.ingramcontent.com/pod-product-compliance
Lightning Source LLC
Chambersburg PA
CBHW041311110526
44590CB00028B/4321